GROW
URBAN
HABITATS

*SEEKING A
NEW HOUSING
DEVELOPMENT MODEL*

GROWING URBAN HABITATS

SEEKING A NEW HOUSING DEVELOPMENT MODEL

William R. Morrish
Susanne Schindler
Katie Swenson

William Stout
Publishers
San Francisco

Contents

Carlton Avenue.

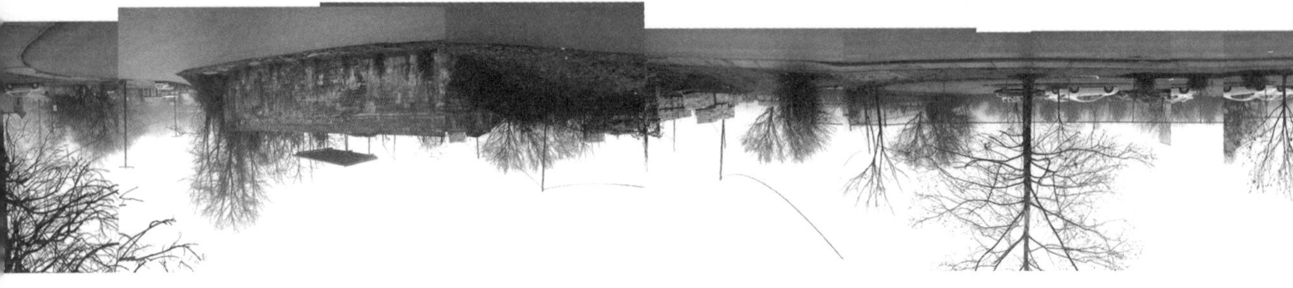

Nassau Street.

Midland Street.

Rives Street.

Sunrise Trailer Court.

Preface

This is a book about using design to improve affordable housing and our cities' neighborhoods. Design is our profession, our trade and our skill. Design is our way of interpreting the world, our way of investigating possibilities for the future. We see design as an act of engagement with the people we are designing for, a process of mutual learning. In the context of housing development, we use the term 'community design' to describe a process that prioritizes input from current or future residents in both individual projects and broader neighborhood plans. This may seem obvious, but to really engage designers and the eventual users in the development of affordable housing and neighborhoods, requires an integrated and inclusive planning, design, and development approach.

When Sunrise Trailer Court in Charlottesville, VA came up for sale in 2003, its residents protested, unwilling to give up the affordable, supportive community they had created for a short-term, maximum-return-on-investment, kind of development. The uproar got the attention of the surrounding neighborhood, and together their voices were loud enough to get the attention of the City, housing activists, and thankfully, Habitat for Humanity of Greater Charlottesville (HHGC). When HHGC made the bold claim that they would develop new housing without displacing the residents, all were greatly assured. The question became: How? What is our vision for our new community and how do we get there?

HHGC, working with the Charlotttesville Community Design Center (CCDC), acknowledged that in order to implement a more equitable form of development they would need to tap into the expertise of designers. Together the two organizations launched an open design competition called Urban Habitats. Urban Habitats became a vehicle for creating an expansive and inclusive dialogue about the best possibilities in urban design for small-home neighborhoods in the United States today. As Overton McGehee, then-Executive Director of HHGC, pointedly wrote in the Call for Entries: "We need your help. Your designs for this neighborhood will be the tools that will help transform Sunrise Trailer Court into Sunrise Park and create a new model for the transformation of an American trailer park."

In response to this call, HHGC and CCDC received 164 boards from design teams from over 37 countries, an outpouring of interest and commitment far beyond any expectations. What was the draw? Why did so many designers contribute their time and ideas to Sunrise? Many architects get interested in architecture because they believe that the built environment has an enormous impact on the quality of people's lives. But often in the course of practice, architects become removed from the tangible, human-scaled impact of their work. Urban Habitats provided an opportunity for architects to confront the enormous challenge of creating affordable housing while engaging the trailer park, a prototypical form of American living, currently in danger of disappearing. At the same time, the competition afforded participants rare insight into the lives of a particular group of people and a particular place.

The goal of this book is to understand how to learn from very local, intimate issues and solutions in community development, as we have done with Sunrise, in order to help other communities in their development efforts. Doris Koo, president and chief executive officer of Enterprise Community Partners, a national nonprofit that provides expertise for affordable housing and sustainable communities, says, "There are a lot of cynics who say, 'Poverty is too big for us to attack.' I've learned that poverty *can* be alleviated building by building, block by block. But at the end of the day, we have to scale up our solutions." As the demand for affordable housing continues to increase throughout the country, there is no doubt that we need to scale up the solutions. We hope that the Charlottesville example, and the examples of the projects described in this book, will inspire you to "trust the wisdom and instincts of struggling families" (Koo) with innovation and creativity, and contribute to this larger goal.

Designer Katie Swenson founded the CCDC in 2004. Urban Habitats was their first large project. After finishing a three-year tenure as a Frederick P. Rose Fellow, Katie saw the opportunity for the Design Center to bring technical and logistical assistance to Habitat and the Sunrise community, and brought together the project team and vision. Today, Swenson is the Director of the Rose Fellowship, a program of the Enterprise Community Partners, working at a nation-wide level to advance the collaboration between designers and affordable housing developers. William R. Morrish, Elwood R. Quesada Professor of Architecture, Landscape Architecture and Urban and Environmental Planning at the School of Architecture of the University of Virginia, was a founding board member of the CCDC. He brought his experience of working with community groups across the country to Urban Habitats to help expand the possibilities of the Sunrise development. Architect Susanne Schindler, who together with Christopher Genter was the first-place winner of the Urban Habitats competition, joined in the effort to explore the lessons learned in the competition in the broader context of affordable housing development in the United States.

We are united in the belief that we, as a design community, can contribute in a more meaningful way to an equitable form of community development. To do so, we need to find new ways to work in concert with community-based partners, especially residents, non-profit developers, and city officials. Our goal today is the same as when we started this project. In McGehee's words: "For many years to come, when someone proposes a land use that would displace trailer park residents, or other low-income people anywhere in the United States, someone may stand up in a public hearing and say, 'There may be a better way to do this. In Charlottesville, Virginia, a trailer park was redeveloped and no one was displaced.'"

This book is dedicated to the residents of Sunrise. The role of the Sunrise residents in the Urban Habitats process cannot be overstated. They literally opened up their homes to the process. They shared their history, their values, their hopes and fears for the future. They hosted barbeques, dances, tours, and breakfasts at Sunrise. We thank them for their warm welcome, their honor of tradition, and their optimism for the future.

Tree lined streets, well kept lawns, childrens8 laughter. This is the Belmont community in Charlottesville, Virginia. Located in close proximity to Thomas Jeffersons' Monticello you can experience the history of his designs in our neighborhood. I was born in I949 at the Martha Jefferson hospital. My parents brought me to my grandparents home on Monticello ave. where they were living. My Dad was a World War II veteran and worked for the C&O railroad. My Mom was an English war bride and worked for the telephone company. One year later they moved to our own home on Tufton ave.,still located in the Belmont neighborhood. I have two brothers and we had so much fun growingh up in Belmont. Our Dad passed away in I958 but we had the love, support and security of friends and neighbors. In I968 I graduated from Lane High school and went to work at K Mart. Early I970 I married and started my own family. There was no way I could think of leaving this loving, close knit place. We rented homes in the area over a ten year period, then we were able to purchase our mobile home and live at Sunrise Trailer court. We are so content here and have been for 25 years. The views are beautiful and ever changing with the seasons. People all over Belmont are caring and kind, more like family members. The older homes in the Belmont area are soothing to the soul because their structural designs are of a long ago era that was the foundation of Charlottesville. I say, " Let's keep as much history around as we possibly can." I will always hold Belmont and its' families close to my heart.

Marion Chapman Dudley
I4I0 Carlton ave. # II5
Sunrise Trailer Court
Charlottesville, Virginia
22902

Introduction
Double-Wide Democracy

On March 8, 2005, Habitat for Humanity of Greater Charlottesville (HHGC), in partnership with the Charlottesville Community Design Center (CCDC), announced an open ideas competition called Urban Habitats. The task at hand was the redevelopment of Sunrise Trailer Court, a 2.3-acre site in Charlottesville, into a project of affordable, compact, and sustainable housing. The organizers did not shy away from setting a high benchmark. The Urban Habitats competition was in pursuit of "a new housing development model."

On July 1, 2005, FedEx, DHL, UPS and U.S. Postal Service carriers deposited 164 packages each containing two 24 by 36 inch project boards into a hot warehouse at the edge of Charlottesville. A CCDC volunteer group spent the day unwrapping and recording these submissions, which included entries from 51 countries outside the U.S., and represented just a subset of 423 original registrations. The 41 student and 123 professional collaborations produced 652 linear feet of illustrations that outlined Urban Habitat design concepts in plans, digital models and sketches.

On September 2nd and 3rd, 2005, after two days of intense jury deliberations, the results of the competition were announced. A public exhibition was opened at the Design Center, and the broader themes and implications of the competition were discussed at the Growing Urban Habitats symposium. The symposium was hosted by the University of Virginia School of Architecture, a project partner, and brought together academics, nationally acclaimed architects and developers of affordable housing, and competition finalists. Habitat for Humanity interviewed the competition's three finalist teams and proceeded to engage two to take the redevelopment of Sunrise forward. As this book goes to print, the implementation of "a new housing development model" is well underway.

The broader themes and implications of the redevelopment of Sunrise Trailer Court form the basis of this book. The significance of the Urban Habitats project for Sunrise lies in finding models for compact homes and gardens that add social, physical and ecological diversity to small-home neighborhoods. Upon this background, *Growing Urban Habitats* outlines opportunities for achieving what we have called the four urban habitat goals: *affordable*, *dense*, *compact*, and *sustainable* housing. These goals are self-evident and nothing new. Implementing them, however, is not an easy task. To achieve these housing goals we advocate an approach that is driven by design.

Design, to us, is anything but an add-on, an option, or a luxury. Everything around us has been designed, and results from choices that have been made. We need to invest the time to understand how these choices are made and what their impacts are. In advocating for design, we are not interested in outlining prescriptive arguments. Rather, design should be seen as a way to test possibilities and to push the envelope that organizes and structures our lives. The choices architects make may not transform society. They do, however, determine what you hear when you wake up in the morning, who you see when you walk to your front door, how much you pay for your utilities. To attain our four goals, we need strategies to actively reframe our choices. The four urban habitat strategies we describe in this book are: *counting again*, *expanding options*, *mixing it up*, and *building for change*.

Put much more simply, and as the Charlottesville Community Design Center announces on its T-Shirts, "Design Matters", and it is well worth the investment.

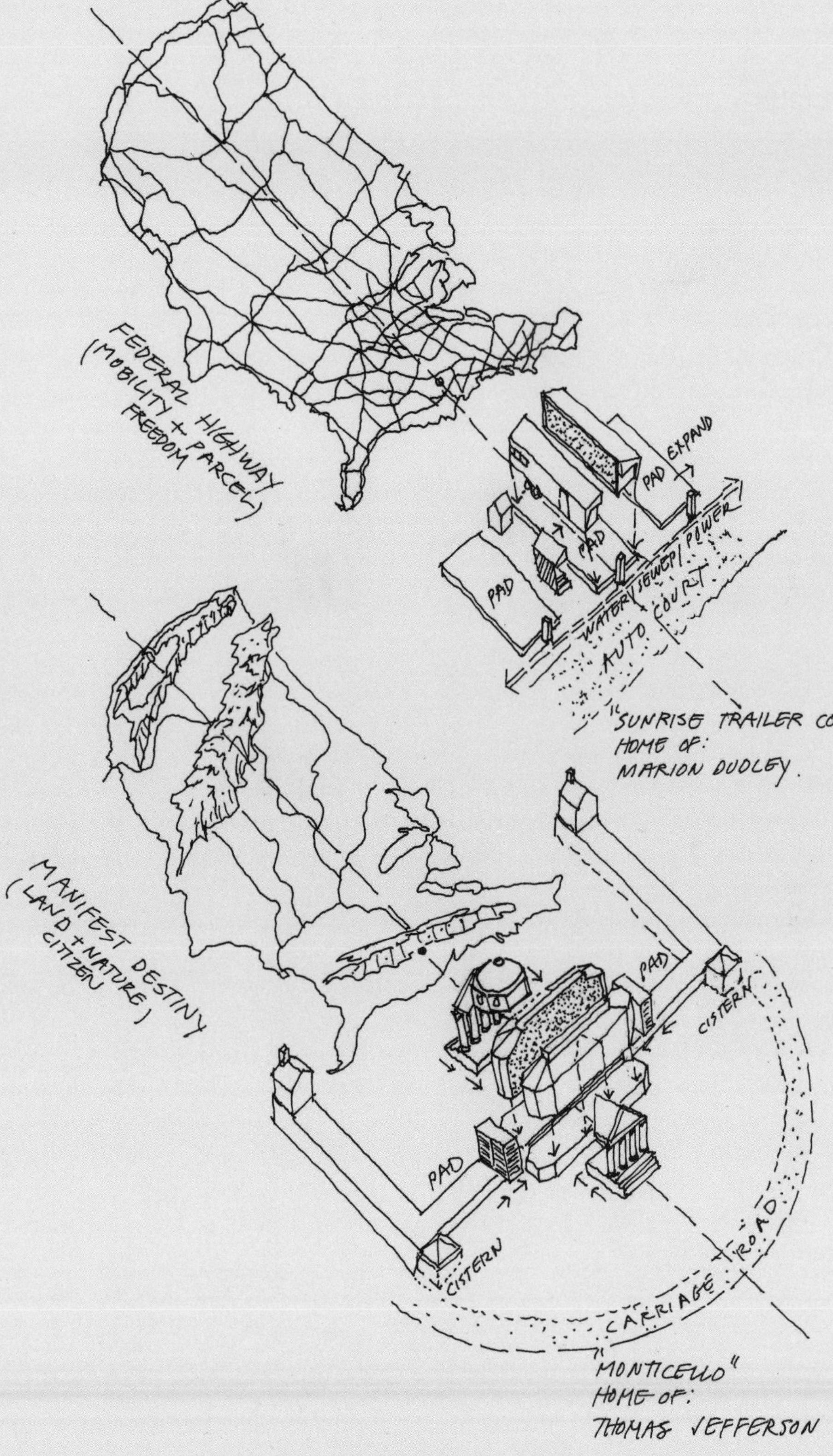

FEDERAL HIGHWAY
(MOBILITY + PARCEL)
FREEDOM

EXPAND
PAD
PAD
PAD
WATER/SEWER/POWER
AUTO COURT

"SUNRISE TRAILER COURT"
HOME OF:
MARION DUDLEY.

MANIFEST DESTINY
(LAND + NATURE)
CITIZEN

PAD
CISTERN
PAD
CISTERN
CARRIAGE ROAD

"MONTICELLO"
HOME OF:
THOMAS JEFFERSON

1—From 1998–2001, William R. Morrish directed a comprehensive planning and urban design study called "Green By Addition. Recycling the First Ring Suburb". It analyzed the existing state and future viability of Minneapolis / St. Paul metropolitan area cities and first ring suburban neighborhoods built 1945–65. Results can be accessed under www.arch.virginia.edu / faculty / WilliamMorrish /

The problem

In 2004, Sunrise Trailer Court, the focus of this book, went up for sale. A for-profit developer made a bid on the property, but the eighteen families living at Sunrise as well as residents of the surrounding Belmont neighborhood, themselves under pressure from gentrification, went up in arms. Sensing an opportunity to make a difference here, HHGC moved quickly with a proposal to redevelop the site without displacing the current residents. The organization was backed by the neighborhood, secured funding from an anonymous donor, and succeeded in acquiring the land. But how to proceed from here? How to implement the challenge Habitat had set for itself?

Recent research has revealed that first ring suburbs, located between gentrifying central city neighborhoods and wealthy second ring suburban communities, contain the majority of a region's affordable housing.[1] Typically, this post-World War II residential fabric is made up of blocks of aging small homes averaging 1,000 square feet in size, interspersed with trailer courts. While not part of a larger metropolitan region, Charlottesville's Belmont, the neighborhood of Sunrise Trailer Court, exemplifies this type of community.

As land prices in these formerly fringe neighborhoods have increased, oversized sites formerly considered uninteresting—trailer parks, greyfields burdened by past industrial use, or sliver parcels with difficult dimensions—have become choice parcels for development. Though hundreds of people may live in a single trailer park, trailer parks usually belong to a single owner who can sell their land with no obligation to the families in residence, making the purchase of a large, contiguous property all the more attractive to developers. The combination of high land, construction and mortgage costs, pushed upward by the area's advantageous location relative to the central city, a mature canopy of trees, and access to community services, threatens trailer parks and their small home neighborhoods with imminent extinction.

Faced with these development pressures, the choices are not easy. If our goal is to build on the qualities of small home neighborhoods while accommodating more families, where do we fit these additional residents? If our goal is to preserve housing stock that is affordable to a diverse population, how do we address rising costs of living and shifting markets? If our goal is to make all housing, the old and the new, more energy efficient, how can we build design incentives into our proposals?

To generate solutions, we need to re-examine some of our static notions about housing development and design. What happens, for instance, when policy makers challenge the regulatory limit of one dwelling unit per parcel? What alternatives are there to requiring two parking spaces per household? How can a home be designed to adapt to change, rather than becoming a burden as soon as a certain period of the owner's life is past? How can occupancy be conceived as something other than the two diametrically opposed options of owning and renting?

Given the project at hand, perhaps we should begin by examining some of our static notions of trailer parks. Perhaps there is something to be learned from trailer parks in general, and from the community that has grown at Sunrise over the course of the past thirty years in particular.

Americans have a love-hate relationship with trailer parks. On the one hand, the romantic notion of an aerodynamic, silver coated, aluminum mobile home represents the ultimate American freedom: the independence of a movable platform with all the

2—Corey Kilgannon, "Trailer-Park Sales Leave Residents With Single-Wides and Few Options," New York Times, 18 April 2007.
3—Cheryl Sessions, ROC USA, cited in: Paul Bradley, "Gaining Ground," in: Shelterforce Online, Issue 149. Spring 2007.
4—http://www.census.gov/prod/2003pubs/c2kbr-32.pdf, retrieved May 2008.

modern conveniences of home, while roaming the American landscape, free from the constrictions of the conventional neighborhood. At the same time, trailers are the ultimate symbol of transience and trouble. Due in large part to the concentration of poverty in trailer parks and the frequently dismal quality of trailer construction, reinforced by movies such as "8 Mile" or images of the massive deployment of emergency shelters post-Katrina, trailers are generally considered the least desirable housing option.

Trailer living might not be as glamorous as the aerodynamic aluminum model suggests, but for many residents, owning or renting a trailer is preferable to perhaps the only available alternative, living in rental multi-family or public housing. A 14-by-75-foot trailer, although limited in size, does afford the same independence and autonomy as living in a single-family house. There is a piece of lawn, it is yours, and there is a front door that is yours too.

Back, then, to reconsidering our static notions about housing: Might the trailer park model actually exhibit features of a more affordable, dense, compact and sustainable form of development? Consider for a moment the following perspective.

Trailer parks represent a form of low-rise, high-density urbanism, something architects have sought with little success for decades as an alternate to both urban sprawl and high-rise living. Trailer parks engender forms of collective living that redefine conventional wisdom about public and private space, often by blending the two, as is manifest in the tight-knit community at Sunrise Trailer Court. Trailer parks demonstrate that compact living can work, very much in contrast to the "bigger is better" mentality that has driven the U.S. housing market for the last fifteen years. Trailer parks implement prefabricated building methods in multi-unit developments. While modular building has been in fashion for years, it has never been successfully incorporated in multi-family applications, except in trailer parks. Finally, trailer parks propose a form of tenure beyond the traditional model of home ownership—which, as we have also recently seen in the mortgage meltdown of 2008, is not tenable for all—by combining the ownership of the home with the leasing of the site.

In reality, despite the potential for innovation, few trailer parks resolve these issues in a satisfactory manner. Clues for a new housing development model, however, are most certainly there. Sensing these latent qualities was one reason for the enormous response to the Urban Habitats competition call.

What can trailer parks tell us about the state of housing in the U.S. in general? When *The New York Times* explored its city's metro-area trailer parks in 2007, it found that since 1990 the average household income had increased by 50% to $48,000, the median age had fallen from 61 to 48, and the percentage of college graduates had doubled to 18 percent.[2] Given current trends in the housing market, stagnating income and the rising cost of living, is it surprising that trailer parks constitute the greatest source of unsubsidized affordable housing in the United States today?[3] Is it surprising that, according to the 2000 U.S. Census, 7.6% of United States households—nearly 20 million Americans—live in mobile homes?[4]

Trailer parks may not be your housing of choice. However, in light of the urgent need to find new equitable housing development models, in particular for existing small-home neighborhoods and trailer parks, we cannot afford not to learn from Sunrise.

Urban Habitats

In re-examining static notions about housing, we became acutely aware of the role of language. "Housing", for instance, has a negative connotation in North America. It frequently goes hand-in-hand with "affordable" or "multi-family" to euphemistically describe low-income, government-assisted forms of dwelling, which, in turn, are considered inconsistent with the promise of the "American Dream." We want to upset some of these biases and long-standing preconceptions that are embedded in the language we use. As a result, *Growing Urban Habitats* is in large part about rephrasing questions and renaming issues. By doing so, we can begin to see the opportunities related to designing housing rather than the perceived problems.

Reframing language began with coining "Urban Habitats". "Urban" and "habitat" were combined to represent the goals of the two competition sponsors, HHGC and the CCDC. *Urban* reflects the philosophy of both organizations toward the future development of their hometown Charlottesville. In the context of rising living costs and continuing sprawl into the surrounding countryside, *urban* highlights the connection between the affordability of living and the many "Smart Growth" planning principles reflected in transit-oriented developments across the country. *Habitat*, on the other hand, is Latin for "it inhabits." The term is rooted in the science of ecology and refers to the place where particular species, human or other, live. In the context of development, *habitat* refers to two critical but often ignored principles for a project's long-term success: involving local residents and working with natural systems.

For HHGC, *Urban Habitats* resonated on several levels. First and foremost, *Habitat* coincided beautifully with the organization's well-established name. Founded in Georgia in 1976 as an ecumenical organization, Habitat for Humanity has since become an organization that builds housing throughout the world. Its key mission is to eliminate substandard housing by providing home ownership, its key strategy is the use of volunteer labor. Habitat targets families earning between 30% and 60% of the area median income (AMI), or a family income of $20,000 to $40,000 per year in Charlottesville, families that would have no chance of home ownership without Habitat. Once selected, families invest 200 hours of "sweat equity" on the construction site and in return receive an interest-free loan to be paid back over 25 years. The land and construction is funded through donations, both in cash and in kind.

While *habitat* tied into the organization's long and well-known history, *urban* reflected the recognition within its Charlottesville affiliate, founded in 1991, that a major change in its mode of operation was necessary: the organization had to move beyond building single-family homes. This had rather straight-forward origins: The cost of land in Charlottesville had simply grown too high to support single-family models, and building further and further outside of the city puts an enormous time and financial burden on families who need to commute to work. Yet, given that unskilled labor performs the bulk of the construction work for Habitat, restructuring the organization to build more urban housing—multi-story, multi-unit building types including households of various income levels—is a real logistical challenge. Adapting goals and transforming operations constitutes a major paradigm shift. *(See Epilogue for a discussion of further HHGC initiatives.)*

For the CCDC, the term *Urban Habitats* captured the essence of its two main missions since its founding in 2004. *Urban* reflects the Design Center's push for participatory development models to improve the quality of life in the city's neighborhoods, while *habitat* stands for building local capacities to develop affordable housing using green technologies. By sponsoring public programs featuring design and building methods employed elsewhere, the Design Center has sought to help local leaders, officials, developers, and residents find ways to implement infill housing using sustainable building techniques and "Smart Growth" development guidelines. As an example, in 2006 the City of Charlottesville and the CCDC organized the first ever Charlottesville Neighborhood Design Day, "In My Backyard!", officially launching the city's 2006 Comprehensive Planning Process. Public meetings were held at six locations, and teams of residents, professional designers, and city planners worked together to craft a vision for the future of the city. The CCDC is funded through grants and donations, or through joint programs, such as the various design competitions it has organized both for developers and the city.

In focusing on participatory design approaches, the CCDC is a part of a growing, nation-wide community design movement advocating more equitable, sustainable, and inclusionary urban development. Community design centers originated in the late 1960s, when grass roots initiatives tied to the Civil Rights movement opposed frequently destructive top-down government planning projects. In contrast, design centers worked to bring change to blighted inner cities by tying investment to active community involvement in the decision making process. Community design centers have since evolved and become less confrontational advocates of design. They are agents of change that involve all parties concerned, including municipalities, private developers, and residents. Today, the term "community design" describes a broad spectrum of socially responsible design practices, ranging from open networks such as Architecture for Humanity, known for organizing rebuilding efforts in post-catastrophic areas; to design-build projects such as Rural Studio based at Auburn University in Alabama; to initiatives such as The 1% Solution, which calls on architectural professionals to donate one percent of their time to pro bono work.

In outlining the competition program, culling through the competition submissions, and seeking out case studies of relevant projects in the United States, *Urban Habitats* proved an ever more valuable way to describe a multi-family housing approach that embraces expanded economic, social, physical, and ecological considerations. *Urban Habitats* is also an effective framework for integrating examples of the current nation-wide efforts to provide compact infill housing prototypes in existing urban neighborhoods. Expanded by an active verb, *Growing Urban Habitats* is about practices for making better places to live, about setting the foundations for it to happen, and about expanding the network of like-minded projects.

Structure

Growing Urban Habitats is intended to serve as both as a source book and as a how-to guide. As a source book of affordable, dense, compact, and sustainable housing, it aggregates Urban Habitats competition proposals and examples of projects from across the United States. As a how-to guide, it is not a cookbook of recipes to follow, but rather a collection of ways to re-think recurring issues in housing design. The book has been written not just for designers—architects, landscape architects, or planners—but for all citizens, civic organizations, housing advocates, elected representatives, municipal officials, academics, and developers undertaking efforts similar to the redevelopment of Sunrise Trailer Court.

We have structured *Growing Urban Habitats* by crossing our four development goals—*What We Want*, and four development strategies—*How We Get There*, to generate sixteen design opportunities. Goals, strategies and opportunities are summarized as a matrix in the table of contents.

Each of the book's four chapters is dedicated to defining and requalifying one urban habitat goal—affordable, dense, compact, or sustainable. In summary, to develop housing that is affordable for its residents, we need to lay *multiple foundations* in terms of financial and community support. Dense housing must always be realized as *integrated density*, that is part and parcel of its existing surroundings. Compact housing can be successful only on the basis of *dimensional diversity*, not repeated uniformity. And building sustainable housing demands both ecology and economy, *the two greens* essential to our lives.

Each urban habitat strategy aims to frame a particular, non-standard mind set for approaching these goals. *Counting again* encourages tinkering with the quantitative aspects of development. *Mixing it up* calls for transgressing traditional categories of use. *Expanding options* leads to new forms of multi-tasking. And *Building for change* describes ways to anticipate what cannot be planned nor controlled.

Each urban habitat goal is considered in light of the four urban habitat strategies. Each of the resulting, sixteen design opportunities describes alternate ways to consider recurring challenges in housing design. For instance, the *Expand Options : Share Boundaries* opportunity in the Compact chapter explores how the walls, fences, and thresholds between households, if intelligently designed, can give each family more space and privacy, not less, even in tight conditions. *Build for Change : Harness Seasons*, to take an example from the Sustainable chapter, looks at how buildings can move beyond their status of energy guzzlers and start generating their own power.

Each design opportunity is brought to life by two case studies. The first is a housing project built or proposed in the United States over the last fifteen years. We focused on American examples only since cultural and regulatory conditions in other countries make the translation to American conditions difficult. Some projects originate in a non-profit setting, while others are the product of for-profit development, and yet others are not projects at all but enlightened state or municipal policies that will allow better projects to be realized.

Many of the case studies demonstrate that lessons are being learned from existing situations, especially from small-scale neighborhoods that have evolved over time. A close look reveals that many of these areas support diverse lives and lifestyles. Frequently, these neighborhoods are the product of non-conforming urbanism. That is, their buildings could not be built according to current zoning code or building laws, since the spaces are too small or oddly dimensioned, or their uses are not allowed. Together, the selected projects reflect the range of efforts currently underway to create better affordable, dense, compact, and sustainable housing. The projects both literally and figuratively push the envelope, illustrating the potential for the phrase "urban habitats" to describe housing options in the changing economic, social, and physical context of our cities.

The second project illustrating a particular design opportunity is a proposal generated for the Urban Habitats competition. The thirteen (out of 164) Urban Habitats competition designs that are presented include the three finalist schemes and the four schemes awarded an honorable mention. The other proposals were selected by the authors based on the originality of the contribution and its relevance to the topics discussed. To tap into the pool of experience brought together by the Urban Habitats competition, we have added an extension to each scheme that traces the trajectory of these architects since 2005. Not surprisingly, many have pursued and have been able to realize projects of direct relevance to the urban habitat goals.

The four main chapters are preceded by the original Urban Habitats competition brief. An epilogue describing the developments at Sunrise Trailer Court since the completion of the competition in 2005 concludes the book.

The Urban Habitats Competition Brief
A Call For A New Development Model

Call For Entries

Habitat for Humanity of Greater Charlottesville, in partnership with the Charlottesville Community Design Center (CCDC) is pleased to announce an open ideas competition for the transformation of Sunrise Trailer Court into a vibrant, attractive urban community called Sunrise Park. In communities where Habitat is accustomed to building single-family homes, the shortage of affordable land requires Habitat affiliates to build at a higher density. Urban Habitats is in search of innovative models that provide sustainable, affordable multifamily housing.

The competition integrates affordable and market rate housing into a medium-density, mixed-income, mixed-use community. The goal is to generate culturally and climatically responsive architecture through a sustainable continuum, from site development to energy efficient unit operation. The proposals should provide compact efficient floor plans that utilize innovative building technologies.

Design concepts generated by the competition will provide the baseline for a new national model of community development. The results will guide non-profit organizations, private developers, or public / private partnerships in the redevelopment of trailer parks while providing affordable housing for the current trailer park residents.

This is an open ideas competition. Individuals, teams, academic studios and firms in architecture and its allied fields are encouraged to enter. Award funds in the amount of $25,000 will be distributed at the discretion of the jurors to a maximum of three Finalists displaying the highest level of response to the program challenges. Up to twelve Honorable Mentions will be awarded without compensation. Finalists will be invited to meet with the Board of Directors of Habitat for Humanity of Greater Charlottesville to discuss their ideas for Sunrise Park. Competition entries will be on public display at the Charlottesville Community Design Center during the month of September 2005. Individual Finalists may be asked to give a lecture in conjunction with the exhibit.

A companion publication using the principles developed in the competition program and demonstrated in selected competition entries will be produced by the Charlottesville Community Design Center in collaboration with the University of Virginia School of Architecture.

Aerial photograph of central Charlottesville

Habitat for Humanity

is a global organization with active partners in 100 countries. Locally, Habitat for Humanity of Greater Charlottesville has built nearly 50 low-income homes with families in Charlottesville, Albemarle, Buckingham, Greene and Louisa. HHGC was established in 1990, incorporated in 1991, and dedicated its first home in 1992. The local affiliate operates within the guidelines of the international organization. Ninety percent of all revenue goes to construction of houses in the abovementioned areas. Like all Habitat for Humanity affiliates, HHGC contributes 10 percent of its revenue to affiliates in other countries. Because construction costs differ, the local affiliate has funded more houses in Nicaragua and Haiti than in Charlottesville and Albemarle.

The Charlottesville Community Design Center

brings together citizens and design resources to promote discussion and debate toward creating an equitable, sustainable and beautiful community. CCDC's objectives include the provision of technical assistance to communities, groups and individuals seeking to promote their vision for the improvement of their neighborhood or community; the demonstration of applied good design through exhibitions, programs and model projects; and the creation of an ethical framework for development using the highest and best standards of design. CCDC works with builders, designers and local government to raise the quantity and quality of affordable housing and to propose practical, innovative, alternative design strategies that promote diversity and inclusion as well as increase energy efficiency and sustainability in all areas of development and urban planning. CCDC supports green building practices and encourages discussion and debate on relevant design issues.

Dear Entrants,

Every year, across the United States, affordable housing is lost and low-income families are displaced when trailer parks in high cost areas are bought for redevelopment. We want to prove that it is possible to transform a trailer park into a desirable, sustainable, and very livable urban neighborhood with diverse uses and income levels without displacing any of the trailer park residents.

Here in Charlottesville, we hope that a new development model for Sunrise Park will enable us to pursue additional similar sites. We propose to do this by using the very market pressures that threaten to displace trailer park residents in growing communities. Here is how it will work: Habitat donors will help fund the affordable housing at Sunrise Park, while the units that are sold on the open market will help fund the affordable housing for the next mixed use community we develop. This is just one of the aspects that we believe is unique about this concept for Habitat for Humanity.

Using the Habitat model at Sunrise, we will create homeownership opportunities for all eligible residents and provide low-cost rentals for the others. Including commercial space and selling condominium units at market value will create a stronger neighborhood and a financially sustainable model we can then use in other areas where low-income families are in danger of displacement. The mixed-income nature of Sunrise Park will fit right in with the growing economic diversity of the Belmont Neighborhood surrounding Sunrise. Young professionals who have fallen in love with our community will be the new neighbors of people who have lived at Sunrise for 30 to 40 years. That combination will form a strong neighborhood.

We need your help. Your designs for this neighborhood will be the tools that will help transform Sunrise Trailer Court into Sunrise Park and create a new model for the transformation of an American trailer park. For many years to come, when someone proposes a land use that would displace trailer park residents, or other low-income people anywhere in the United States, someone may stand up in a public hearing and say, "There may be a better way to do this. In Charlottesville, Virginia, a trailer park was redeveloped and no one was displaced."

Many people in Charlottesville know Sunrise as the trailer court with the great view of Monticello. In the future, people will know Sunrise Park as the innovative community with the great view of Monticello. And perhaps, when they think of good architecture in Charlottesville, both Monticello and Sunrise Park will come to mind.

Sincerely,
Habitat For Humanity Of Greater Charlottesville
Overton McGehee, Executive Director

Program Challenges

Entries will be judged for program compliance and the level of response to the following challenges:

:Design a vibrant, attractive urban neighborhood within the constraints of the suggested program

:Generate culturally and climatically responsive architecture

:Implement a sustainable continuum from site development to energy efficient unit operation using EarthCraft House®

:Create a community that integrates mixed-income and mixed-use principles within the guidelines of the Charlottesville Planned Unit Development Zoning Ordinance

:Design a diverse range of market rate housing and commercial space using compact floor plans

:Develop and utilize economical innovative building technologies

Jury Members

J. Max Bond Jr., FAIA, Partner,
Davis Brody Bond, New York
Lynne Conboy Vice Chair, HHGC,
Charlottesville
Teddy Cruz Principal, Estudio Teddy Cruz,
San Diego
Marion Chapman Dudley Resident,
Sunrise Trailer Court, Charlottesville
Nevil Eastwood Director of Construction,
Habitat for Humanity International
Julie Eizenberg AIA,Principal,
Koning Eizenberg Architecture,
Santa Monica
James P. Grigg AIA, Board Member,
HHGC, Charlottesville
Kendra Hamilton Charlottesville City
Council
John Woodriff Belmont Carlton
Neighborhood Association, Charlottesville

1—320 Bob Minzesheimer, "'Mr. Jefferson would be proud': Charlottesville is No. 1," USA Today, March 29, 2004

Goals

Affordable and Compact

Across the nation, Habitat for Humanity is struggling to fulfill its mission to provide affordable housing for low-income families due to the shortage of inexpensive, undeveloped land. Fast moving development has pushed Habitat affiliates to seek more creative solutions as it becomes increasingly difficult to build affordable homes.

A 2004 article in USA Today heralded Charlottesville, Virginia, as the most desirable place in the country to live in.[1] The sole concern or disadvantage the article cited is the relatively high cost of housing fueled by an influx of new residents to the area. Indeed, though the city's population has remained essentially constant over the past two decades, the population in surrounding Albemarle County has grown from 61,400 in 1986 to 90,400 in 2005, and nearby counties of Greene, Fluvanna, and Louisa have experienced similarly dramatic increases. As a consequence of this increased market demand, real estate values have risen to a point that it difficult for low-income families to afford the purchase of a home in our city or county. Workers have been forced to move away from the city's core in search of affordable housing, increasing their transportation costs. The lowest-income American families spend nearly 40% of every dollar earned on transportation, a phenomenon that emphasizes the need to increase housing density within the city.

Compact development is a fundamental challenge of the competition program. Habitat for Humanity will increase the allowable site density for Sunrise Park. Under the provisions of Charlottesville's Planned Unit Development (PUD) Zoning Ordinance, Habitat will develop an innovative mixed-income, mixed-use community that offers appealing market rate housing with compact efficient floor plans plus office and commercial retail space.

Sustainable Design

Habitat for Humanity of Greater Charlottesville will incorporate the best practices in design and construction with a culturally and climatically responsive architecture at Sunrise Park. Habitat's mission not only provides affordable home ownership opportunities to low-income families, but also assures that those families can afford the maintenance and operation costs of owning a home over the long term. The financial savings achieved through energy efficient design and construction are especially important to low-income families who can spend up to 17 percent of their income on energy bills. Successful designs will respond to the distinct climate of the region, minimize the negative impact of construction, encourage the use of public transportation and limit the use of natural resources.

The EarthCraft House® green building program is the new standard for sustainable development in the Charlottesville region. The recently developed EarthCraft House® multifamily housing guidelines will serve as the baseline for the sustainable aspect of the competition program. EarthCraft House® defines the following areas for consideration: site planning, building envelope and systems, lighting and appliances, resource design and building materials, waste management, indoor air quality, indoor and outdoor water management, construction and user operations.

Site Description and History

Sunrise Trailer Court, a 2.3-acre site in the Belmont Neighborhood of Charlottesville Virginia, sits at the edge of a commercial / industrial area near downtown Charlottesville's Central Business District and Interstate 64. Bounded by Carlton Avenue to the north, Nassau Street to the east, Midland Street to the south and Rives Street to the west, the property consists of six contiguous parcels: two parcels with 23 mobile home spaces, three parcels with three rental units consisting of one house and one duplex apartment, and one vacant parcel. A modern warehouse / office building sits across Carlton Avenue, and another six-acre mobile home park faces the site across Nassau Street. Modest single-family homes line Rives Street and Midland Street. The site slopes moderately from north to south, and the immediate area is currently zoned for mixed-use development.

The parcels occupy an entire city block except for two corners. A small walk-up convenience store sits to the southwest, while two significant detached residences occupy the northwest corner. One of these, the Young Office Building, is a relic of the J.S. Young Company, a tannin extract plant that opened in 1916 across Carlton Avenue on the present-day site of the Barnes Lumber Company. (A Spanish-style house that housed the company manager has since been demolished). The brick structure—one of the only Jacobean Revival buildings in Central Virginia—is protected from demolition thanks to its listing on the National Register of Historic Places as part of the Charlottesville Multiple Resource Area. The half-timbered house just to the east of the Young building also holds historic significance, and Habitat intends to preserve it as well.

New duplexes and multifamily housing units have been built on Carlton Avenue just west of the site. The H.T. Ferron Company's concrete plant lies diagonally across Carlton Avenue and east of Nassau Street. The plant mixes concrete and produces concrete block, and the concrete delivery trucks it dispatches combined with other nearby commercial and industrial uses generate considerable heavy truck traffic on Carlton Avenue and Nassau Street. The property lies 2,000 feet from the Rivanna Water and Sewer Authority's wastewater treatment plant on Moore's Creek.

In 1955, Sunrise Trailer Court was developed by Julius "Red" Lively who has lived in Charlottesville all his life. His family owned most of the land from Meade Avenue down to Moore's Creek. When he returned from the Army in 1947, he began building houses. Lively says, "I took a wild gamble," starting a trailer court where he used to cut hay.

In 2003, Mr. Lively put Sunrise Trailer Court on the market. The property offered a highly sought-after building site within the city limits. Habitat began to investigate a development model where it could replace the housing, increase the density and not displace any of the current residents. While Habitat researched the financial feasibility of their proposal, a commercial development group put Sunrise under contract, stipulating that the residents of the trailer park would be evicted 120 days after rezoning to make way for their upscale redevelopment of the site. With the danger of being displaced, relocation became a serious problem for many Sunrise residents. Other trailer parks in the area are full, and the age of many Sunrise trailers makes it illegal to relocate them (in the cases where they could physically sustain a move). Further, many Sunrise residents cannot afford to pay the market rent of $600 to $700 per month for an efficiency apartment.

In 2004, the Belmont Neighborhood Association announced their opposition to the displacement, causing the development group to withdraw its plan and

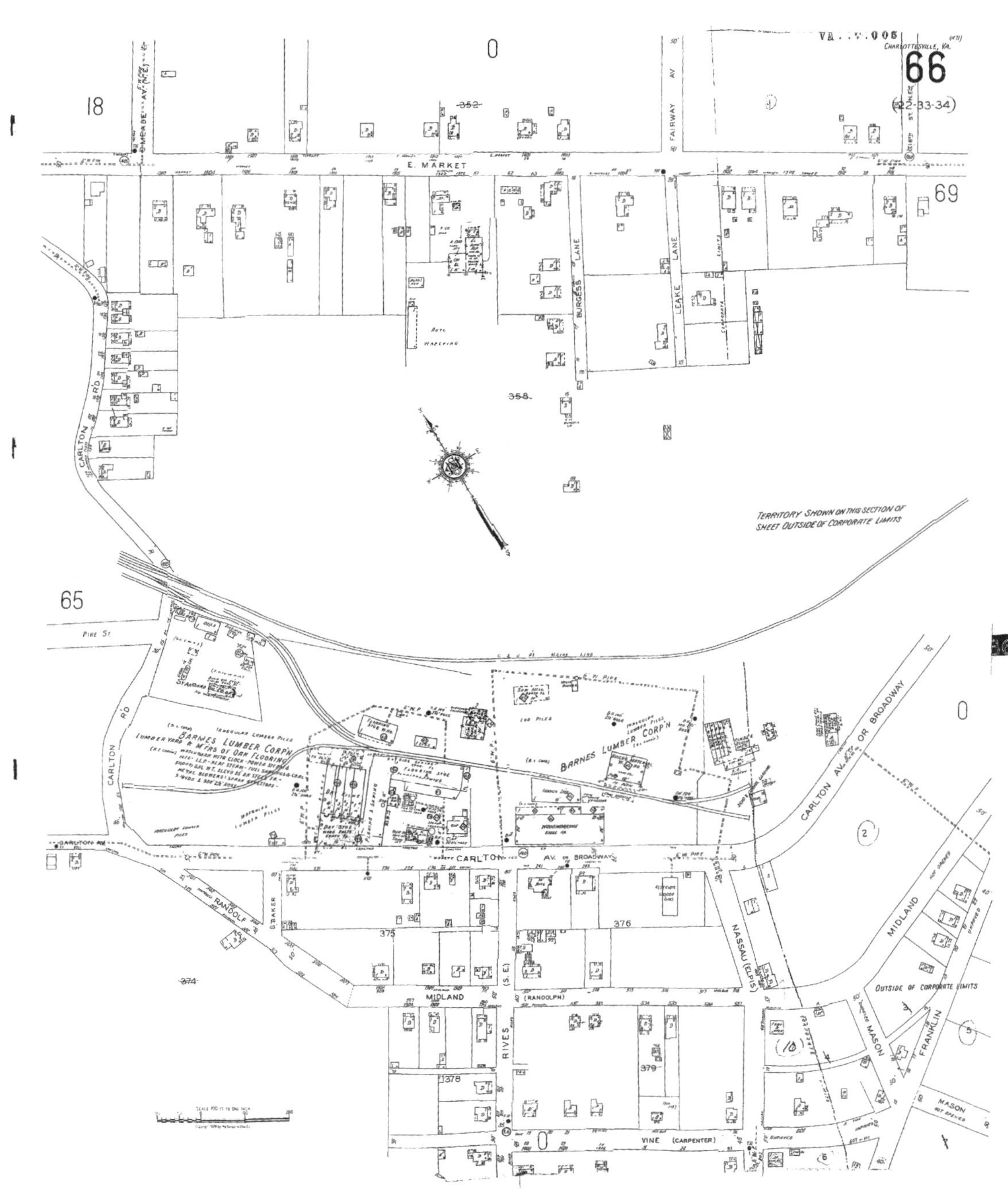

Sanborn map of 1950.

turn the contract over to Habitat for Humanity of Greater Charlottesville. Habitat purchased the property in November 2004, with the promise to provide affordable housing to the current Sunrise Trailer Court residents. None of the current residents will be expected to pay more than 30 percent of their income in rent or mortgage payments.

18 families live in Sunrise's trailers, and each will be given the opportunity to live in Sunrise Park. About half of the residents are elderly and some have lived there for many years. The trailer homeowners rent the spaces their mobile homes occupy for $235 per month, making it the least expensive trailer park rent in the area.

Like many cities and towns, the City of Charlottesville has recently experienced major increases in housing costs and an influx of new residents looking for homes in a compact urban setting. As Urban Habitats was gearing up, the City finished a revision to the city-wide comprehensive plan that sought to integrate smart growth and sustainability policies and regulations. With the help of neighborhood groups and citizens, the city completed the plan and prepared a policy platform for accommodating market forces and social

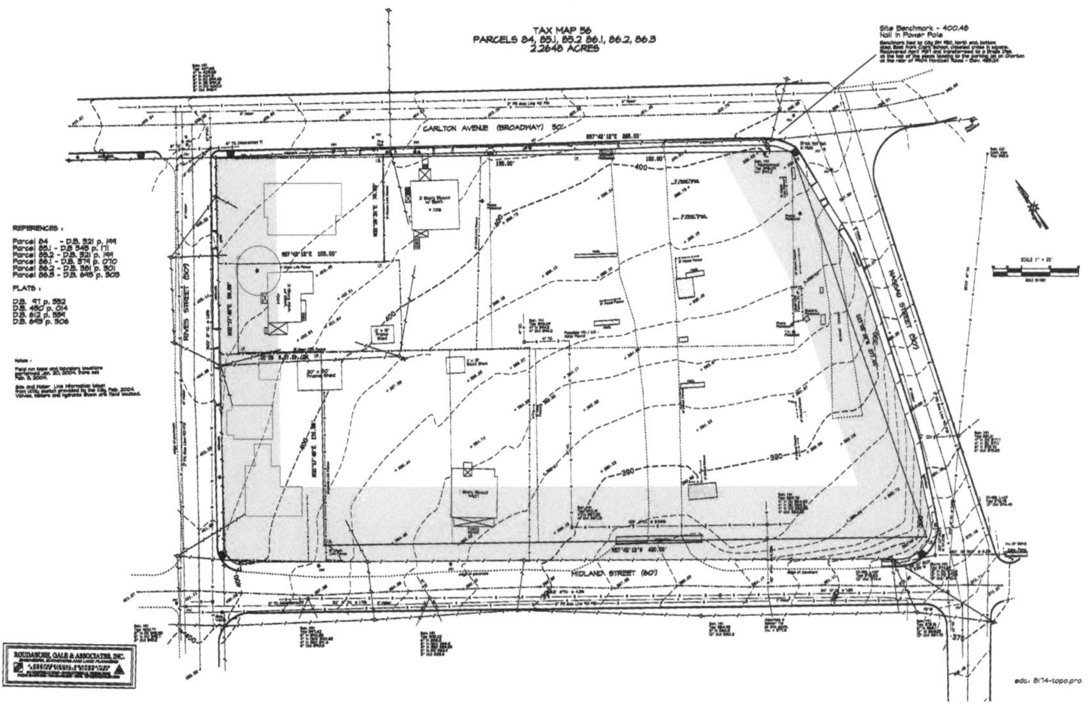

Site survey of 2004, showing existing parcels, buildings, and topography.

challenges. The plan called for rezoning the city's gray-field commercial properties, empty light-industrial brownfields, trailer courts and large residential parcels—at least those located on or adjacent to major city arterial corridors and containing transit routes and commercial activity. The resulting increases in density are intended to accommodate a combination of infill development, including mixed-use medium commercial and multi-family housing.

One of the sites affected was the Sunrise Trailer Court. Initial calculations suggested that the city's development polices would allow the building of up to 72 units on the 2.3-acre site. This maximum projected build-out provided the baseline for the Urban Habitats program —a decision that added to the perception among civic leaders, neighborhood residents, and local housing providers that the competition was a crucial step for translating the intentions of the revised plan into reality. The program demonstrates the maximum build-out for the site given the existing Planned Unit Development zoning criteria in the City of Charlottesville. The program requirements have been determined by Habitat for Humanity to be the baseline for meeting the expectations of the Sunrise Park project.

Aerial photograph of 2000, showing Sunrise Trailer Court between industrial uses, small homes, and trailers.

Program

Figure-ground plan of existing condition. Dashed line indicates the extent of the site.

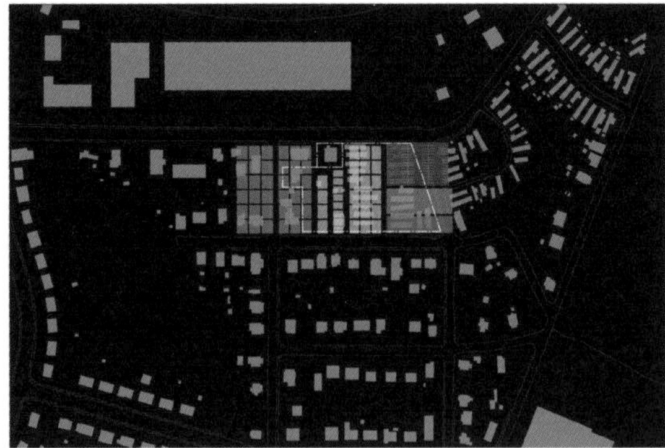

Overlay of competition program in square feet. Market-rate housing (red), Habitat housing (orange), parking (grey), open space (green), commercial space (blue).

Affordable / Habitat Housing

Habitat for Humanity Homeowner Units: These must be simple for volunteers to build. The 3-bedroom units may be one-story (1170sf) or two-stories (1270sf). The cost of building materials and subcontracted services should be considered. These will be sold to households that earn $16,000 to $30,000 annually. Minimum number of units required: 18.

Habitat for Humanity Rental Units: These are one-story (600sf) efficiency units provided for elderly or disabled Sunrise Residents. Units should be designed to Habitat's Accessible Standards and may be built by volunteers or contractors. Minimum number of units required: 8

Affordable Condominiums: These units will probably be built by contractors, but volunteer labor could be explored. The 3-bedroom condominiums (1200sf) will be sold to households that earn $30,000 to $50,000 annually. Minimum number of units required: 4.

Total (maximum) number of Habitat units: 36.

Market Rate Housing

Condominiums: These units will be sold on the open market to provide a diverse income mix to the neighborhood and assure a sustainable development strategy. These units may be one and / or two-stories. The condominiums will be sold to households with an annual income of $50,000 and up. Number of units required: (18) 2-bedroom units (1200sf), (18) 3-bedroom units (1400sf).

Total number of market rate units: 36.

Commercial Office / Retail

Commercial space should be suitable for retail, small business or social service offices. Total floor area required: 10,000 sf.

Site Development

Community Landscape: The landscape components may be built by volunteers and/or contractors. The plan must include at least 15 percent or approximately 15,000sf of community space in order to obtain Planned Unit Development rezoning for the 2.3-acre site. A larger percentage of green space is encouraged. The plan also must include a small playground for children who are too small to walk to Rives Park without a parent. Bicycle racks should be provided. Note: parking is not included in this calculation.

Parking: Parking requirements encourage the use of public transit, reduce construction costs for on-site parking structures, and reduce cost of living expenses related to transportation for the residents. The residents of Sunrise Trailer Court have easy access to public transportation, minimizing the amount of parking needed on site. Curbside parking, sufficient for commercial uses, may be added along both sides of Carlton Avenue. All on-site parking must be at grade, either in open lots or under second story construction.

Total number of on-site parking spaces required: 90.

115
115
OCT
1607 400th

VEGA
05
79
2007

View of the pool, center of the new Sunrise.

View of the trailer park, approaching from Rives Street.

konyk
Trailer Park

The Urban Habitats competition proposal by konyk of Brooklyn, New York makes a beautiful case that trailer parks have qualities that need to be built upon, not disregarded. konyk points out that trailer parks are the greatest and most accessible way to provide affordable housing in the United States today.

In fact, trailer parks hold the clues for achieving the four urban habitats goals. Trailers are affordable by virtue of their serialized construction. Trailer parks exemplify a type of dense, low-rise urbanism. Because of their precisely calibrated dimensions, trailers prove that compact living is possible. Finally, were the methods of prefabrication to embrace state-of-the-art, energy-saving technologies used, trailers would be today's show-case sustainable dwellings.

What trailer parks need, konyk argues, is an image overhaul.

For the re-vamped Sunrise, the architects have selected a slender Thunderbird to replace the bulky single-wides, and instead of the oversized cars, each resident drives a spiffy, space- and fuel-saving Smart. With its spiral ramp ascending around a Caribbean-style swimming pool, the architects were surely aware it would not be selected for realization. But with its literally over-the-top approach—the views from the ramp must be spectacular—the image of the ramp and the pool sticks in our minds and we find ourselves wondering: Why not?

In this way, the project lets us question long-standing assumptions about trailer parks in particular and housing in general. Isn't the inherent mobility of a trailer park's residents a good thing in light of the highly mobile lives we all live? Shouldn't we celebrate the possibilities of construction even when dealing with affordable housing?

Honorable Mention

Team Members
Craig Konyk, Timo Koeppe, Jonathan Louie, Ivan Sorensen

Statement
We base our proposal on the premise that as a model of affordable and sustainable housing, the American Trailer Park is almost OK. Our proposal is to improve upon the existing model of the Trailer Park, adding amenities and support facilities as well as integrating a new idea about the landscape and urban living. Our hope is to create an environmentally sustainable community.

The Trailer Park, like the Drive-In Movie Theater, is a uniquely American invention. The most common example of the "machine in the garden", the Trailer Park embodies a direct relationship to nature, a sense of community, suburban / urban frontierism and the allure of temporal living. We feel that the Trailer Home represents the most democratic and accessible model of home ownership. It is affordable and adaptable. What is more, the trailer constitutes a perfect urban module; the multiplication of the unit forms a first town or pre-urbanism. And at a cost of under $60,000 for each new housing unit, the trailer home represents the best value over any other available housing model, both in terms of cost and ease of site delivery.
We propose using the Airstream International CCD Model, the interiors of which are designed by the San Francisco architect Christopher C. Deam. This model, which borrows design features from Japanese Capsule Hotels, is a modern update on the classic Airstream model. And with a manufacturers' suggested retail list price of $57,233, it represents, we think, the most affordable and accessible solution for low- to moderate- income housing.

Jury Comments
The jury likes the spirit of this design. Even though it does not address the realities of the programming, it reminds us that not only people are being displaced but also a typology that has been dear to American culture. As the jury said, "Competitions are about invention. Let's not forget about joy."

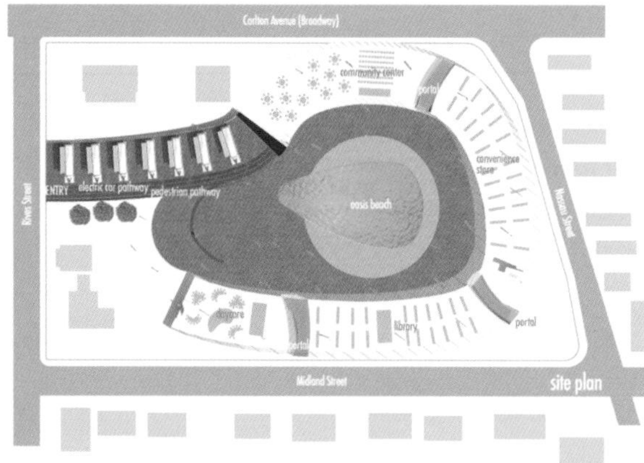

Ground floor plan.

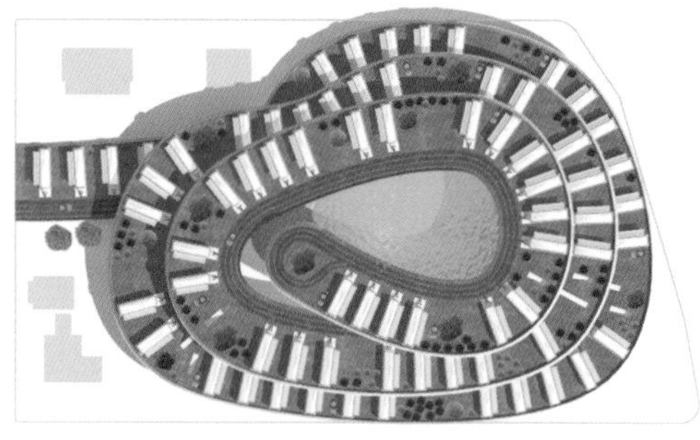

Roof plan.

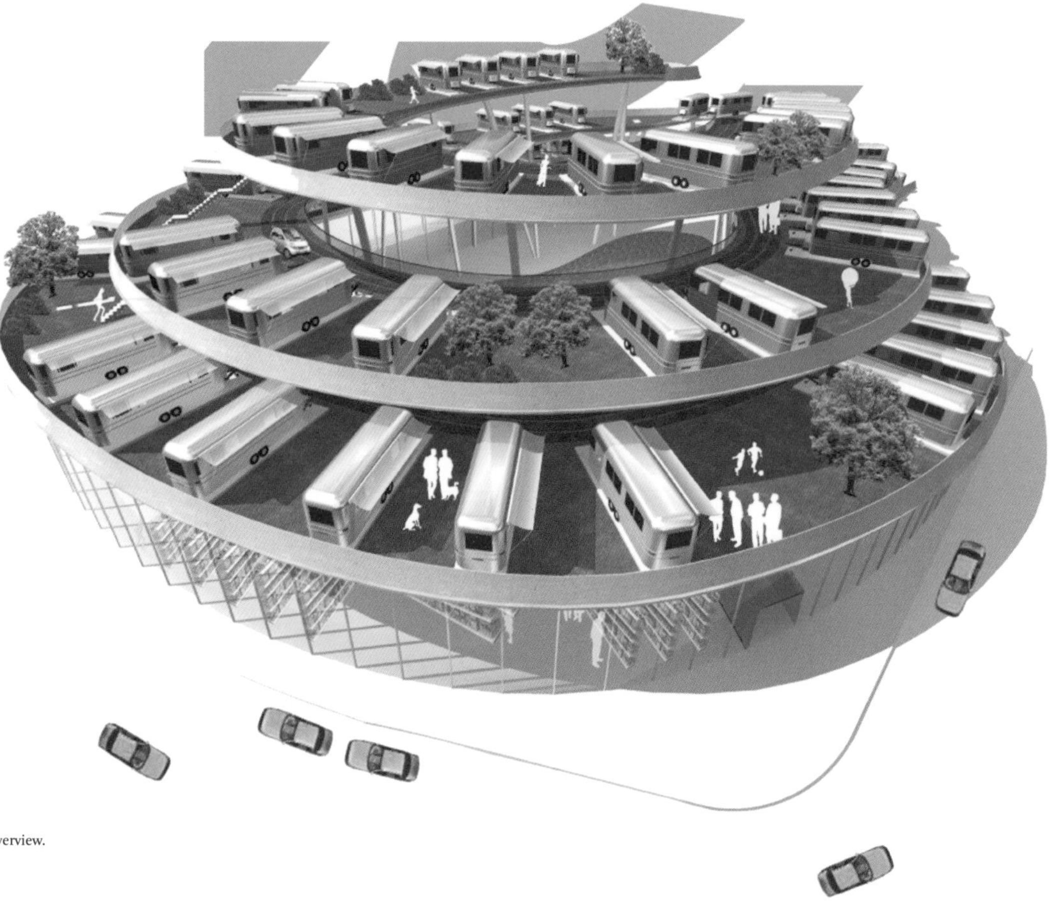

Overview.

Extension
konyk

konyk was founded by Craig Konyk in Brooklyn, New York in 1989. konyk seeks innovative approaches to architecture at multiple scales, multiple senses. New programs, new arrangements and new domestic situations create openings for novel approaches to architecture and its participation in urbanism. konyk seeks to exploit these new opportunities and allow them the liberation of self-expression.

What role does / did the Urban Habitats competition play within your practice?

In general, in our practice we strive to propose somewhat unconventional ideas and see if we can realize them.

Competitions allow us to propose ideas that are not normally associated with the discussion of what constitutes an "architecture". The Urban Habitats competition allowed us to liberate an idea that had been percolating in the studio for a number of years, the idea that any extant semi-urban construct should be considered on its own merits. In this case, we felt that the American Trailer Park doesn't have to be viewed as a negative. In fact, it has a rich and storied postwar history.

Have you been able to further develop the concepts put forward in your entry?

We are pursuing our interest in prefabricated houses, for instance with the UP!house, a minimal dwelling that is derived from automotive fabrication methodologies. We have continued to explore different related housing types, such as the startUPstudios project for San Francisco, developed for the Octavia Boulevard Infill Housing Competition in 2005, and the Fail-Safe Housing proposal for New Orleans for the Tulane / Architectural Record sponsored Multiple Housing Competition. In terms of new forms of cohabitation, we recently developed an idea for the weekly arts guide Time Out New York for housing we called "Commune-ism", where four families shared one building, each with separate private quarters, but sharing public spheres—a city block compressed into a building.

Have you been able to realize any projects that are related to the Urban Habitats project, be it in scale, approach, client, philosophy?

We are designing two artists' residences with a gallery space in an existing warehouse shell in Greenpoint, Brooklyn—coincidently for the same building that was used for the "Commune-ism" project. We should be under construction by the early fall of 2008.

In 2005, the Octavia Boulevard Housing Design Competition sought proposals for a 15-by-120-foot site in San Francisco available due to the demolition of an elevated highway. konyk proposed 72 startUPstudios, incubator live-work spaces that share lobbies and other amenities.

BELOW
Aerial perspective of the startUPstudios.

BOTTOM
Impression of the building's lobbies and cafes at street-level.

Chapter 1—

Affordable Multiple Foundations

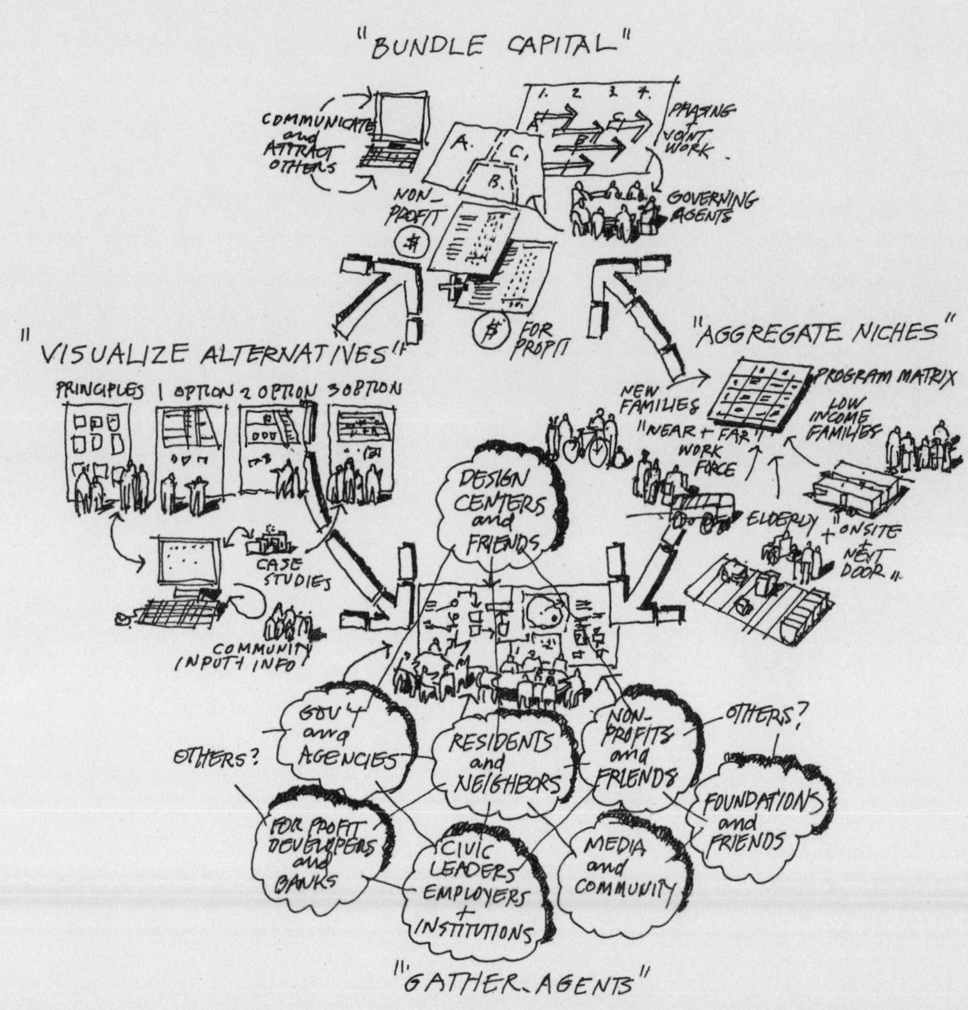

More often that not, groups come together with the purpose of stopping things rather than the purpose of starting things. One of the challenges that we face as architects is to frame that debate; to take the energy groups gather to prevent something from happening and mobilize it for the creation of a fundamentally different proposition, the creation of an innovative solution.

William Williams, Architect and Associate Professor, University of Virginia, Growing Urban Habitats Symposium, September 2005

Most new development projects lack a community process, even when rezoning is required. In the best case, a typical community design process might suggest the following trajectory: Call a neighborhood meeting to gather concerns and goals from the neighborhood. Provide pizza and soft drinks. Designer and developer listen to the neighborhood concerns. Designer returns to office and works hard to satisfy the neighborhood concerns, while creating a proposal that also satisfies the many other development criteria. As the project continues, the development team continues to make hard choices, sharpening their pencils to the point that the neighborhood may not recognize their input in the final product. Neighborhood gets angry, developer gets frustrated.

Growing urban habitats, however, needs productive community involvement, as the process of transforming non-standard sites into affordable homes and gardens is a complicated one. It takes considerably more up-front work than developing a standard, merchant-built project, both in terms of design study, and programming and financing. To strike the right deal, city officials, residents, architects, and developers need to work together to explore options. And most likely, the funding will only work by combining multiple sources, including: bank loans, government grants, foundation gifts, social service programming budgets, neighborhood social capital, volunteer labor and family sweat equity, to name just a few. The challenge is to deploy these various resources in service of a shared vision that will maximize social and ecological benefits. This is what we mean when we talk about laying multiple foundations.

So, what if we forget the pizza? What if we consider that development is not a series of sequential "hearing" steps, but rather an active and open design process that helps the various constituent interests step back and frame the larger questions, such as "How do we really want to live? What are the qualities of the community that we want to create? How can we work together to make a complex project happen?"

This chapter outlines design opportunities related to laying multiple foundations.

Working with people we haven't worked with before

Recent development initiatives in regions that have lacked the attention of planners provide excellent examples of the strong vision and active community engagement involved in laying multiple foundations. Proposed changes to zoning procedures put forward by Casa Familiar, a human services organization active in the San Diego border neighborhood of San Ysidro, and recent housing developed by the Native American tribal Ohkay Owingeh Housing Authority in New Mexico, show that building innovative affordable housing frequently requires re-designing the underlying regulatory and financial framework.

The San Diego neighborhood of San Ysidro is characterized by rapid ad-hoc growth unaccounted for by current zoning regulations.

The San Diego neighborhood of **San Ysidro** is located on one of the world's busiest international borders, between the United States and Mexico. Its population is primarily of Hispanic origin, the buildings are a mixture of small homes and service businesses on narrow lots. San Ysidro has little vacant land but is experiencing rapid growth. Given this situation, **Casa Familiar** is aiming to re-jig the policies that govern how housing gets built. Led by director Andrea Skorepa and designer David Flores, the organization has been collaborating with architect and Urban Habitats competition juror Teddy Cruz, principal of **Estudio Cruz**, since 2003 in order to enable the gradual densification of a 25-block area, and avoid large-scale development which would likely displace current residents.

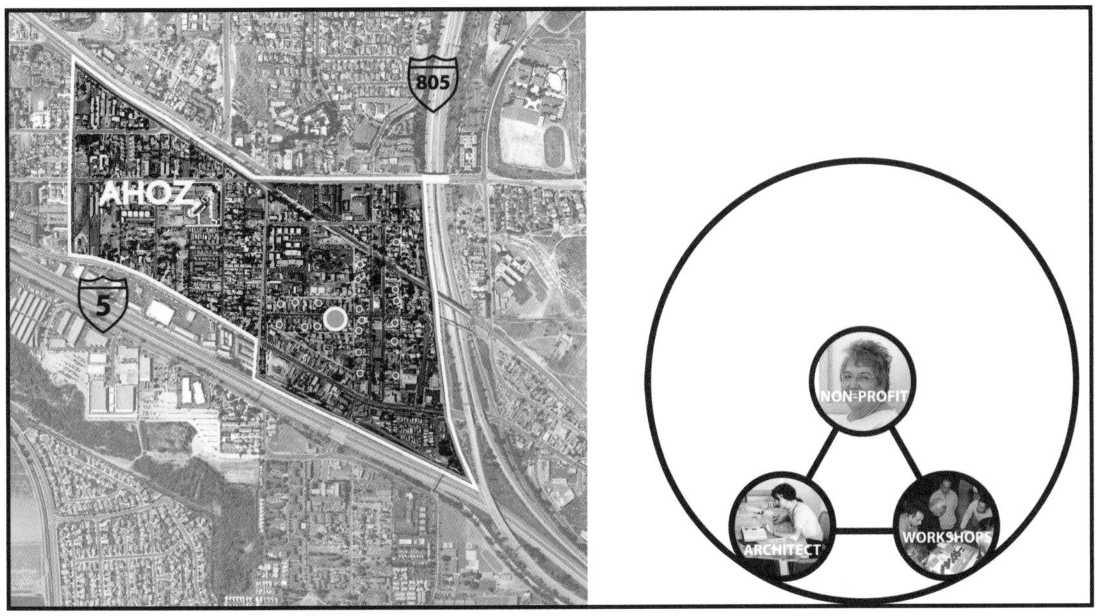
805
AHOZ
5
NON-PROFIT
ARCHITECT
WORKSHOPS

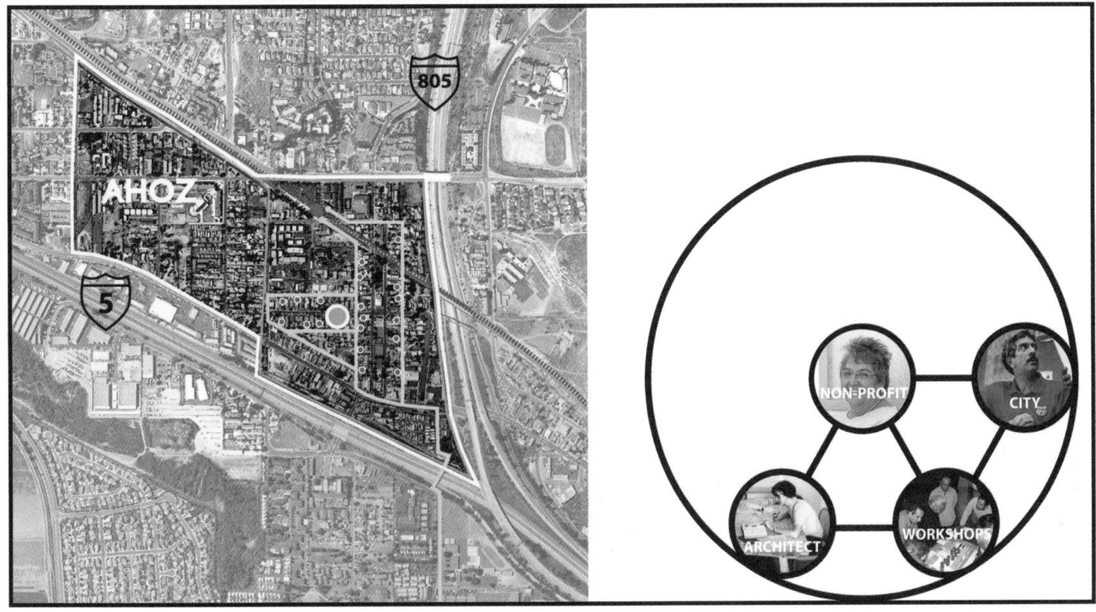
805
AHOZ
5
NON-PROFIT
CITY
ARCHITECT
WORKSHOPS

Estudio Cruz' collaborations with Casa Familiar reveal how by not allowing for the gradual alteration of existing properties, current zoning regulations actually favor large-scale new construction and encourage the gentrification of the neighborhood. Cruz has developed an alternative approach: he sees the existing complexity of the small-home neighborhood, where residents strive to add living and work space to their homes, as the starting point for further development. This approach is both messier and more opened-ended than a clean-slate method, as it requires examining the changing needs, lifestyles and life cycles of the neighborhood's primarily low-income families. Only then can the needs be expressed in architectural form, and a project realized through community organization.

To accomplish this agenda, Estudio Cruz and Casa Familiar reposition the roles of the City, the developer and the non-profit organizations. They are seeking to insert a specific zoning process known as an overlay district to support the community's step-by-step redevelopment through what they refer to as "bottom-up agency." The proposal is currently being discussed with City officials. It is likely to be adopted, and if it is, all infill development projects within the overlay district would be managed locally by a non-profit agency.

In San Ysidro, Casa Familiar would lead the process for design, construction and growth based on four "micro-policies." These form the quantitative and qualitative foundations for short-term construction projects as well as long-term growth. The steps would be as follows: First, Casa Familiar coordinates the documentation of key neighborhood information, for instance, by mapping existing additions to residences which have been built by owners without first having obtained a permit. Second, it works with City Hall to recalibrate land use policies and development regulations, acting as a kind of little city hall, with the goal of legalizing much of the pre-permit construction while envisioning future growth and enabling more mixed-use opportunities than would otherwise be possible. The third step is providing design assistance to the owners, in order to take advantage of alternate construction techniques and nonstandard unit layouts. Finally, Casa Familiar acts as a lender, breaking down large loans into multiple micro-loans, and organizing social programs to assist families working in their home. In summary, Casa Familiar, as facilitator and manager, is laying the multiple foundations that will enable San Ysidro to grow in an equitable way.

OPPOSITE, TOP
San Ysidro, Micro-Policy 1
In a first step, the non-profit Casa Familiar works as a think-tank and documents the neighborhood's existing non-conforming uses, including all non-permitted additions and mixed-uses.

OPPOSITE, BOTTOM
San Ysidro, Micro-Policy 2
In a second step, the municipality allows a new category of zoning. It legalizes "ad hoc" buildings through an Affordable Housing Overlay Zone (AHOZ) and authorizes their replacement by new ones.

NEXT PAGE, TOP
San Ysidro, Micro-Policy 3
In a third step, Casa Familiar operates as "little city hall", facilitating the design and construction of new additions. The municipality pre-authorizes drawings for plug-in prototypes and allows the non-profit to manage the pre-approved construction permits.

NEXT PAGE, BOTTOM
San Ysidro, Mirco-Policy 4
In a final step, Casa Familiar operates as a facilitator of economic growth. It manages micro-credits by taking on the liability of a large construction loan. From this umbrella loan, it transfers funds to participating residents, converting sweat equity into economic value.

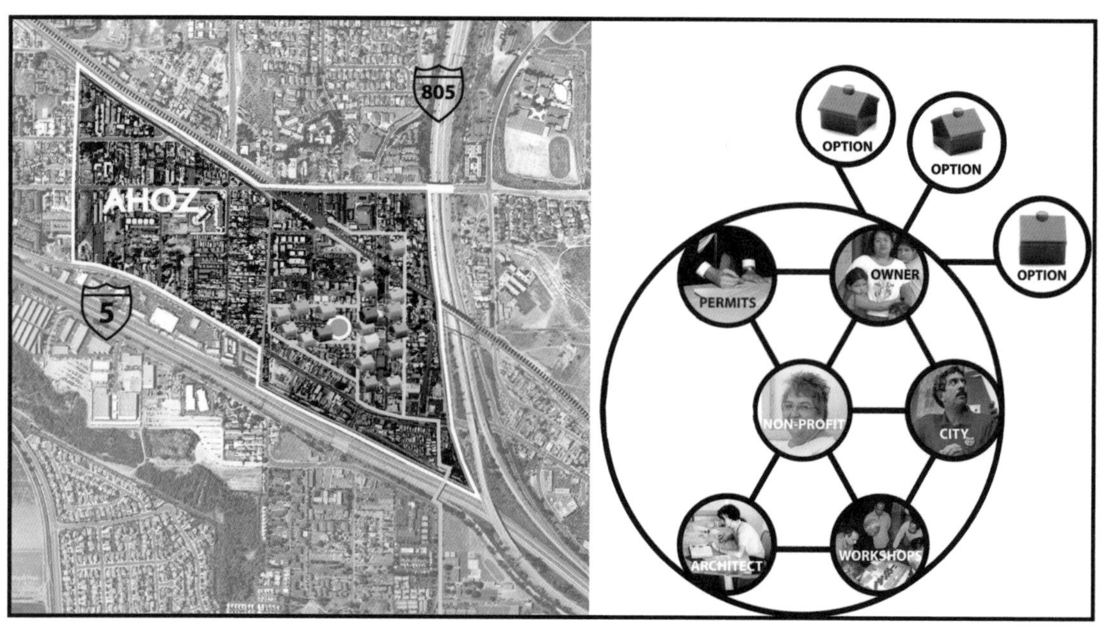
805
AHOZ
5
OPTION
OPTION
OPTION
PERMITS
OWNER
NON-PROFIT
CITY
ARCHITECT
WORKSHOPS

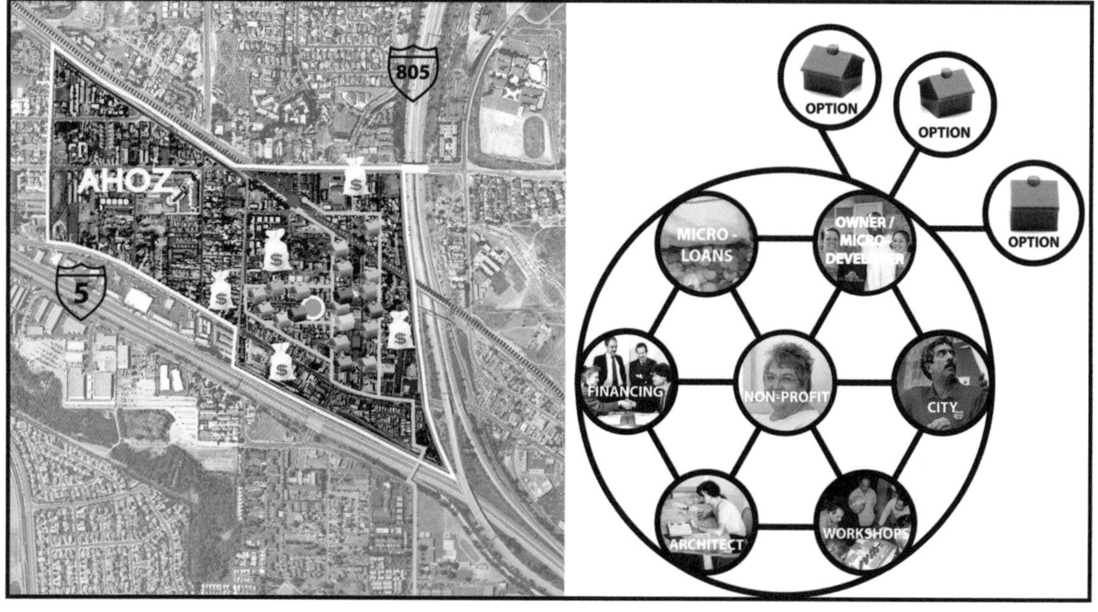
805
AHOZ
5
OPTION
OPTION
OPTION
MICRO - LOANS
OWNER / MICRO - DEVELOPER
FINANCING
NON-PROFIT
CITY
ARCHITECT
WORKSHOPS

BELOW
The tribal trust lands of northern New Mexico are characterized by sprawling, single-family development. Tsigo bugeh village, shown below, sets new standards for multi-family living.

In Northern New Mexico, too, there are changes affecting how housing is being built and financed. **Tsigoh bugeh village** is a complex of 40 townhomes and a community center completed in 2003 at Ohkay Owingeh, a reservation on tribal trust land, located 30 miles north of Santa Fe, New Mexico. The Pueblo is located in the Española Valley on prime agricultural land at the confluence of the Rio Grande and Rio Chama. A sprawling, automobile culture has come to dominate life here, and tribe members depend on cars to get to jobs and schools.

Tsigo bugeh Village was a first for the tribal **Ohkay Owingeh Housing Authority**: the first housing development experience, and rental, multi-unit housing at that. The key motivation for the project was to use quality rental housing to reduce the number of families on waiting lists for housing, a situation made much worse because access to conventional mortgage lending for families living on tribal trust lands is very difficult. Two key figures behind the project were Tomasita Duran, a tribe member and executive director of the Housing Authority, and architect Jamie Blosser of Santa Fe. Blosser's participation was funded by the Frederick P. Rose Architectural Fellowship, which promotes the value of quality design and green building in affordable housing.

The first task was to lay the foundation for a culturally and environmentally sustainable design. The tribe engaged in a larger planning effort and in 2004 completed a master plan, designed with a community-based process by Moule & Polyzoides Architects and Urbanists of Pasadena, California. Its land use plans incorporated pedestrian-oriented villages and Smart Growth principles. The plan builds upon the ancient, community-oriented settlement patterns of the Ohkay Owingeh by proposing more compact and walkable urban patterns that respect tradition, and provides a sense of cohesiveness through design guidelines for new construction and rehabilitation. For Tsigoh bugeh Village, the challenge was to inspire future residents to see the potential of multi-family housing. At first, most were skeptical of living in such close quarters, as they had grown used to the double-wide trailers and single-family HUD bungalows spread over tribal land on 100' by 100' lots.

The design team proposed a layout and massing that were inspired by the original buildings at the Pueblo, located half a mile north of the new Village, one of the oldest continuously occupied places in North America.

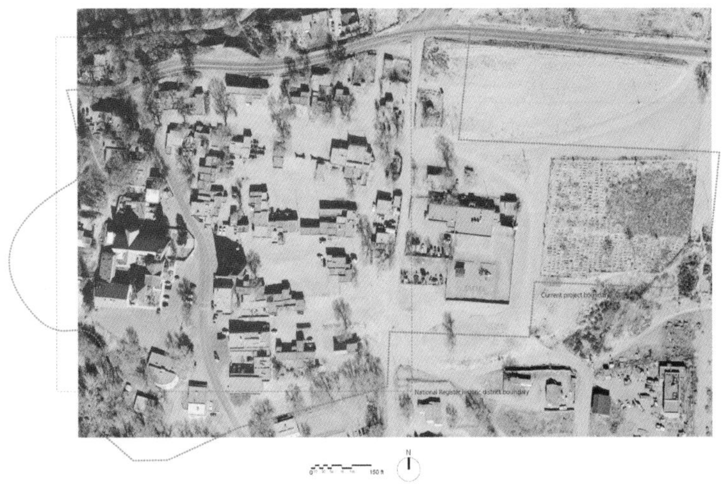
N
150 ft

future single family homes
future commercial
summer solstice
equinox
plaza
community center
market
future community use
community park
plaza

Like the traditional ceremonial plaza, the new main plaza was aligned directly east-west, to the equinox. The traditional design was perceived by many tribal members to be outdated, however. Blosser and Duran proceeded to engage the tribe's elders. By bringing questions related to family, social and spiritual values into the discussion, the residents began to understand the benefits of the layout and contributed to it. Blosser recalls,

During the community design meetings, we learned that on the traditional feast days the women typically worked in cramped kitchens preparing food for hundreds of people, which was then served throughout the day in cramped dining and living rooms. We designed open floor plans to accommodate more flexibility on these busy days.

The project architects, **Van Amburgh + Pares** of Santa Fe, translated these goals into plans for buildings and open space in a language that refers to traditional pueblo architecture, yet responds to present-day needs in terms of accessibility, unit size and layout. The plan also allowed for such elements as hornos, the traditional bread ovens built of adobe and stone, to be built throughout the new plaza, to encourage baking bread and pastries for the feast days.

The second task was to lay the project's complex financial foundations. It took seven different financing sources to come up with the more than $4.8 million required to build the project, which comprises rental housing at both market-rate and subsidized levels for those earning between 40 and 60 percent of the area median income (AMI). Blosser recalls the key role that federal funding played in this process, but underlines how these funds were used in unprecedented ways:

None of it could have been done without seed money from the Native American Housing and Self Determination Act and the Rural Housing and Economic Development grant. With that kind of seed money we were able to raise more than $2.3 million in investor equity. We were also able to come away with less than 5 percent long-term debt. That allowed us to then tailor rents to the tribe's needs.

Duran figured out how to move from HUD-focused housing to working with new partners and leveraging funds. As an example, the New Mexico Mortgage Finance Authority's RiskSHARE loan had never been used on tribal land,

OPPOSITE
Aerial view of the historic Pueblo. Red line indicates current rehabilitation project boundary.
Blue line indicates National Register historic district boundary.

OPPOSITE BELOW
The site plan for Tsigoh bugeh Village was inspired by the layout of the historic Pueblo. Like its ceremonial plaza, the Village's main plaza is oriented to the equinox. Its axis converges on the community center with the axis of the minor plaza.

BELOW
Van Amburgh + Pares Architects' sketches facilitated the discussion of key design ideas with future residents. All dwellings front onto a plaza, and unit interiors are generous and open from front to back.

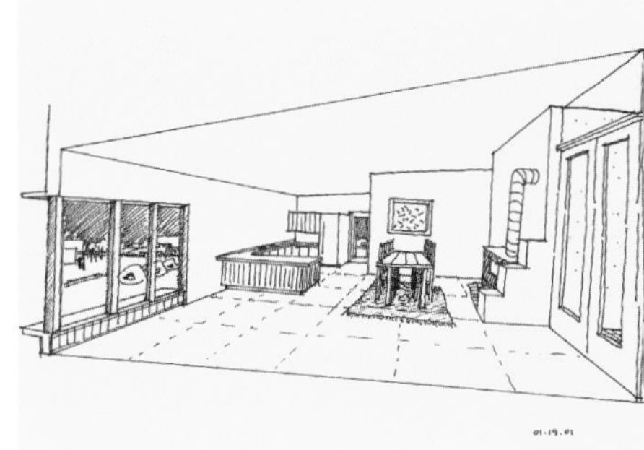

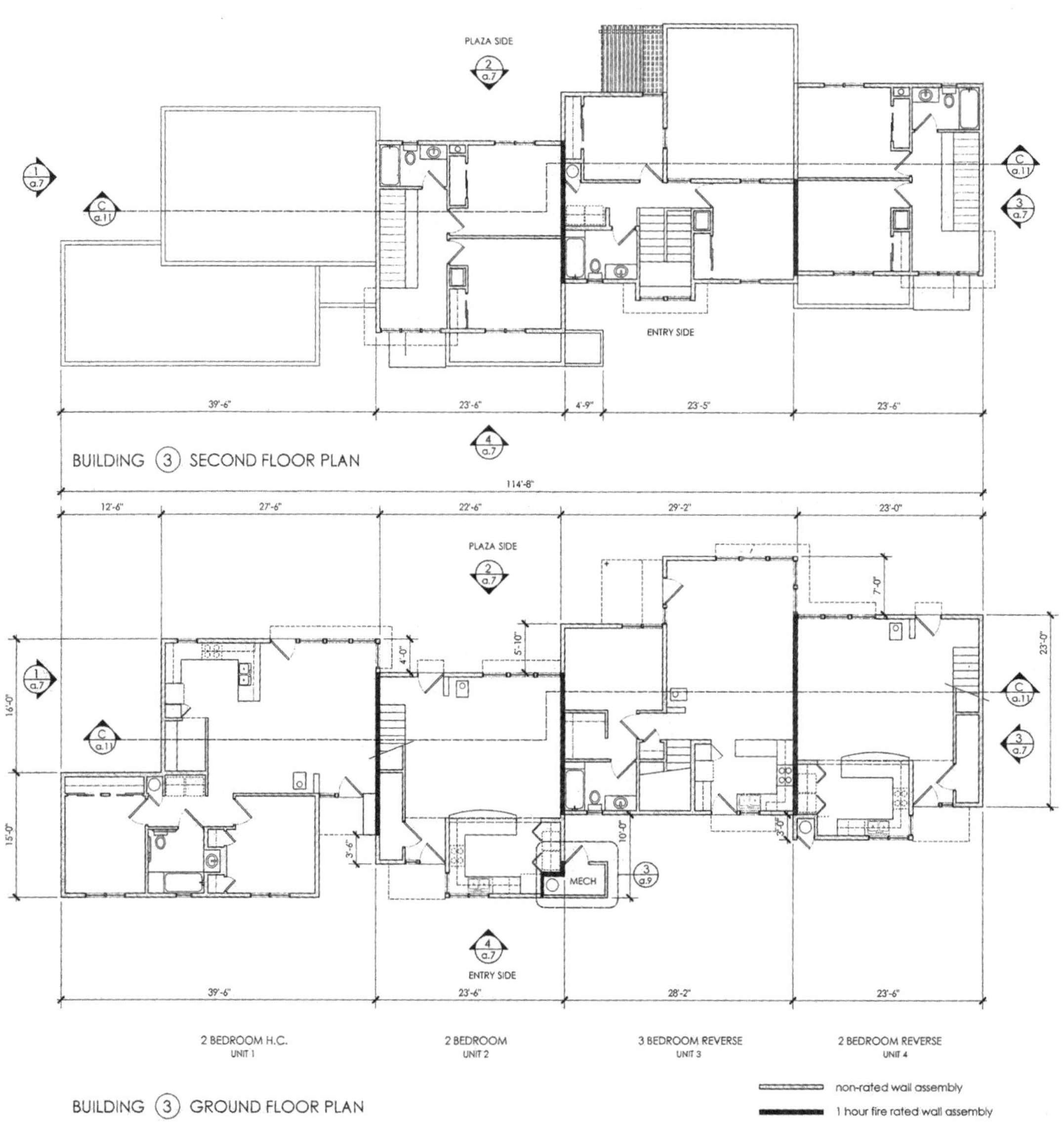
PLAZA SIDE
ENTRY SIDE
39'-6"
23'-6"
4'-9"
23'-5"
23'-6"
BUILDING (3) SECOND FLOOR PLAN
114'-8"
12'-6"
27'-6"
22'-6"
29'-2"
23'-0"
PLAZA SIDE
MECH
ENTRY SIDE
39'-6"
23'-6"
28'-2"
23'-6"
2 BEDROOM H.C.
UNIT 1
2 BEDROOM
UNIT 2
3 BEDROOM REVERSE
UNIT 3
2 BEDROOM REVERSE
UNIT 4
BUILDING (3) GROUND FLOOR PLAN
non-rated wall assembly
1 hour fire rated wall assembly

and HOME federal funds had never been used on a tribal project in New Mexico. A lot of work was required to communicate to the lenders what lending on tribal trust land involved, especially regarding the issues of sovereignty and collateral. At the same time, many tribes don't look fondly upon outside investors, and a great deal of trust had to be built.

Because the Village must operate within projected costs, it has been closely managed by the housing authority since occupancy. This is not typical for Ohkay Owingeh, since previous HUD projects were based on a home ownership model. As a result, there has been a learning curve for both the residents and the housing authority as to how to "use" their new village. For example, there was an initial high turn around rate among residents unaccustomed to multi-family living. Today, five years after completion, the turnover has stabilized.

Looking back at the process, Duran lists the key foundations for the success of this development: "Aspirations for high-quality, culturally significant, community-driven development; willingness to explore uncharted, untested financing areas; understanding of and patience for long term planning; [and] accountability to the community." Blosser summarizes, "The village was successful because we opened a discussion of underlying cultural values and were able to manifest some of them in architecture." The way Tsigoh bugeh Village incorporated community input has set a standard for future development by the Tribal Council.

OPPOSITE
Tsigoh bugeh Village combines different unit types in each building, including accessible two-bedroom flats as well as two- and three-bedroom townhouses.

BELOW LEFT
View of the main plaza from the community center.

BELOW RIGHT
The traditional hornos, used for baking.

Count Again
:Gather Agents

Collateral, or why you can't pull this off on your own.

Putting together an urban habitat project is a political and financial balancing act. You need ambassadors for your project, from as many different corners as possible. Count again until you have assembled a diverse base of active supporters. How?

:Gather those who are there.

You can't get around working with the neighbors. So: Get them involved. Go door to door. Know who has which story to tell. The folks living across the street need to become advocates. Does the neighborhood have an organization? Does it have meetings you might join? On a more pragmatic level, your neighbors are an important part of your market pro-forma. They might become future occupants, or customers of new services. They might become advocates for this type of development in other parts of their neighborhood. They could attract others, not yet living here.

:Find those who would like to be.

You're building a new community. Those who will be living there in the future should have as much of a say about its qualities as the neighbors who are there already. Involve your future residents as early as possible. Share your ideas with large local employers, as well as the city (and its schools, hospitals, fire and police departments), and housing and social services agencies. Ask them about their housing needs. They might get be interested in becoming involved and can direct their employees to your project. Work with local real estate agents. Let them educate you about demographics, market trends and client requests. Inversely, educate them about your project's unique market opportunities.

:Go public.

Get all those on board who have no personal stake in the project at all, but have the clout to make a difference, or simply think that what you're doing is great. Public opinion is shaped beyond the confines of a neighborhood. Educate your local journalists. Covering the development of an urban habitat project is not their typical beat.
Work with city officials from the start. Help the mayor and city council members see your project as a crucial learning moment for a wider public. Involve philanthropic organizations, business and the university. Make sure that they understand your project. Spend the time and money to build a well designed website that grows with the project. The website is a fundamental tool for making sure that the right information is being used to judge your work. It will expand your reach to the a wider community and to others across the country. The investment is worth it.

Urban Habitats Competition ***Building Alliances***

Gathering the agents for the redevelopment of Sunrise trailer court was a multi-layered process that started with the CCDC's desire to help the emerging process. As Katie Swenson, founder and former director of the CCDC recalls,

I learned about Habitat's purchase of Sunrise in the spring of 2004 when I was a Rose Fellow working for Piedmont Housing Alliance. As far as I know, there had never been such a large scale affordable housing project in Charlottesville and I was compelled by the scope of the project, the location and beauty of the site and the spirit and strength of the residents. I called Overton McGehee and told him about the idea behind the emerging Design Center and asked if we could be helpful. Having worked for three years on a community design process at 10th and Page which resulted in single-family housing (which started out 'affordable' but later in the project got more and more 'unaffordable'), I was interested and compelled by the Sunrise mandate to increase the density without displacement of the residents.

Often times, architectural professionals wait for the phone to ring with a new commission. In contrast, community-based work requires designers to actively look for needs in the community, and how to help bring resources to those needs. Community Design Centers provide a framework for this approach to civic engagement, large scale and small scale. Organizing a design competition proved an excellent framework to gather the agents for the redevelopment of Sunrise. One of the publicly voiced concerns about design competitions in general, and especially "ideas" competitions, is that the process is a waste of time. In fact, some architectural professionals feel that design competitions solicit free work from architects and belittle their professional contribution.

With this in mind, HHGC and CCDC focused in particular on the community building and public dialogue generated by the competition and the lasting benefits of using design as a tool for building better neighborhoods. The process of crafting the program engaged stakeholders in understanding the culture, climate, topography and ecology of the site, while also addressing the challenges and opportunities of affordability and density. The competition also prioritized the value of good ideas with a significant cash purse (a total of $25,000) as well as investment in public exhibitions and a symposium to communicate the design proposals to the broader community. The competition and symposium brought in a national jury of talent

OPPOSITE
The competition jury gathered agents from diverse backgrounds. Julie Eizenberg, AIA (back to camera) discusses the proposals with Lynne Conboy, Chair of the Board of Habitat for Humanity of Greater Charlottesville. To their right are Sunrise resident Marion Dudley and Jim Grigg, AIA, a Habitat board member. Standing are David Meckel, jury chair and competition advisor, and Teddy Cruz.

and attracted architects from 34 countries. The City loved the attention being paid to Charlottesville and Habitat loved having its issue—the preservation of affordable housing—gain exposure. Almost any public process will draw criticism, even a privately funded competition such as Urban Habitats, but that criticism can actually make the project better by forcing the organizers to make their priorities clear.

OPPOSITE
The residents of Sunrise Trailer Court meet the Urban Habitats jurors and acquaint them with the site. From left to right: James Grigg (back to camera), Kendra Hamilton, Julie Eizenberg, William Morrish, Katie Swenson, Marion Dudley, Teddy Cruz, Hank Koning, David Meckel and collaborators, John Woodriff, Lynne Conboy (both back to camera).

In the process, grant writing and fundraising may seem like an onerous task, but it is, in fact, a chance to pitch the value of the idea. Knowing the need, knowing the opportunity, it was possible to engage the funding community to join in making the project happen. As an example, The Blue Moon Fund, a Charlottesville-based foundation focused on sustainable urban development, came in as an early supporter of the Urban Habitats project. Blue Moon provided a matching grant to enable the Design Center to solicit further financial support from an anonymous foundation, the Enterprise Community Partnership, and Allied, a local concrete supplier. The University of Virginia offered to provide the venue for the jury and reception.

The Belmont-Carlton Neighborhood Association (BCNA) provided support to the Sunrise residents from the very beginning. Contrary to the perception that neighborhoods do not want affordable housing to depreciate property values, the BCNA supported the continued economic diversity of the neighborhood, voiced its concern over the displacement of Sunrise residents, and presented a clear voice to the Charlottesville City Council in support of new affordable housing. As the competition progressed, the neighborhood president joined the competition jury and acted as a liaison to the neighborhood association.

Finally, it is hard to overstate the role that the residents of Sunrise played in the process: the residents started by actively protesting the sale of Sunrise, then fully supported Habitat's role, welcomed the Design Center, and the competition. They relished in participating in the process. The residents exuded a sense of pride in their community that was contagious—what made them so happy? It is a trailer park after all, why is it such a special place to live? In addition to advocating for their housing, they seemed to be generally interested in articulating what made Sunrise special, as if the lesson was not in the housing, dollars, or development, but in understanding the essence of a great neighborhood.

Mix It Up
:Aggregate Niches

Supply and demand, or why you need a good program.

Build and they will come? Not necessarily. See the local market as a mixed menu of standard needs and non-standard niches. Replicating what's already there may be a step backwards. Instead, find those non-standard niches.

:Be aware of what's there.

Yes, loft-style condominiums are all the rage with young professionals. True, townhomes tend to be occupied by families. Building more loft-style condominiums and additional town homes might seem like a safe bet. There are expectations, conventions, funding mechanisms and expected resale value, and they all reinforce each other.

But before you follow the trends that have been set, turn your assumptions around. What about that family who would love a large flat with no stair and dreads gardening? What about the young single who longs for his own little place in order to plant his foot on the ground?

Rather than projecting those lofts and those townhomes onto your site, let your site guide you. Each parcel has a unique set of physical characteristics that can help transform meeting basic needs into creating attractive niches.

:Create all that isn't.

Talk to people. Are their current and future housing needs being met? Do they really have a choice as to where they want to live? Some residents are facing the challenges of aging in their home, would like to downsize, but have few choices for relocating in their neighborhood. Others might be looking for that starter home, don't mind it being small, but need it to be well located and safe to come home to. How can you combine these niches to reinforce each other?

:Produce a proforma.

Know what you want, be ready to tell the story, and run the numbers. Create a graphic to show how funding is being used and needs are being met. Address initial construction and ongoing maintenance costs. Use the spreadsheet to engage others, promote creativity, and identify key points for investment.

Urban Habitats Competition
Writing the Program

After a year of hard work by neighborhood organizations, city officials and professionals, the Charlottesville City Council passed a radically new comprehensive plan in January, 2001. The new plan is based on Smart Growth principles that encourage the production of sustainable, transit-friendly, medium-density housing. Within this city-wide plan, individual overlay districts are used to create a building 'envelope' outlining the dimensions for new development. One of the overlay districts includes Sunrise Trailer Court.

The new overlay district stipulates that if the developer is to receive all the density "bonuses" allowed by city regulations, a site the size of Sunrise, formerly zoned as a combination of light industrial, residential and commercial, might contain as many 72 housing units. Without this new city-wide plan, HHGC would not have had the building envelope to generate enough new market rate housing to subsidize the development of replacement homes for the trailer court's residents.

What gets built inside that building envelope provided by the new zoning, however, remains vague in architectural terms, and most often disappointing in recent developments. It is important to recognize that setting up the goals and writing a program of uses for a new development is in and of itself a design exercise: How do we begin to suggest the qualities of the places we are building? How well does the development serve its primary users, the residents, and how does it contribute to our larger urban fabric?

Writing the program became an exercise in challenging assumptions. Conceiving a mixed-income, mixed-use development meant learning to aggregate niches. Before engaging in a competition for Sunrise, HHGC had assumed a site layout consisting of 28 Habitat attached townhouses along Midland Street and 32 market-rate, multi-story condominium units with commercial spaces along Carleton Avenue. This approach was based on building types that had recently been employed in Charlottesville, and would have excluded niches not yet served by the housing market. The task of writing the housing program, therefore, was to open the possibilities for novel types, and conceive of a mutually beneficial number and type of units. These parameters were determined by the CCDC and HHGC in response to the needs of Sunrise Trailer Court residents, requests received by HHGC, and those of young families relocating to Charlottesville to work at the University of Virginia. Among this last group, the Belmont neighborhood

OPPOSITE
Competition juror Teddy Cruz presented "The New World Atlas" as keynote speaker at the Growing Urban Habitats Symposium in September 2005.

BELOW
On one of several panels at the symposium, UVA School of Architecture Professor William Williams, Urban Habitats First Place finalists Christopher Genter and Susanne Schindler, along with Julie Eizenberg, AIA, discuss the issues of building for a sense of community.

BOTTOM
Over one hundred people attended the day-long symposium to discuss and learn about the issues of sustainable, affordable multi-family housing. Professor Robin Dripps moderates the panel on compact architecture and landscape architecture with David Baker, AIA and members of the Metropolitan Planning Collaborative.

is particularly popular for its central location and small, compact homes. As a result, the program sought to capture this underserved market for 1,200 to 1,500-square-foot family homes.

Another key issue in writing the program was determining the number of parking spaces required per unit. Studies during the programming phase showed that reducing the requirement from 2 to 1.25 spaces per unit would eliminate the need for a costly parking structure. The City agreed to this change as officials were interested in using the competition to study the implications of a reduced parking count for future planned unit development projects. Once this goal was set, the question became a design issue: how to design for the car as part of the project's open space. The program authors felt that this was an important question for the competition to explore so that city officials and neighbors would be able to envision options, and in turn become supportive of a lower car count.

Besides accounting for housing and parking, the program authors decided to incorporate 10,000 square feet of space for commercial or community uses. Doing so was an issue of some debate, since it was unclear whether the location would support uses such as a day care center or office space. However, the partners felt compelled, as a matter of principal, to set mixed use foundations for a project. Finally, it was important for the CCDC and HHGC to clearly describe the project's overall qualitative goals, such as a site design to maximize the benefits passive cooling and heating.

OPPOSITE
The first of two days of jury deliberations in July 2005 began with an overview of Charlottesville by UVA Professor William Morrish at the Charlottesville Community Design Center, located in a storefront on the city's downtown mall. The day culminated with a public viewing of all entries at the University of Virginia School of Architecture, where citizens were given the opportunity to vote for a favored scheme.

Expand Options
: Visualize Alternatives

The vision, or finding a way to work collaboratively.

Frequently, it is difficult for the parties involved to understand what is at stake. Designers, developers and users all seem to be speaking different languages. Visualize alternatives together in order to reveal pivotal choices, their overall impact and tactics for integration.

: Frame.

You need to map out a vision to help you navigate through this non-linear process. A vision isn't a final product; it is a set of goals and principles. A vision is created by ordinary citizens working with inventive leaders, who together develop a set of binding ideas. These ideas will then frame the questions to be addressed and name the means by which the solutions will be generated. In short, a vision defines the project's community working relationships during and after the project is built. What is it that the new residents will feel that they own and desire to maintain? How can they improve on what has been built over time?

: Highlight.

Bring all the aspects important to you to the fore. Cost, of course. But cost has long-term and short-term parameters. So how do you underline these parameters? Costs invariably overrun. So what is your Plan B? What will carry the project forward? Who will manage the project and how?

Roll out a big sheet of white butcher paper to develop a spread sheet that compares alternative plans. Highlight how each addresses the issues of design, program, finance and implementation. The best strategy is most likely a composite of borrowed elements from the various different alternatives.

And as if this were a medical condition: Get a second opinion. Invite design and development professionals to help you analyze your options and suggest alternatives. You may have missed the most innovative, low-cost strategy out there.

: Materialize.

Some people read plans. Others see only numbers. Perspective renderings are lovely. A physical model always helps. In short: materialize a project's quantitative and qualitative characteristics using all of these, and many other, forms of communication. Get the assistance of a graphic designer or communications professional. They can help you organize the information so that anyone can navigate the project's ideas and component parts. Put this information on a website that you can easily update yourself, and continue to do so as changes are made.

Urban Habitats Competition
The Jury Process

Staging an international design competition was motivated by the fundamental desire to visualize as many different alternatives as possible for the redevelopment of Sunrise Trailer Court. The organizers' hopes were not disappointed: the Urban Habitats competition drew more than 170 entries from all over the world. Actually evaluating the implications of all of these alternatives, however, was only possible because the nine-person jury had been composed to encompass different fields of expertise. As a result, over the course of one tiring, but satisfying July weekend, they were able to select three finalist proposals.

OPPOSITE
Final jury deliberations focused on ten entries. Charlottesville Community Design Center interns, Urban Habitats advisors and Habitat for Humanity staff members were allowed to observe, but not comment, on the jury proceedings.

Put another way: Composed of internationally renowned architects, city government, Habitat board members and local residents, the jury process was successful precisely because the group understood that the vision for Sunrise went beyond the physical qualities of the site—the real issue at hand was how design would engage the needs, desires, and history of the community. The diversity of the jurors' backgrounds, positions, and outlooks—along with a mutual sense of respect, admiration, and ability to listen—made for a vibrant, constructive conversation and a jury process that was a true community-building event.

Since the jury was drawn from a variety of backgrounds, differences of opinion emerged during the selection process. For example, while the residents tended to prioritize social aspects of proposals—such as green space and livability—the developers and architects focused more on the practical and technical challenges. This sentiment was echoed by a local architect, who commented that the jury process "seemed driven more by ideas than a hard look at reality." Despite differing views of "reality," the honest and open discussions led a number of jurors to comment on the comfortable dynamic that developed over the weekend. Ms. Marion Dudley, a Sunrise resident, went so far as to say that, "from day one, they were like family."

A long-time Charlottesville resident and a natural leader within Sunrise, Ms. Dudley admits to being shocked when she was first asked to be a juror in an architecture competition. She took on the responsibility, however, because "it wasn't just me—it was the whole trailer court that I was doing it for." Unlike development projects that present communities like Sunrise with already established plans at the first public meeting, Sunrise residents were involved from the onset of the project, which provided them with the rare

SUNRISE PARK

opportunity to shape their future. For example, Sunrise residents took part in three community meetings, spelling out development goals that included affordability, energy efficiency, and access to outdoor space. Subsequently, they were invited to comment on the program draft. Ms. Dudley's participation as a juror further solidified her community's influence. She informed the other jurors about the area's subtleties, elaborated on the community's roots, and brought the jury back to reality if the conversation became too heady with design theory. As nervous as Ms. Dudley might have felt about accurately representing her community's views, she was absolutely delighted when she found out that a couple of her neighbors had also favored the first prize winner out of all 164 entries.

OPPOSITE
Marion Dudley and Kendra Hamilton (back to camera) individually review and identify entries for features of interest to be brought forward for discussion with the group.

The success of the Urban Habitats process lies in its affirmation of community-based collaboration and design. Last year, neighbors were fighting the development; this year, they are part of the redevelopment team. The local community is learning that change can be positive as long as the community works together toward the best outcome. Ms. Dudley says, "I know these places that they'll put down here will be a welcome change—they'll be nice places—but it's going to take me a long time to adjust to it." Change is never easy for a tight-knit community. By improving the quality and quantity of affordable housing while respecting the inherent history, values and culture of a place, however, change will become a positive force.

Build For Change
: Bundle Capital

Equity, or:
What can we sustain?

Securing multiple sources of funding to develop affordable housing is inevitable. Tax credits, direct public subsidies, for-profit investment, charitable donations, volunteer labor. Between all of these variables, how can you ensure the financial stability over the lifetime of your project?

: Overlay investments.

Forget about each funding resource underwriting just one program need. Instead, think about how each investment might overlay with others, such that each can spread its impact across the project and produce added benefits through common efforts. Some of the senior housing needs might just happen to be similar to the needs of family housing.

: Share Programs and Energy.

Think about how your team might evolve from a group that manages a capital development project into a partnership operating a living community. Look into the future to identify potential income. This might come from renting for-profit commercial space or running a child care center within your development.

: Build big with details that add-up.

Realize that your vision should be big, but that the steps to getting there will be small. The use of volunteer labor, for example, might impact your program by limiting buildings to three stories in height. Not a problem. Once you fine tune the construction method, the project will roll.

Urban Habitats Competition
Funding Sunrise

OPPOSITE
At the conclusion of the Growing Urban Habitats Symposium, presenters and participants were treated to a barbeque hosted by the residents of Sunrise Trailer Court. Peter Anderson of Anderson Anderson Architecture dances with Sunrise Trailer Court resident Mary Conley to music by the Hogwaller Ramblers.

From the first day of discussions between the CCDC and HHGC on the competition design and development program for Sunrise, the process of tying the various cost factors and financial issues into an interconnected bundle influenced many program decisions for Sunrise.

As an example, Habitat for Humanity brings unique resources to the development table, including both volunteer labor and funding drawn from donations. This housing is generally targeted at households with incomes between 30% and 60% AMI (area median income), or, in Charlottesville, a family of four earning between $20,000 and $40,000. To broaden its reach for Sunrise, HHGC talked to another Charlottesville-based non-profit housing provider, Piedmont Housing Alliance (PHA). PHA focuses on serving households within the low- (less than 50% AMI) to moderate-income (less than or equal to 80% AMI) bracket, using federal, state and local funding sources. In addition to developing housing, PHA provides loans to individuals and other developers, so their agenda directly complements HHGC's. The goal of their conversations was to jointly develop and operate the low-income family units to satisfy both organizations' mandates.

The development of a mixed-income housing project must take into account the requirements of market rate housing development. The HHGC Board used the Urban Habitats competition process and its results as an educational process toward that goal. The competition reshaped the understanding of what it means to design and develop a 72-unit sustainable, affordable, and mixed-income project. The professional quality of the competition submissions and the national case studies presented during the symposium attracted local developers to join HHGC efforts. Several local developers have been brought into the project as advisors to help the HHGC Board form a new for-profit development arm called Creative Housing. Its goal is to generate a low-income housing subsidy through the profit generated by the sale of housing to households with incomes between 80% and 120% AMI. *(See Epilogue for more information on Creative Housing.)*

Using sustainable design practices has yet another set of funding implications: One of the primary reasons for using green building and site planning strategies such as passive heating and cooling is to reduce the operating costs for Sunrise residents. However, the strategy had an additional unforeseen benefit: on the basis of this goal, HHGC received a

major gift from an anonymous donor reducing the purchase price of Sunrise Trailer Court by half. HHGC set an investment return of $700,000, which was far less than the return a standard for-profit developer would have expected. In this way, the profit that would have gone to a developer, or toward retiring the debt on a higher purchase price, was rechanneled to reduce homes prices and into green investments.

In short, bundling capital treats the financing of a project like Sunrise as if it had a triple bottom line. It involves new non-profit resources, while enhancing for-profit viability with the long-term cost-effectiveness of sustainable development, to bring social, financial, and ecological returns.

OPPOSITE
Katherine Conley, left, chats with Catherine Lynch of Metropolitan Planning Collaborative.
The evening picnic gave Urban Habitats finalists and Sunrise Trailer Court residents an opportunity to meet each other informally.

OPPOSITE, BELOW
The Hogwaller Ramblers.

BOTTOM
And another beautiful Sunrise sunset.

Chapter 2—

Dense Integrated Density

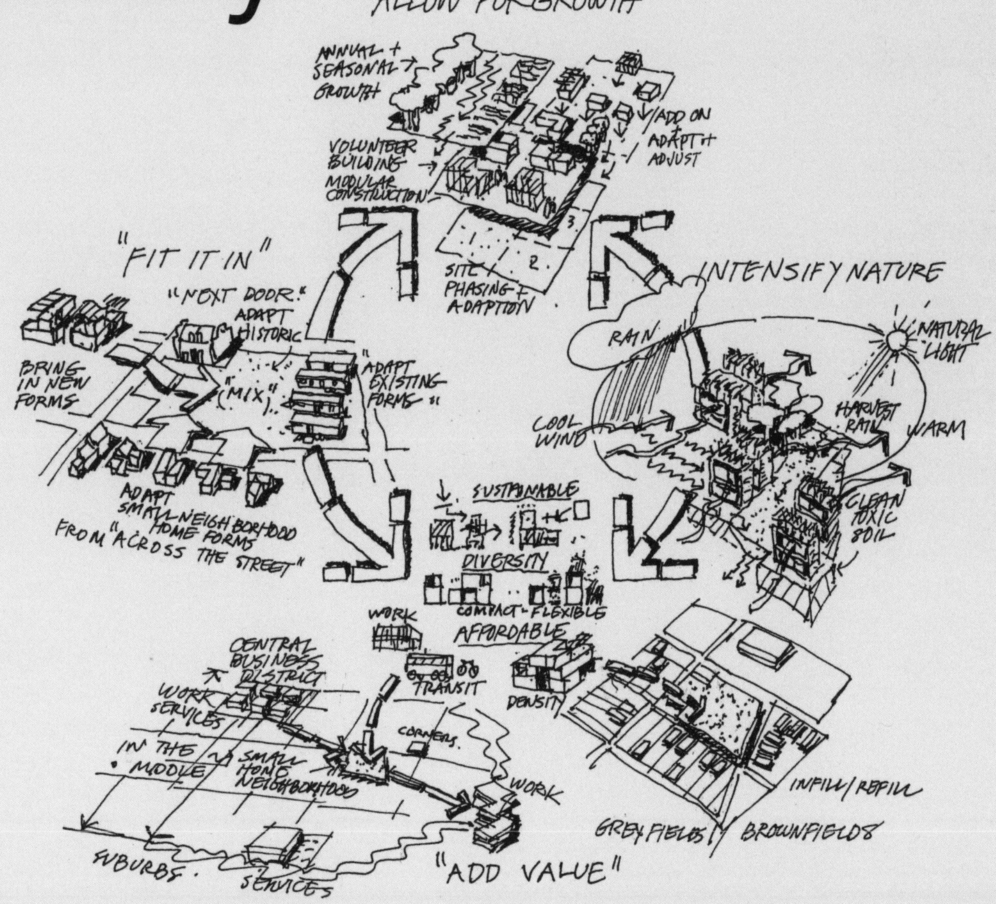

We are arguing about "Smart Growth" like it's a choice. But take the San Francisco Bay Area. It has limited space and we're supposed to add 200,000 dwellings by 2020. Streets, services, parks, schools. Typically we don't put houses on top of those things. Perhaps it's a thought that should be given.

David Baker, David Baker Associates, San Francisco,
Growing Urban Habitats Symposium, September 2005

Growing urban habitats means building on existing neighborhoods. Unfortunately, just mentioning the possibility of increasing the density of a neighborhood is likely to trigger negative reactions among its residents. Simultaneous images of poorly operated public housing and walled-off luxury condominiums inhabit their responses. Accordingly, their fears are contradictory: on the one hand, there is the fear of dropping property values: Affordable housing? Not in my backyard! On the other hand, there is the fear of rising property taxes that would price current residents out of their homes: Luxury condominiums here? Never! Additional concerns come along for the ride: increased automobile traffic, loss of already scarce parking spaces, loss of natural amenities, increased noise, and overrun public schools. This defensive reaction to "density" plays out in neighborhoods across the country.

Meanwhile, regulatory agencies, private sector developers, and residents alike are recognizing that given their pre-existing infrastructure and social cohesion, existing communities may provide the best foundations for further growth. Accordingly, forward looking state and city agencies, working with neighborhood organizations, think tanks and advocacy groups, are taking on the challenge of encouraging denser development in existing urban areas. Among their goals is to stop the stream of unpredictable, time-intensive one-off zoning variances required for building at a higher density when no comprehensive policy is in place.

One of the larger-scale legislative efforts is the "Smart Growth" legislation passed in 2004 as Chapters 40R and 40S of the Massachusetts General Laws. Through 40R and 40S, the state provides municipalities with cash incentives for creating zoning overlay districts in areas close to existing transit lines, as a means of promoting mixed-income housing development. Where other state-mandated density laws trump towns' permitting processes, this legislation provides towns with funds, proportionate to the number of new permitted dwellings, that they can then invest at their own discretion. In addition, the state offered to help cover the costs generated by new children entering the public school system, acknowledging that these costs were not likely to be offset by the property taxes from affordable housing. By the spring of 2008, Massachusetts had approved 19 districts with a total of almost 7,000 new units of housing.

This chapter outlines some of the design opportunities related to policies for integrated density.

The Right Stuff

Los Angeles is an excellent place to discover ways to integrate density. The Los Angeles metropolitan region is filled with explorations of medium-density housing prototypes, distinct from the urban row houses, social housing blocks and apartment buildings found in East Coast cities like New York or Philadelphia. Los Angeles' development reveals how important it is to read history while projecting for the future, for, quite simply, urban habitats cannot grow in a vacuum.

Gardner 1050 is an example of recent architecture in Los Angeles that builds on the city's long history of medium-density housing.

There are several reasons for the richness of urban habitat models in Los Angeles. One was the need, in the early 20th century, for clusters of affordable housing, especially for the burgeoning film industry's working class. The second was the desire to build at a medium-density that would be conveniently located and yet open to the "Mediterranean" climate. On the one hand, ingenious developers produced what has become known as the Courtyard Houses: a clustering of patio units stacked into two-story ensembles, frequently dressed in the style of Spanish hacienda architecture that was part of Hollywood set design. *(For an example, see Maltman Bungalows, p. 86)* At the other end of the design spectrum, a group of architects trained in the emerging modern architecture of Europe developed other models of integrated density: they discovered, incorporated and reinterpreted South-Western pueblo architecture, traditional Japanese design and the emerging Southern California lifestyle of indoor and outdoor living. They created unit layouts that integrate exterior living spaces, and tested the possibilities of new building systems and materials, such as tilt-up concrete. This group's key works include Irving Gill's Horatio Court West in Santa Monica (1919), Rudolf Schindler's Pueblo Ribeira in San Diego (1923), and Richard Neutra's Strathmore Apartments in Westwood, Los Angeles (1937).

In the 1950s and 60s, housing production in Los Angeles was influenced by a group of architects interested in incorporating new industrial processes developed during World War II into affordable housing for returning veterans and their new families. This included the Case Study House program (1945–66) which sponsored experimental housing, and included key designs such as the steel house by Ray and Charles Eames which could be assembled by hand in three days. This rich history feeds into the work of architects such as Koning Eizenberg, Michael B. Lehrer, and Pugh + Scarpa, who continue to push the idea that multi-family housing is an urban habitat, not just a block of housing units. *(For Koning Eizenberg, see p. 79; for Pugh + Scarpa, see p. 179)*

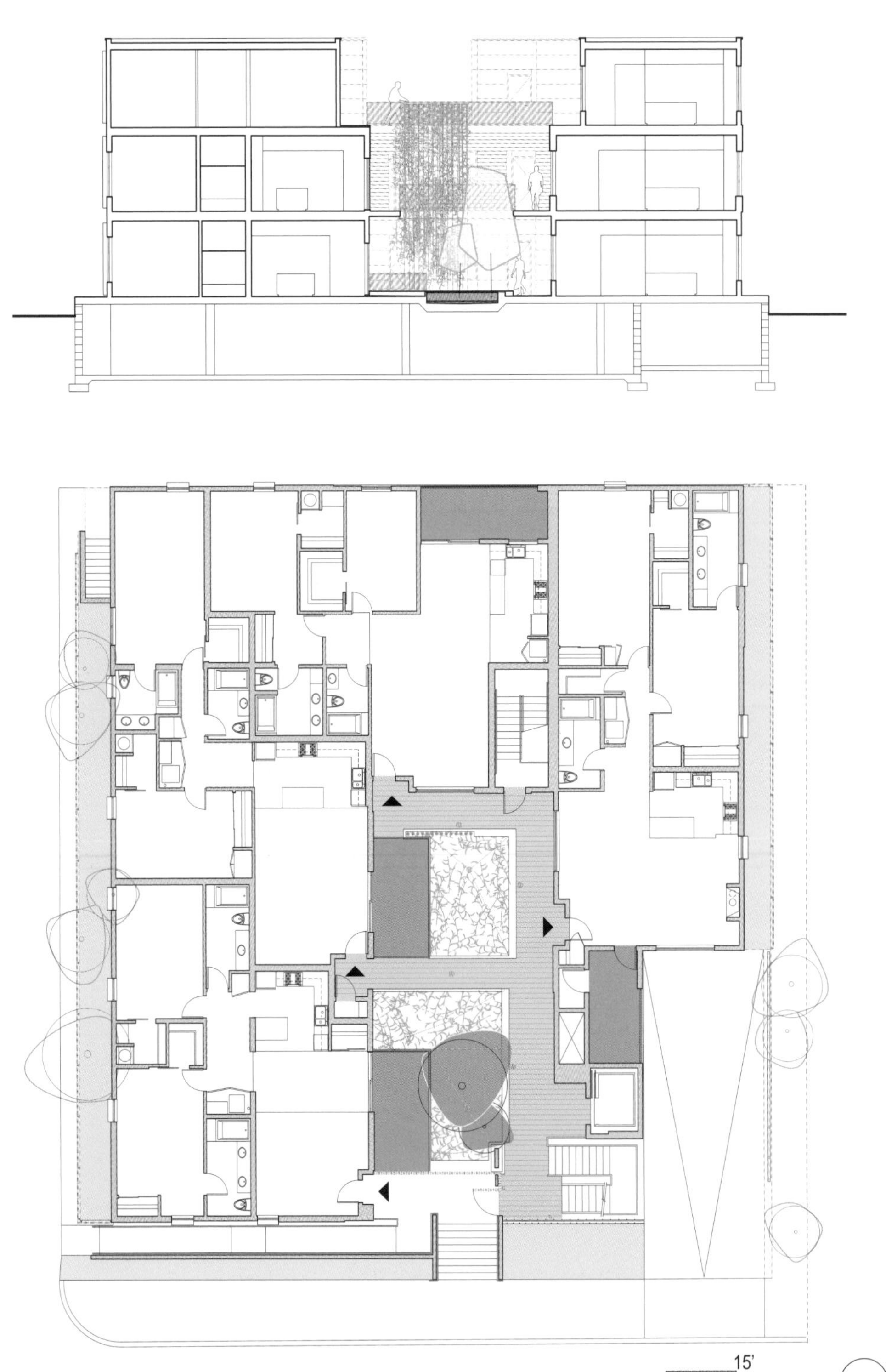
15'
0
5'
25'

OPPOSITE
Ground floor plan and cross section. By organizing the building around a courtyard, all units can have multiple exposures and enjoy cross ventilation.

LEFT
View of the galleries in the courtyard. View of the building from the street.

BELOW
Aerial photograph showing Gardner 1050 located between commercial uses along Santa Monica Boulevard and residential uses to the south.

A recent iteration of the city's historical precedents is **Gardner 1050**, a market-rate condominium building designed for Habitat Group Los Angeles, a private developer, by the Los Angeles-based architecture firm **LOHA**. Located in West Hollywood in a transitional area wedged between a commercial strip and a residential neighborhood, the 10-unit building intelligently revisits the courtyard typology. LOHA achieved integrated, livable density by carving out quality open space. At three stories in height, the U-shaped configuration allows all units to have at least two exposures, enabling cross-ventilation and maximizing day lighting. The courtyard also creates a clear hierarchy of shared and private space. The layout of each unit is unique, yet all living areas are entered directly from the courtyard or its related galleries, and the bedrooms are located towards the rear. Each unit has access to a private patio or deck, and parking is accommodated below ground. Since the building does not exceed the density allowed by zoning in the area, or violate setback stipulations, it did not require any variances. Because the neighbors were in favor of more housing, there was no opposition to the project either.

But integrated density does not always come so easy. As with the other urban habitat development goals, it requires members of public agencies, funders, developers, architects and residents to swim further upstream in the development process and engage in intense negotiation. It will take visualizing options, bundling finances and testing unusual design solutions to translate the goals into built form. Above all, achieving integrated density requires forthright talk about the trade-offs involved.

Hancock Lofts, a mixed-use, mixed-income project on a 2.1-acre site also located in West Hollywood, is another example of recent innovations in housing in Los Angeles. Completed in late 2008, it provides an excellent case study in getting the public on the side of integrated density. The project's public-private partnership involved the City of West Hollywood,

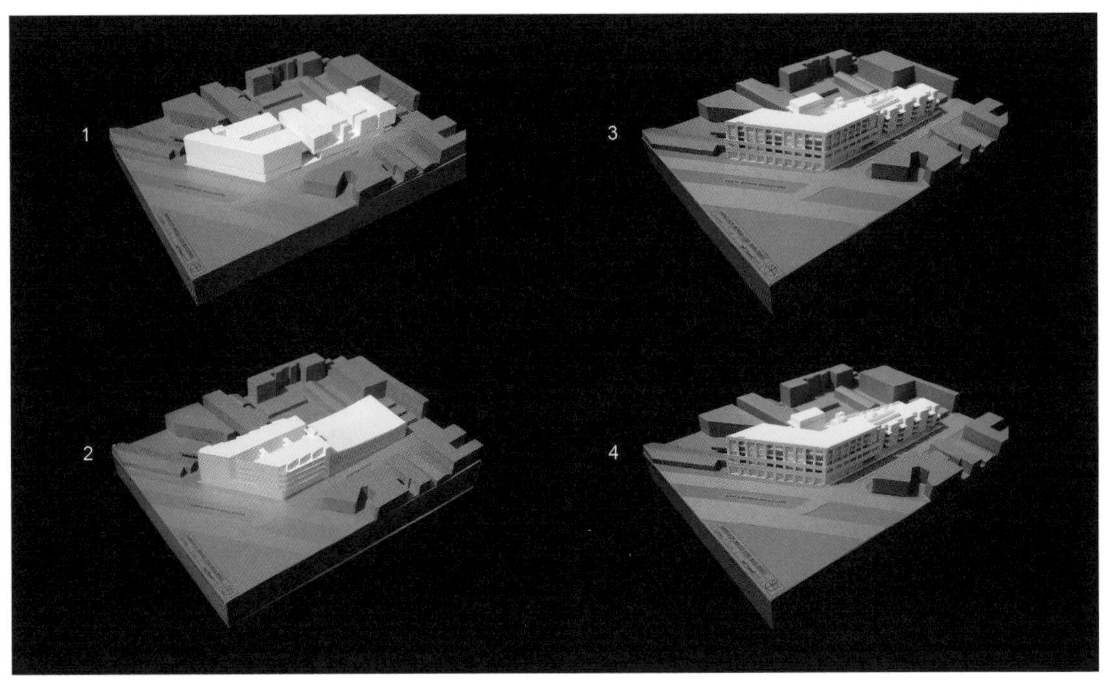
1
2
3
4

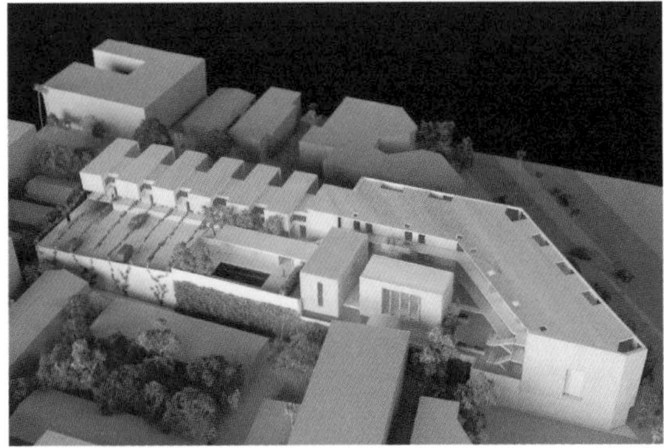

owner of the surface parking lot and responsible for building a new public parking facility there, and the private developer, CIM Group, who was to finance the residential and retail development. Together with **Koning Eizenberg Architects**, the developers initiated a comprehensive public process to determine exactly what density would be socially appropriate and financially feasible for the prominent corner of Santa Monica Boulevard and Hancock Avenue.

At the Growing Urban Habitats Symposium held at UVA in September 2005, architect and Urban Habitats Competition juror Julie Eizenberg presented the following thoughts on the process:

So the city had a community process. It was a fairly structured community process, and the developer was asked to come in with a couple of different scenarios. One was to maximize the units. One looked at how you could maximize parking to supplement the parking shortage in the neighborhood. Another scheme had some parking and fewer units.

The community pushed for a height limit and an active street front along Santa Monica Boulevard. A compromise was found in part because of CIM Group's commitment to the site and willingness to accept a narrower profit margin: the developer went the extra mile by reducing the number of units and engaging in a more expensive construction method for the parking garage. The community, on the other hand, accepted fewer public parking spaces. Although the duration of the public process and the lack of compensation for the architects led Eizenberg to describe it as "extremely frustrating", it ultimately led to a project that satisfied the parties involved.

This trade-off was only successful because the architect translated the varied program into a convincing structure. The building organizes 31 condominiums, seven affordable rental units as required by the City, more than 11,000 square feet of retail and 217 parking spaces, of which 90 are public. How? The architects satisfied expectations and inverted them all at once. The expectation: The sidewalk is continuously fronted, by retail on Santa Monica and the affordable units along Hancock. The inversion: Three levels of parking are stacked behind, above and below the scrim of housing on Hancock. The public and affordable parking is located below grade with the remaining parking above and residential units tucked in between.

OPPOSITE, ABOVE
Models of Hancock Lofts as developed through the community process.
1 Maximizing the number of housing units
2 Maximizing the number of parking spaces
3 Hybrid
4 As approved, with four floors only

OPPOSITE, BELOW
Model views of building from front and back.

BELOW
Aerial photograph with the site highlighted.

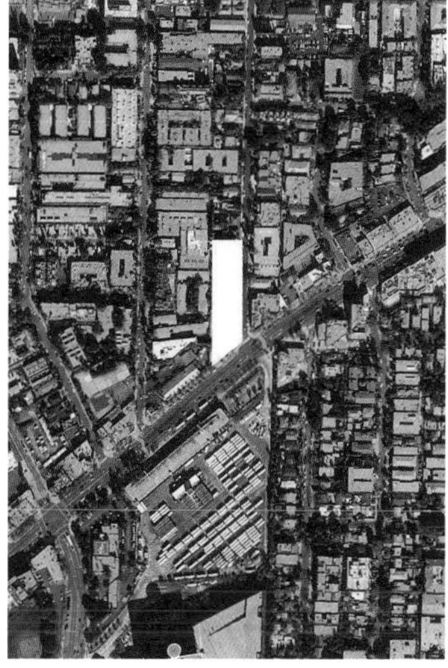

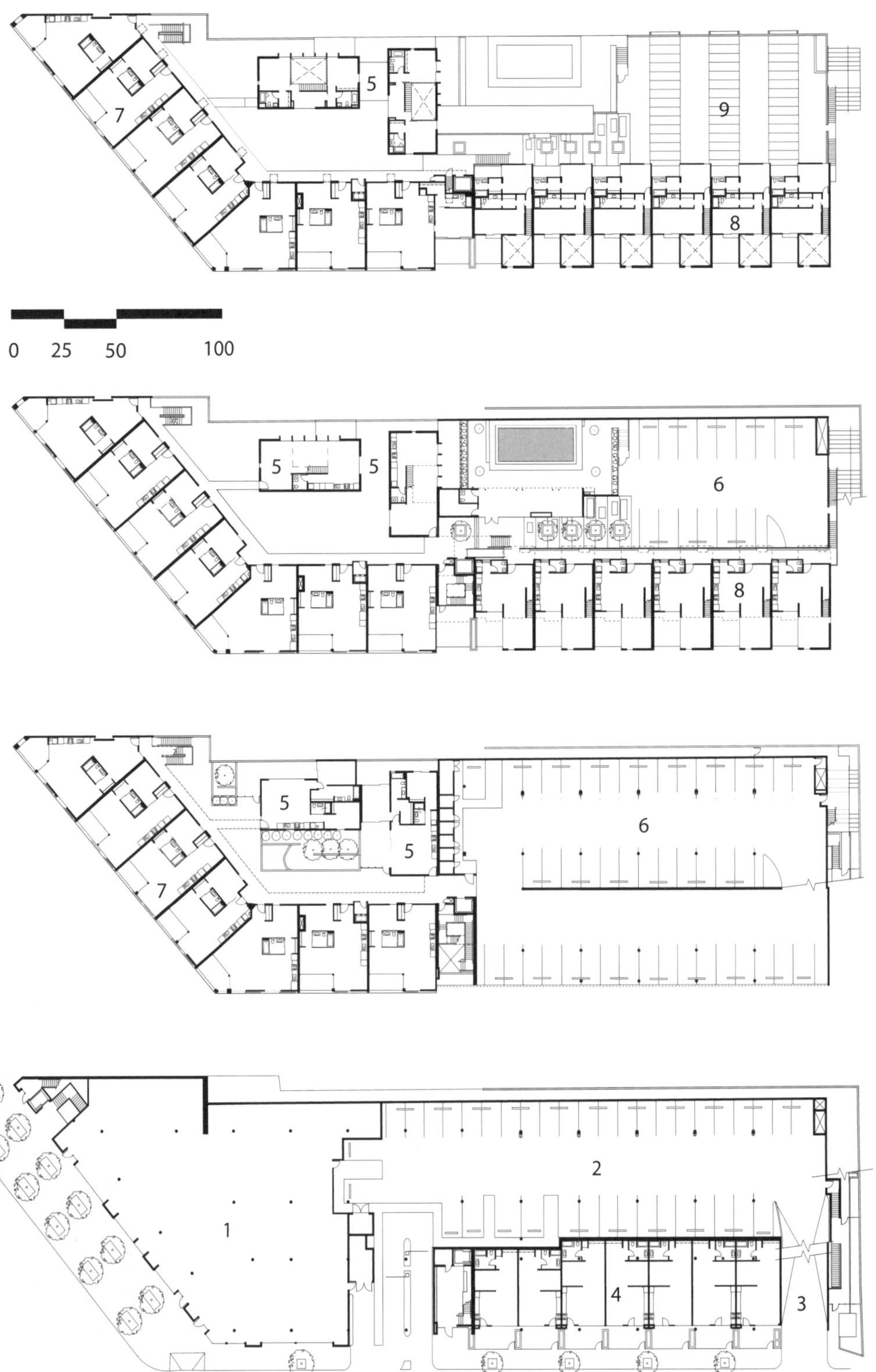
0
25
50
100
1
2
3
4
5
6
7
8
9

Thus the majority of the cars, the least attractive part of the program, are buried, out of sight, within the building. At the same time, the parking structure creates the artificial ground for a generous shared roof garden and swimming pool.

Eizenberg's key reflection on the process of integrating density with Hancock Lofts refers back to the importance of laying multiple foundations:

You would think that the developer would start this whole exercise by thinking about style, because if you're going to live in the city and are talking about urban stuff, the Mediterranean is a good place to look to get people together. But you may find that Mediterranean doesn't suit a contemporary lifestyle once you add cars into it and look at contemporary construction techniques. If you start with the wrong stuff, you get the wrong stuff—it doesn't matter what the trend is.

Designing integrated density is about defining this right stuff, right from the start. Getting it realized requires a back and forth process and most definitely calls for unconventional solutions. Looking into the history of a city is not about imitating styles. Rather, as Gardner 1050 and Hancock Lofts beautifully show, it is about building on what is there to generate new forms of living.

OPPOSITE
Hancock Lofts, floor plans.
1 Retail space
2 Public parking
3 Up to residential parking
4 Rental units
5 Cabana units
6 Residential parking
7 Flat
8 Garden units
9 Arbor

BELOW
Section through the building, showing how the rental apartments create street-level activity along Hancock, hiding parking below, behind, and above.

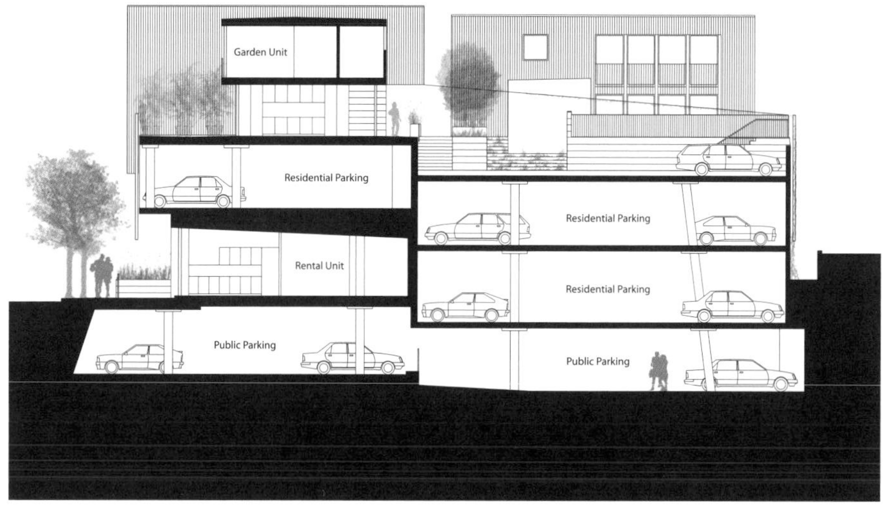

Count Again
:Add Value

The D Word, or how to deal with density.

Increased density may constitute the most difficult issue to deal with when trying to build new housing in an existing neighborhood. The challenge is to show current residents that the proposed development will add value, not destroy it. How do you go about doing just that?

:Forget units per acre.

Think instead about how to qualify what you are proposing. Describe what you're proposing not in numbers, but by demonstrating how residents might live and work in the proposed project. How might the project help local families remain in the community? How might it increase housing choices?

:Talk trade-offs.

Be frank about trade-offs. There are always trade-offs involved when adding value.

Additional residents may indeed increase traffic. But their presence also puts additional eyes on the street, resulting in a safer neighborhood. Additional residents may strain public institutions, such as schools. But they also increase the tax base, creating a louder political voice when demanding public investments in the neighborhood. Additional children may indeed play on the streets and create a ruckus. But new families also increase the likelihood that shared amenities will come to the neighborhood. A corner store, a day care center or a public transit stop needs a critical mass of users to support it.

:List the local menu.

Neighbors' first assumption is that a proposed project will be occupied by "total strangers": people who are not like them moving in from somewhere else. Developers for their part tend to ignore the "local menu," that is, potential residents already living within plain sight. Addressing the common goals of existing and new residents is a frequently overlooked development opportunity, one that can capture a broader market than is typically assumed.

City of Los Angeles ***Small Lots Ordinance***

Municipalities are starting to revamp regulatory guidelines to allow for denser, more diverse housing within existing neighborhoods. For instance, in December 2004, the City of Los Angeles adopted a new Small Lots Ordinance that altered its zoning codes to allow the construction of new "fee-simple" townhomes in areas generally zoned for apartments or commercial developments. Prior to this change, the City's zoning code prohibited the development of townhomes unless they were part of a condominium association. Building condominiums, however, raises developers' insurance fees, and permitting is frequently hampered by neighbors opposed to multi-family housing. The new ordinance, in contrast, encourages detached homes on small lots by reducing the minimum lot size and side yard requirements, and allowing lots without direct street frontage. The ordinance wasn't designed to make the city denser per se, but to simplify the development process for smaller developers and create opportunities for affordable home-ownership. The ordinance allows for the transformation into housing of around 1,650 vacant land parcels and 850 substandard multifamily buildings throughout the City of Los Angeles.

To explore the design opportunities for housing under these new regulations, Enterprise Community Partners joined with the City of Los Angeles to mount a design competition in late 2005 called Small Lots-Smart Design. The goal was to develop a series of prototypical designs that future homeowners and landowners could use as off-the-shelf solutions. While there is no "typical lot" in Los Angeles, the competition was based on subdividing a probable 42-by-155-foot lot to accommodate three units and on-site parking.

OPPOSITE
Fung + Blatt's CityHoodHome (6 units at 7 degrees) tests the design opportunities created by the Small Lots Ordinance. View of buildings from the street.

BELOW LEFT
Site plan.

BELOW
Floor plans of a two-family unit.

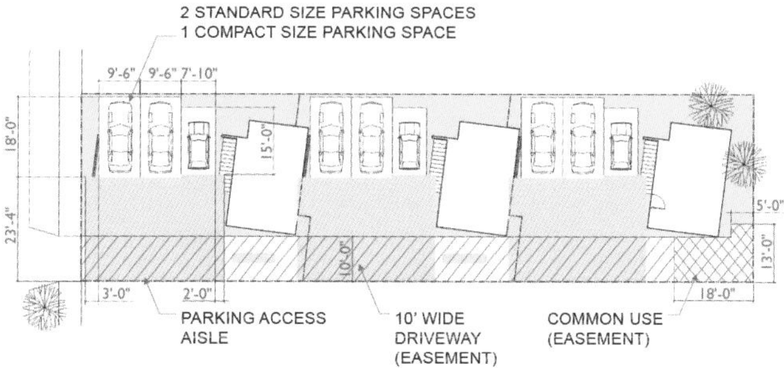

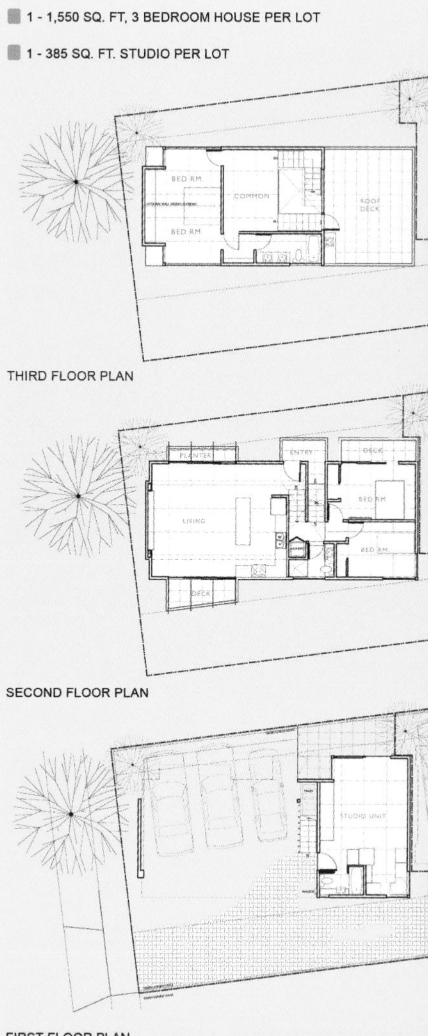

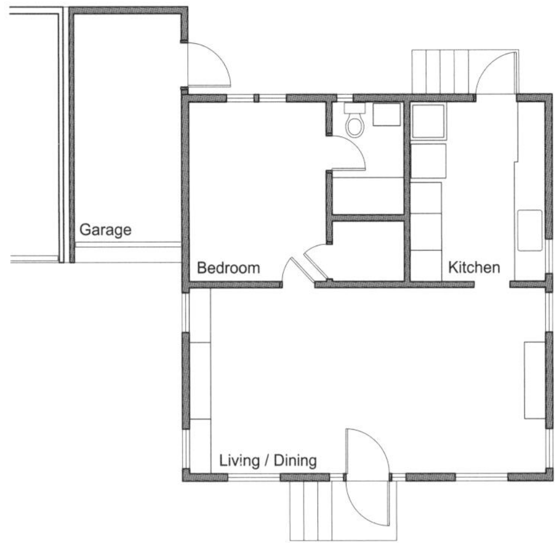

The Small Lots Ordinance provided the legal framework to convert the 1926 Maltman Bungalows from rentals to individual properties.

LEFT
Floor plan Type A.

BELOW LEFT
Floor plan Type B.

BELOW RIGHT
Floor plan Type C.

BELOW
Site plan.

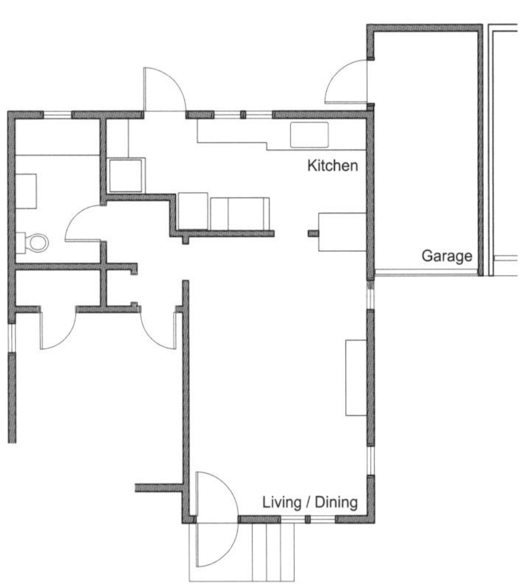

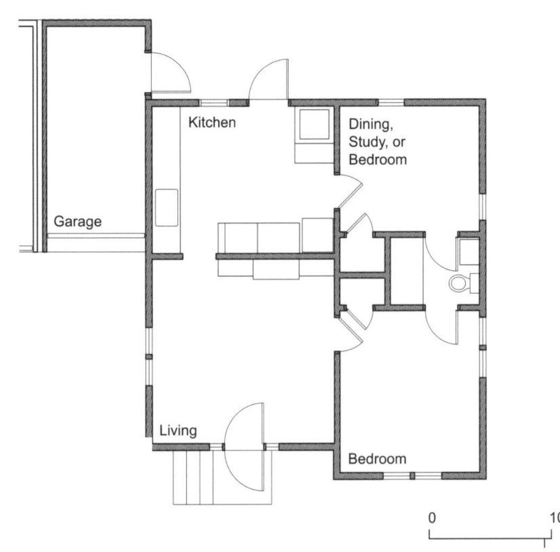

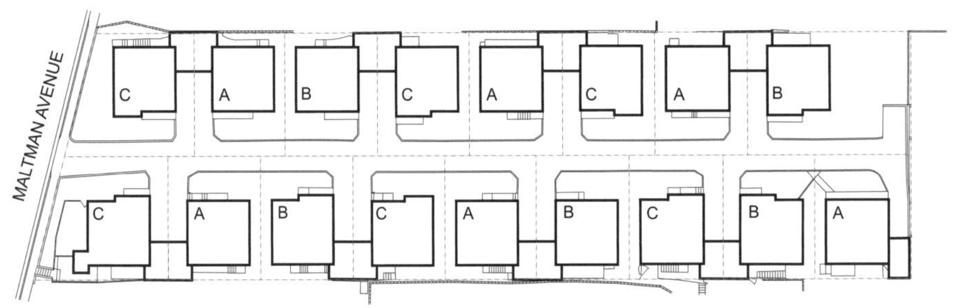

In their proposal **CityHoodHome**, winner of the competition's Mayor's Award, architects **Fung + Blatt** rotate three attached two-unit homes by seven degrees, ensuring visual privacy for all units while allowing ample light into their interior. To date, none of the competition proposals have been implemented, although developers have shown interest. Fung + Blatt are taking the initiative into their own hands and plan to realize their design in the Highland Park neighborhood in the near future. *(Also see the competition proposal by CK-Architecture, p. 204)*

By April 2008, permits for more than 1,000 units had been filed with the City's Planning Department. As Jane Blumenfeld, a Principal City Planner of Los Angeles and an initiator of the ordinance, explains, "It's been enormously successful. [...] This thing is so simple, people can understand it without lawyers." Many small projects are being filed directly by owners and many are located in lower-income neighborhoods, just as the initiators had hoped. Other Small Lots projects are more high-end and add fewer units, not more: in one instance in Silver Lake, eight single-family homes are being built where 13 condo units would have been permitted. Either way, the fact that the developments consist of "single-family homes" or duplexes or triplexes has dramatically reduced the number of appeals, since neighbors no longer feel threatened by the development of new "condominiums."

In many ways, Los Angelenos are simply learning to develop new architectural prototypes for an old urban tradition of clustering homes on compact sites. Organized around garden courts and tucked-under parking spaces, these small-lot designs update Los Angeles's early 20th-century courtyard houses, whose staying power has obscured their more humble roots. Recently, renovations have converted some of these courtyard houses into upscale residences, at times using the Small Lots Ordinance to change a former rental property into a number of individual properties. An example is the award-winning conversion of the **Maltman Bungalows** by architects **Drisko Studio** and developer / contractor Civic Enterprise. Built in 1926, the 17 houses each measure only 26 by 26 feet. The team left living rooms, bedrooms and baths in their original configurations, but removed the dividing walls to the kitchens in order to pull the back porch into the interior. As an additional amenity, they added garages between pairs of houses. The Small Lots Ordinance, therefore, provided the key policy for the re-use and preservation of housing that may otherwise have been demolished for more standard solutions. Needless to say, reusing existing structures is a key strategy of sustainable development.

BELOW, FROM TOP TO BOTTOM
View of the bungalows. Bungalow interior. Aerial view.

OPPOSITE AND BELOW
Looking closely at how space is used at Sunrise and in the larger Belmont neighborhood was central to the Metropolitan Planning Collaborative's design approach.

NEXT SPREAD
MPC's framework plan for Sunrise.

Large scale commercial uses along Carlton Avenue present an opportunity to site retail uses on the northern edge of Sunrise.

Both Sunrise Trailer Court and the surrounding residential neighborhood have yard space of an almost rural nature: gardens blend to lawns to driveways without discernable boundaries.

Multiple, flexible use of open space such as driveways, parking, recreation, and pedestrian paths optimizes the use of limited land area.

Metropolitan Planning Collaborative ***Sunrise***

Second Place Finalist

Team Members
Aaron Young *Architecture and Urban Design*
Catherine Lynch *Urban Planning*
Georgia Borden *Urban Planning*
Richard Ramsey *Landscape Architecture*

The Urban Habitats competition proposal by Metropolitan Planning Collaborative (MPC) proposes a loose strategy formulated as a framework to add value to an existing site. This framework plan, to be realized according to demand, builds explicitly on existing building types and the relationships between them:

The eclectic and "small home" character of Belmont led us to explore high density, low-rise clusters of houses, rather than large scale multifamily buildings. Breaking the site down into zones, each with a slightly different architectural typology, allowed us to propose a diverse mix of housing, while maintaining a high degree of porosity and stunning mountain views.

MPC's framework plan allows for standard floor plans and also proposes new ones. While the standard 60-foot-deep, double-loaded commercial building speaks the same language as its neighbors across Carlton Avenue, the buildings along Nassau Street are narrow, two-story homes inspired by the existing trailers. Free standing houses with attached garages line Midland Street. The landscape, a network of shared and private outdoor spaces, is continuous and plays a crucial role in tying together the variety of building types. As the team writes:

When low-rise high-density projects are designed, they necessitate an understanding that the old models of hierarchical frontages (front, back, side and side) are less effective in solving the complex relationships that such proximity demands. Therefore, one aspect of this project became about testing the relationships

Integration of 1 and 2 story homes provides an organic street elevation reflective of the eclectic residential neighborhood south of Sunrise.

Second-story boutique office space along Carlton Avenue (e.g. medical, counseling, legal, non-profits, etc.) can be converted to additional condominium units if demand requires. These offices will also supply additional foot traffic to support ground floor retail uses.

New retail uses along Carlton Avenue such as a deli or small restaurant and a daycare center will serve residents of the community and the 650 employees of LexisNexis located on the northern side of the street.

The existing building stock is retained, renovated and even added onto in an effort to maintain the residential patterns present on the site, as well as to reuse- rather than discard, valuable material.

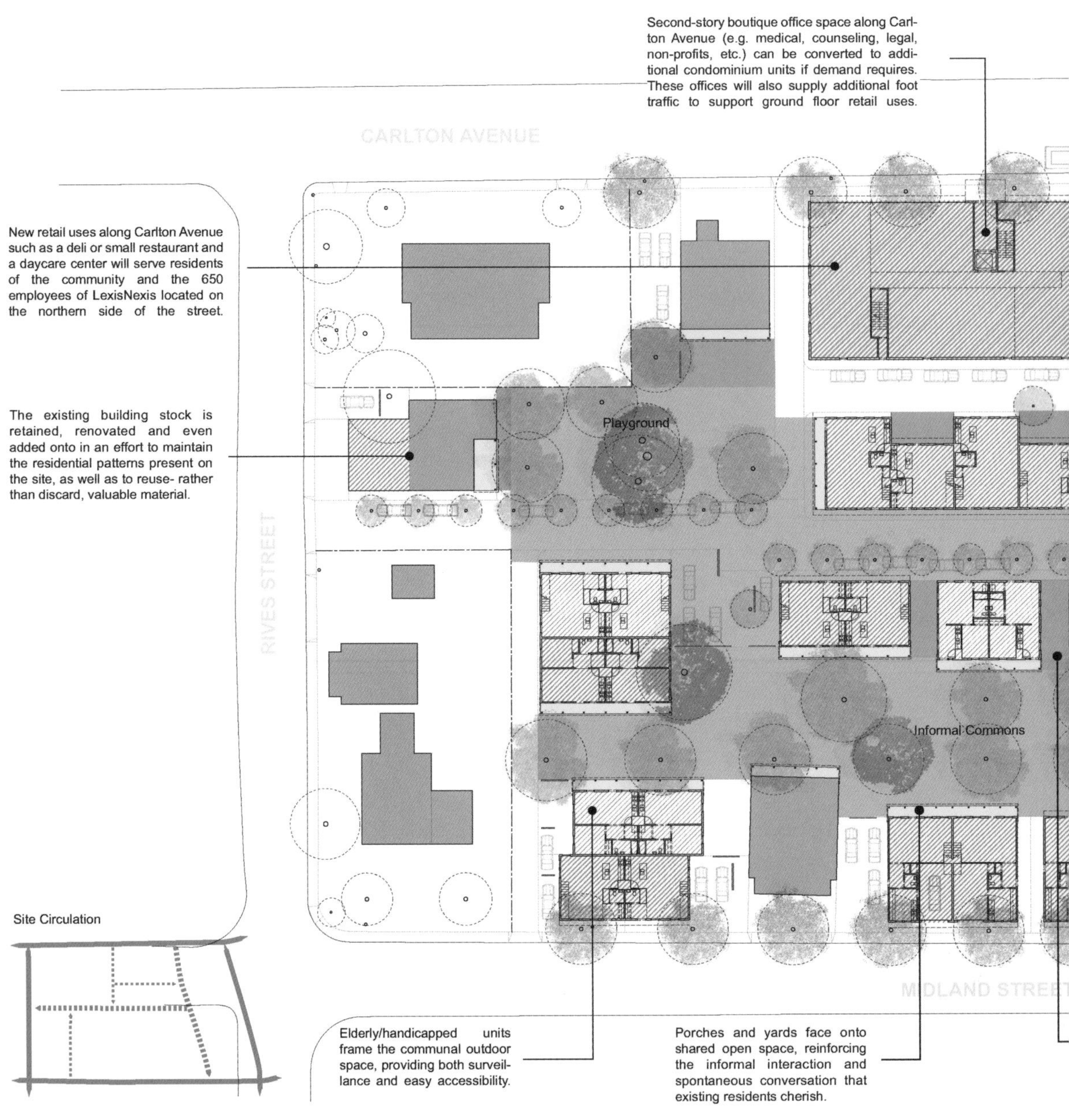

Elderly/handicapped units frame the communal outdoor space, providing both surveillance and easy accessibility.

Porches and yards face onto shared open space, reinforcing the informal interaction and spontaneous conversation that existing residents cherish.

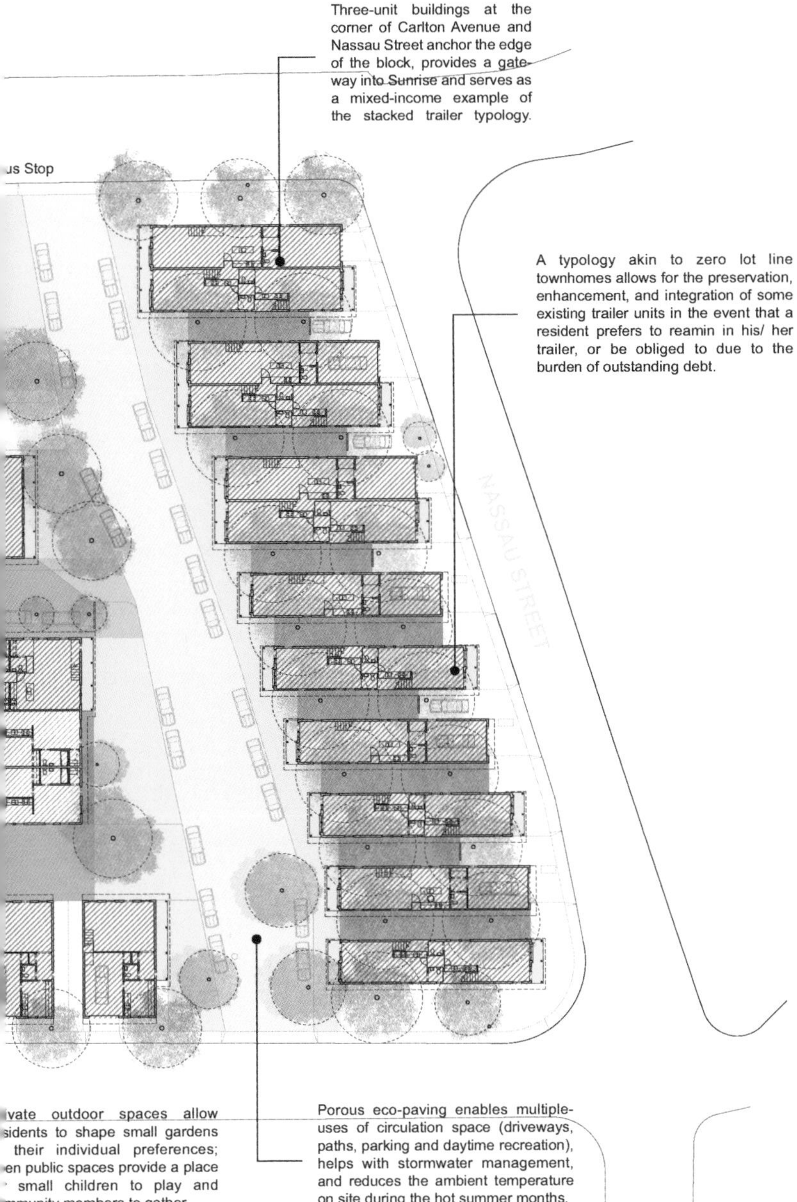

Statement

No sunrise is exactly the same as the next. And similarly, no trailer park is identical. Like each sunrise, each trailer park has its own identity and defining characteristics. The challenge then, is to create a replicable model for the redevelopment of trailer parks across the United States while simultaneously maintaining the strong sense of place and community that already exists in the Belmont neighborhood of Charlottesville.

Re-new, don't re-invent. The Sunrise plan seeks to leverage the trailer park's assets—a strong sense of community, compact housing, multiple and flexible use of open space, and a spectacular mountain view. Additionally, the Sunrise plan aims to leverage existing infrastructure—sanitary layout, internal vehicular circulation patterns, and trees —while better weaving the block into the physical fabric of the larger neighborhood.

Flexible design is sustainable. Sunrise is a replicable framework that allows for a variety of residential typologies to be "plugged in" depending on climatic, cultural and financial constraints. Providing a mix of building uses and neighborhood amenities, it is designed to attract an economically diverse group of residents who value community life.

Jury Comments

This design has a strong orientation to the existing site and sensitivity to the desires of the residents. Jurors commented on the easy, relaxed, Southern personality of the site plan. The attention to phasing will allow current residents not to be displaced from their trailers until well into the construction process. Jurors also noted that, while other designs used one approach architecturally, this design was not prescriptive as to architectural style, clearly referencing known prototypes and suggesting possibilities within the modern idiom. This design encourages a diversity of scales, incomes and architectural languages.

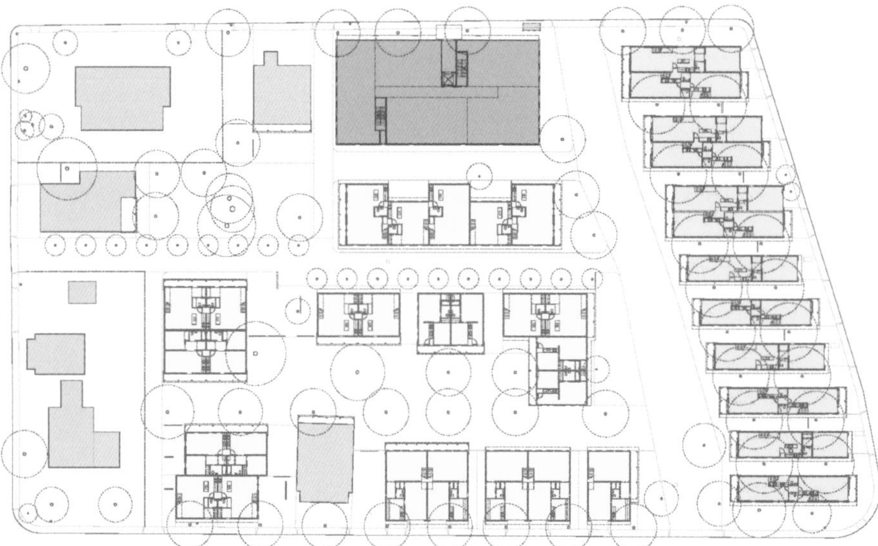

Flexible organizational strategy
By organizing the site according to typology, respecting fairly standardized floor plate depths and building heights, the framework plan accomodates any number of different architectures.

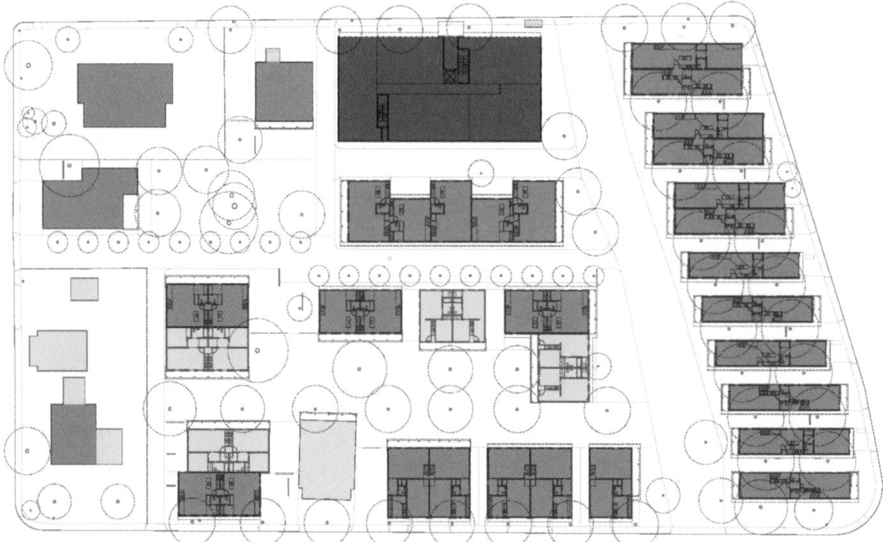

Building heights
Building heights are used to shield the intererior of the site from busy city streets as well as to frame the communal spaces within.

▪ 5 stories ▪ 2 stories ▪ 1 story

between housing types that could blur those distinctions. The notion of multiple fronts to the flexible framework also enabled us to explore the opportunities for public and private open space to have new or different relationships.

A key element of the open space in this plan is: the "woonerf." The concept of the woonerf originates in the Netherlands and describes a type of "shared street" where pedestrians and cyclists have legal priority over automobile drivers. This central space, inspired by the existing access road of the trailer park, functions simultaneously as a street, a parking lot, the main community gathering space and as a rainwater catchment area. Functions typically found incompatible with one another are encouraged to coexist. By organizing parking by hours of use instead of relying on designated parking spaces, contiguous areas of open space become available as play areas during the day when cars are typically off-site.

A major benefit of this framework is the flexibility it allows for building out the development. It assumes that the market will determine what gets built when, as well as what the architecture will actually look like. It is a highly pragmatic approach to adding value: the designers opted for allowing for and even embracing the vagaries of taste, budget and timeframe, rather than imposing a strict order or set of conditions upon the site.

OPPOSITE
MPC highlights critical aspects of their development strategy in plan. The framework allows for different building types, while determining their building heights.

BELOW
Examples of architecture and landscape that could result from MPC's framework plan.

NEXT PAGE
The framework is based on integrating different forms of ownership and uses, while defining the relationship different types of open space.

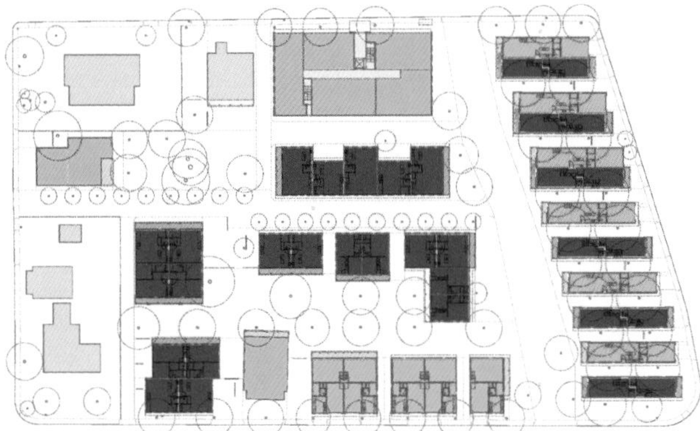

Ownership
Market rate and Habitat for Humanity units are weaved throughout the block, creating a truly mixed-income community.

- Habitat Housing
- Market Rate
- Not Included in Redevelopment

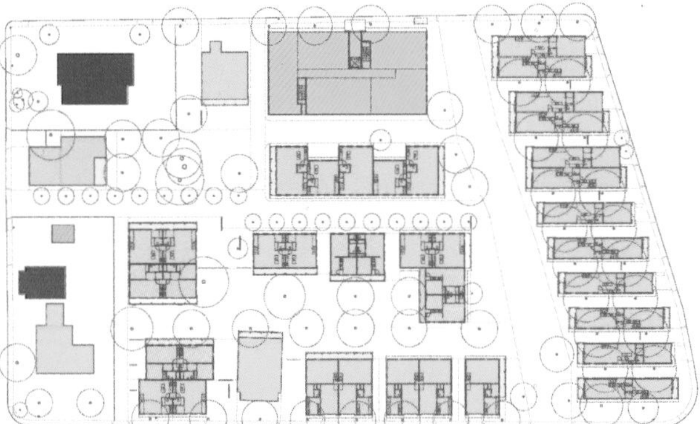

Building Use
Large scale buildings facing the LexisNexis campus on Carlton Avenue step-down to smaller scale residential units along Midland Street.

- 1-story eldely / accessible rental
- 2-story residential
- 5-story mixed use
- Retail
- Office

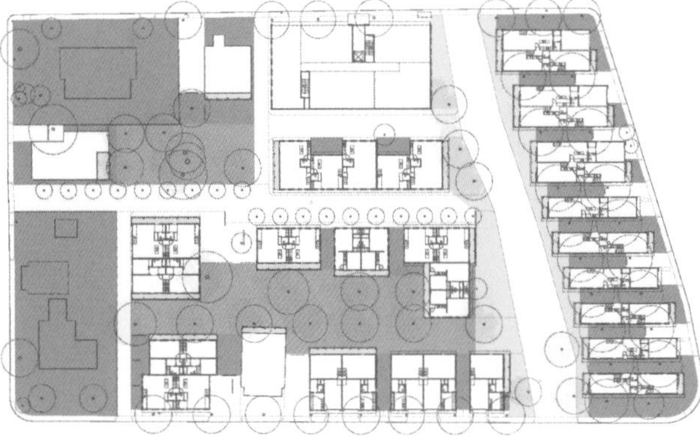

Open Space
Hierarchy of open space ranges from private gardens connected to town home units, to communal pocket parks for tot-lots and barbeqyes, to multi-purpose driveways and parking zones that crisscross the block, to public space for commercial use along Carlton Avenue.

- Private open space
- Communal open space
- Public interior street

Extension

Metropolitan Planning Collaborative

MPC is a multi-disciplinary collaborative working out of Washington, DC, New York, Boston and San Francisco.

What role does / did the Urban Habitats competition play within your practice?

Urban Habitats was the first competition that the members of MPC entered together. The competition design team included Richard Ramsey, a landscape architect from New York. After MPC was selected to elaborate their entry for Habitat for Humanity, Richard decided to pass the landscape design responsibilities to Beka Sturges. Although this was their first joint project, all members of the team had participated in previous design competitions either individually or in other groups. MPC's Urban Habitats competition experience reinforced, for them, the belief that interdisciplinary design creates a more thoughtful, well-formed outcome.

For Aaron Young, an architect and urban designer, Sunrise offered the opportunity to bring together the multiple experiences he has had working as an architect over the past 12 years. Having built a number of single-family homes, and planned developments of over 1,500 multifamily residences, the scale of housing within the urban plan for Sunrise is situated at a middle ground within his professional experience. He appreciates the fact that Sunrise has been driven by Habitat for Humanity's mission, with for-profit considerations reinforcing design decisions, but not controlling them.

For Beka Sturges, the straightforward and responsive way Sunrise has addressed issues of affordable housing and gentrification is exceptional in her professional experience as a landscape architect. Commitment to context, sustainability and local ecologies is familiar to her from other projects, but this is the first time she has seen such an emphasis on high quality open space for a mixed-income housing development.

For Cathy Lynch, an urban planner and mixed-income housing developer, Sunrise presents the opportunity to further explore green design, methods of community engagement, implications of volunteer-built housing, and the chance to participate in community building as a designer rather than a developer.

For Georgia Borden, an urban planner, "inter-disciplinary" design has too often been "assembly line design"—where projects get passed from one professional to another without a tremendous amount of dialogue. While the more cross-disciplinary collaborative approach to both the competition and the project itself has, at times, yielded strong differences of opinion, she believes that the discourse and negotiation involved has led to a much more robust solution.

The team received informal comments from design professionals at the Urban Habitats symposium that their entry did not go far enough toward illustrating a specific landscape or architectural design—that perhaps their emphasis on a design framework came at the expense of architectural and landscape design. One of the best parts of an ideas competition is that it forces participants to develop clear, strong ideas in a short period of time. While they would have loved to develop both the landscape and architecture further, they felt that their strength as an interdisciplinary team lent itself best to the development of a flexible planning framework.

Have you been able to further develop the concepts put forward in your entry?

By being retained by Habitat for the further master planning effort for Sunrise, MPC has been able to hone many of the basic principles put forward in the original competition entry: building on the trailer court's assets, establishing a connection between the site and the Belmont neighborhood, and leveraging the strong sense of community among current Sunrise residents by strengthening their multiple and flexible use of common spaces.

Have you been able to realize any projects that are related to the Urban Habitats project, be it in scale, approach, client, philosophy?

MPC completed a sustainable, eco-friendly subdivision plan for 100-acres of farmland in Maryland. The owner of the land, formerly used by his family for dairy farming, had the objective of creating an innovative mixed-use subdivision that would enhance the semi-rural setting rather than distract from it. The final design used the natural topography and view corridors as a starting point for the design concept. Hedgerows, vegetated buffers, retention ponds, and minimal roadways were then used to segregate one lot from another.

Mix It Up
:Fit It In

The C Words, or what we mean by context and community.

When discussing the physical design of new housing in existing neighborhoods, the most frequent demand by current residents is that the new development "fit in." Context and community are the terms most frequently used to do so. How to go about clarifying what we really mean?

:Describe "context".

How to add new to old? The most frequent demand neighbors make of a new development is that it "fit in" to the "context." The context, however, is rarely described. There are neighborhoods where the scale, typology and orientation of houses are all very much alike, and continuing to build in this vocabulary may be the best choice. But there are many neighborhoods characterized by a wide variety of buildings and uses where fitting in may require some more soul searching.

Context is frequently invoked as a short cut to describe easily recognizable architectural features: a form of roof, a type of porch, a common color. Simple replication of these elements distracts from finding out what really works.

What are the positive features of your site, what may benefit from a rethinking? Just because some buildings are already there, must they set the benchmark for all others? Just because a building is old, is it automatically good? Alternately, some old buildings have fallen into disrepair and are considered an eyesore. Might they be worth reusing all the same? Describe the pros and cons of the existing neighborhood. Describe what is missing and why what works, works.

:Define "community".

Like "context," "community" is frequently invoked to lend an air of legitimacy to development and design decisions. There is hardly a new development that does not claim to be building community. Talking about community always sounds good, but who actually benefits?

Articulate what "building community" means for your project. Who does it include? Who does it exclude? Does it mean "non-profit" or "grass roots" or "small-scale" or something entirely different? Are you building "a community" which is distinct from its surroundings or are you building homes that will be a part of a larger neighborhood?

Defining community is the first step to managing expectations and creating a project that will live up to them.

City of Portland, Oregon
Living Smart Project

The City of Portland, Oregon's Living Smart Project is a good example of how proactive policy that includes design solutions can address the concerns of context and community in an urban neighborhood.

Portland is known for its growth management. The city's regional Urban Growth Boundary (UGB), in place and continually adjusted since the late 1970s, protects outlying open spaces and agricultural lands from development. As a result, the city proper has been subject to a sharp rise in land prices in the past 30 years, while witnessing tremendous growth in homes built on small in-fill lots. In a number of neighborhoods characterized by 5,000 square foot lots, the historic plot size and zoning regulations allowed for development on 25- by 100-foot-deep parcels, and 15-foot-wide houses helped meet the city's need for entry-level single-family homes.

This boom in narrow house construction, however, led to strong opposition among citizens who felt that the infill development was out of scale with the surrounding neighborhood. In addition, these developments frequently triggered the demolition of existing houses to allow for the site's subdivision. Despite the opposition, the City Council reaffirmed its commitment to

OPPOSITE
Aerial photograph of two narrow houses realized in South Woodstock by a builder who used the pre-approved plan by Vargas Greenan Architects.

BELOW
The two homes seen from the street.

LEFT
First floor plan alternates. The house can accommodate either a garage or an office.

OPPOSITE
Second floor plan.

BELOW
View of the side yard between the two houses in South Woodstock.

the Urban Growth Boundary in 2003 by continuing to support narrow-lot, infill development. It did, however, restrict the subdivision of lots to vacant properties and added new design requirements pertaining to dimensions, openings and materials used.

The Living Smart Project was launched specifically to address the design aspects of this challenge, and City Commissioner Randy Leonard committed to holding a design competition in 2004. The challenge to design a 15-foot-wide, three-bedroom house drew more than 400 submissions. The City published selected designs in two readily available catalogues. It took the initiative a step further, however, and set up a permit-ready program, conceived as an incentive to builders to actually implement the good designs. Two proposals were chosen from among the competition winners and developed to the level of buildable plans. Builders can now obtain these designs from the City, commit to the architect's specifications and details and get a fast-tracked approval and a 50% discount on the city's fees.

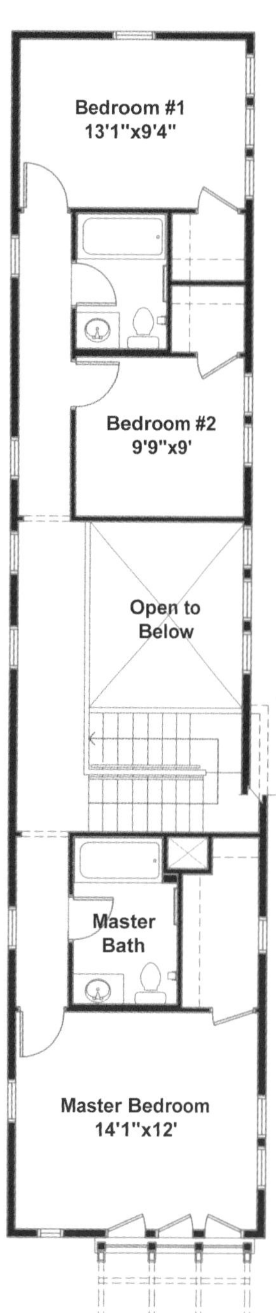

By the summer of 2008, ten homes had been built through the permit-ready program. Located in a range of neighborhoods, the homes were selling well for the builders and at around $320,000, are considered low in price by market standards. As an example, the private builder Prairie View Homes built two homes in the South Woodstock District based on a design by **Vargas Greenan Architects** of Berkeley, California. In terms of subsidized housing, the City has tried to network with affordable housing developers in the hopes that they, too, would use the plans. To date, however, no initiative has resulted from this effort, in part because coordinating the construction of several small parcels is much more time consuming for a developer than managing a larger project on one site. As Russ Turkus, Senior Administrative Specialist of the Department of Development Services notes, by providing the plans, the City is inadvertently placed in the role of project manager and intermediary between the designers and builders, which is especially laborious when designs are implemented for the first time.

The additional effort on the part of the City seems to be paying off, however. Neighborhood opposition to narrow houses on subdivided lots has subsided—mainly because existing houses are no longer being demolished. The City plans to include several more designs in its permit-ready program and is in the process of upgrading the energy efficiency requirements.

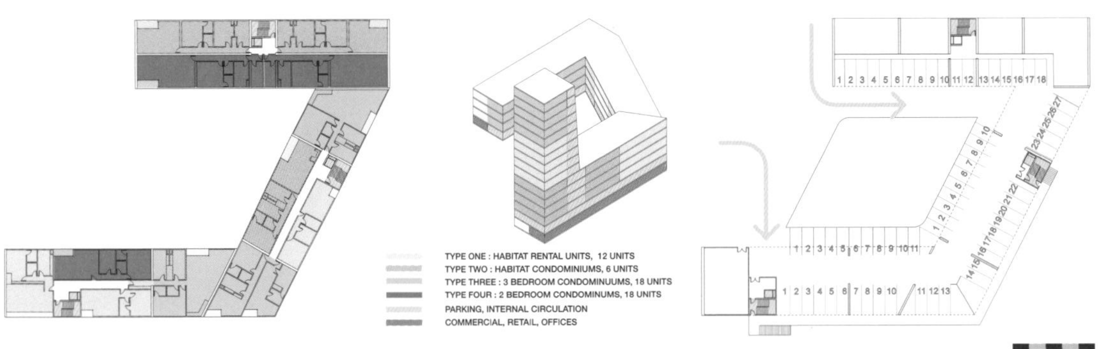

Condominium building: typical floor plan, unit distribution, and ground floor plan.

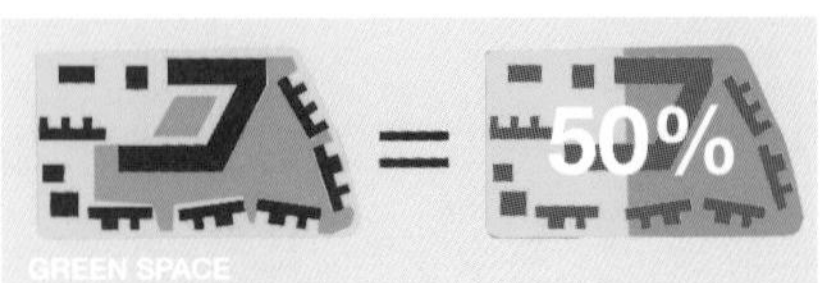

Higher buildings create more open space.

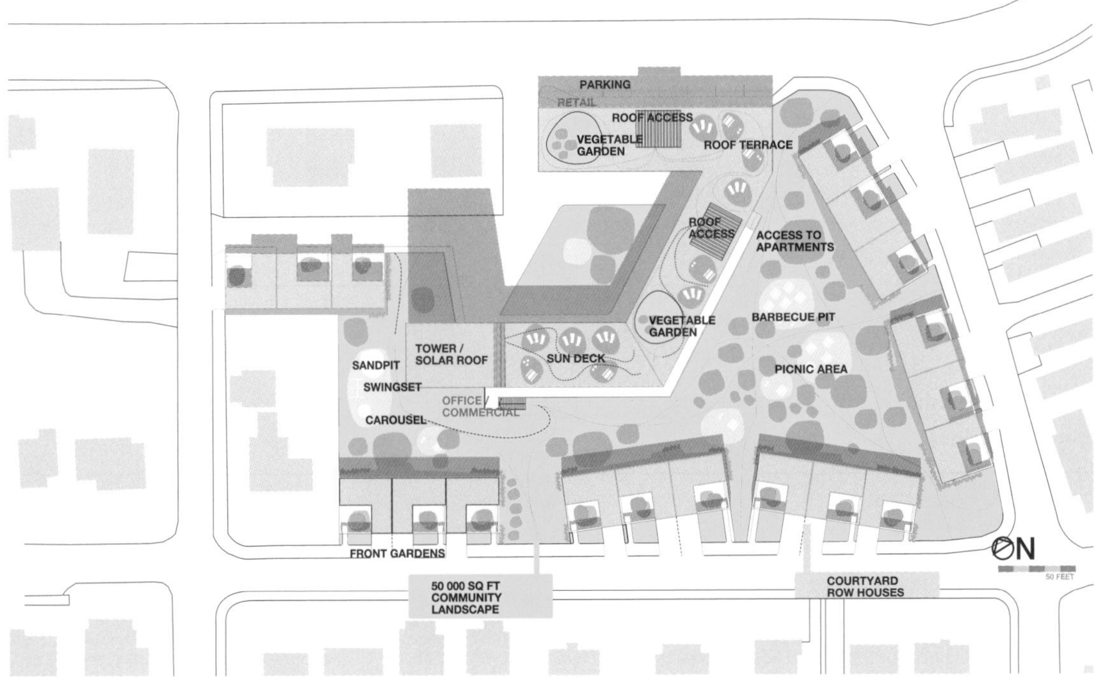

Site plan.

Boyarsky Murphy Architects
Sunrise Park

The Urban Habitats competition proposal by Boyarsky Murphy Architects of London, shows that in terms of context, new need not look like old, and that, in terms of community, different constituencies can overlap. Rather than offering a uniform treatment of the site to achieve higher density, the scheme does so by building high at one end of the site and low at the other. By trading modest height for open space, Boyarsky Murphy create a large, centrally located lawn.

While the condominium, rising up from a four-story base to a 16-story tower, is targeted at Habitat rentals and market-rate units, the 15 two-story courtyard houses along Nassau and Midland Streets are to be built and occupied by Habitat homeowners. Similar to the scheme by Genter Schindler *(see p. 160)*, the various constituencies making up the new Sunrise community are given distinct housing options, yet they come together in the shared open space. In contrast to the Genter Schindler scheme, where the two open spaces are to be used by the residents only, here the lawn is accessible to the larger Belmont community.

The scheme ties into the existing context and community by locating small-scale housing along the streets that surround the Sunrise block. The design team does so by creating a new type of courtyard house to mediate between the street and traffic in front and the recreational landscape behind.

The proposal gives the notions of context and community a spin, however, one that shows that architecture can be contextual and community-oriented without looking familiar at first. While the condominium tower may not have any precedents in terms of height in the Belmont area, the architects felt there was a need for this kind of building. "The condominium building [...] will provide an urban landmark to give a new identity and visual cohesion to the neighborhood. It is an icon for Habitat's new development strategy." Architecture belongs to all who can see it, and must contribute to both the context and its communities accordingly.

Honorable Mention

Team Members
Nicholas Boyarsky, Nicola Murphy, Andrew Lyon, Joakim Skajaa

Statement
This proposal seeks to provide a new urban neighborhood that works creatively with density issues and a diverse range of housing types. The proposal is based on the premise that fifty percent of the site is given over to community landscape. This is achieved by restricting car access to the site and by developing two new typologies: courtyard row houses for affordable housing and a figured, mixed-income condominium. To urbanize the site, we have reinforced the street by positioning the courtyard row houses facing outwards along the perimeter of the block. Grouping the courtyard houses into threes strengthens their urban form and helps to invite and frame entry to the community landscape.

The condominium building is raised off the ground to provide for parking and visual continuity across the site. The form of the condominium carves a sequence of public spaces. It will provide an urban landmark to give a new identity and visual cohesion to the neighborhood. It is an icon for Habitat's new development strategy.

At the heart of the scheme is some 50,000 square feet of community landscape: the means of crossing the site by foot, a place for children to play in safety, for senior citizens to enjoy at their leisure and for all the residents to enjoy visually. Retail outlets and commercial spaces open onto the landscape.

Jury Comments
This proposal suggests a more urban approach to the development of the site. The jury was engaged by the clear distinction between private open space within the courtyards and the expansive urban public space of the park. The jury thought that the development landscape in Charlottesville may not be ready for such a dramatic leap, but they want to make the community aware of the potentials of this development model.

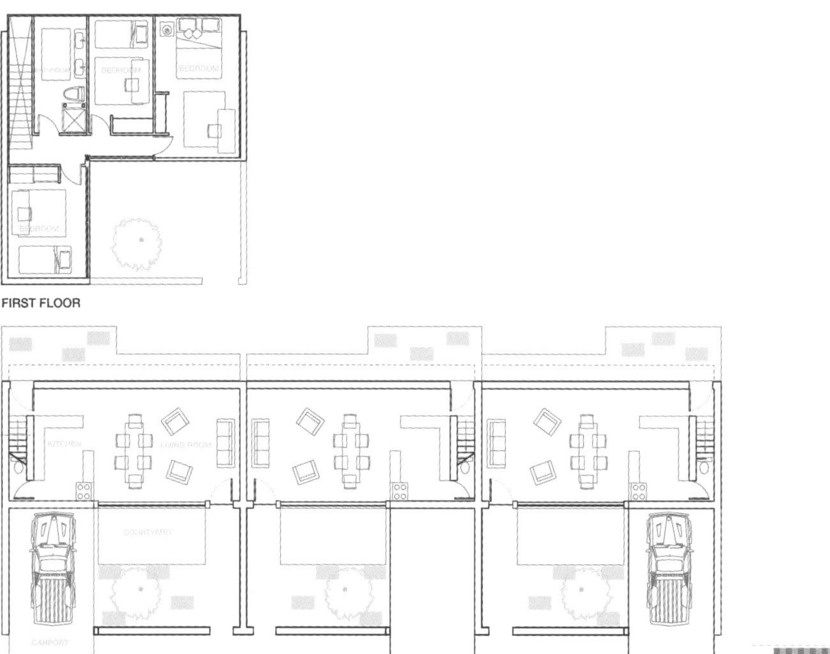

Floor plans of Habitat house.

View of the central community open space.

Extension

Boyarsky Murphy Architects

Boyarsky Murphy Architects was formed as a partnership by Nicholas Boyarsky and Nicola Murphy in London (UK) in 1994. The firm has successfully worked in the fields of housing, urban design, renovations, interiors, prefabrication and smaller cultural and educational buildings. Nicholas Boyarsky has taught at several universities and since 2007 has been director of Syracuse University's London Architectural Study Program.

What role does / did the Urban Habitats competition play within your practice?

It was a great opportunity to test some ideas we've been working on. One is the question of how to accommodate a mix of different densities on one site. The other is how to minimize the impact of the car—a particularly American condition, of course. Both are issues of density, and involve the old question of whether it is possible to use more vertical elements in order to create more quality open space in return.

Have you been able to further develop the concepts put forward in your entry?

We are currently working on a new project for a medium-sized eco-community in the UK consisting of 400 residential units. The whole development will be powered by an anaerobic digestor which will make the development 90% self sufficient in terms of electricity and heat. Housing units will be of zero carbon construction. Waste water will be recycled. It will be a prototype for future developments across the country.

Have you been able to realize any projects that are related to the Urban Habitats project, be it in scale, approach, client, philosophy?

Yes, the Sliver House. Completed in 2006, the single-family house was built on a wedge-shaped site formerly occupied by a single-story wine vault that served the adjacent pub. It is literally wedged between the party walls of this pub and a Victorian terrace, with a frontage of only 3 m (9 feet) and 8 m (24 feet) in height. This infill building is one way to accommodate additional housing on nonstandard sites within an existing neighborhood. Although the Maida Vale part of London certainly isn't comparable to Charlottesville's Belmont in terms of density, it proves that by fine-tuning and extensive code work, even in tight conditions, it is possible to create a sense of spaciousness and a connection between the inside and out.

BELOW

The Sliver House was built into a nine-foot-wide slot between two party walls. View of the street front.

FOLLOWING SPREAD, FROM LEFT TO RIGHT

Floor plans.

View of the Sliver House from the back alley.

View from the living room onto the patio.

Axonometric.

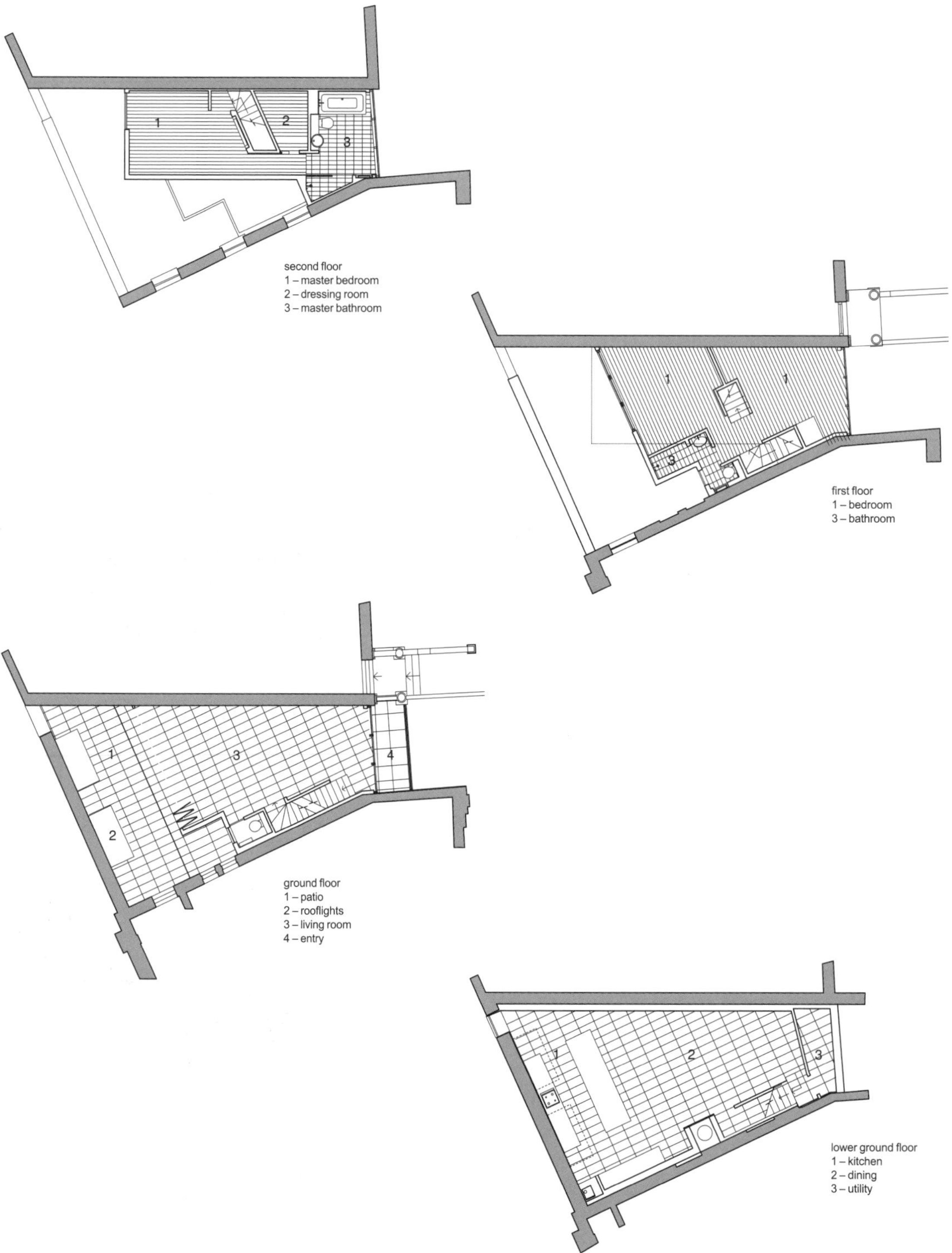

second floor
1 – master bedroom
2 – dressing room
3 – master bathroom

first floor
1 – bedroom
3 – bathroom

ground floor
1 – patio
2 – rooflights
3 – living room
4 – entry

lower ground floor
1 – kitchen
2 – dining
3 – utility

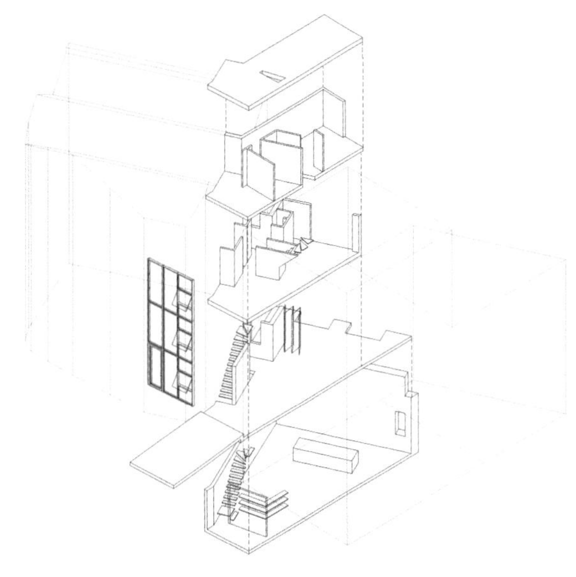

Expand Options
: Intensify Nature

Open Space, or how to live the in-between.

The more you build, the less open space you have, or so the thinking goes. Really? In reality, higher density may actually allow you to intensify the experience of nature. How to approach this mutual reinforcement?

: Make all of it useable.

Zoning codes use the term "open space" to refer to that part of a parcel that is unoccupied by buildings. Most zoning codes stipulate the percentage of a parcel that is to remain open, frequently distinguishing between "useable open space" for recreational use, and the rest for use as access, set-back or parking. Instead of sticking to these categories, make all of your open space useable and make it all an integral part of the development's residential environment.

: Capture the buffer.

Standard site planning practice frequently renders open space little more than a buffer between buildings or a set-back from the street. This results from fire code requirements, not considerations about the functionality or quality of such spaces. Consider laying out your parcels differently. This space can be more than a paved and empty boundary. It can allow for plantings, give access to sunlight and provide a cool breeze. If this is not an option or you are dealing with a single parcel: what can you do with that sliver of land?

: Look beyond the parcel.

Your parcel may be limited in size, but there is certainly lots more land around it. Look beyond the immediate confines of your site. How does its topography relate to its surroundings? What are the views? Where is the wind coming from? Where are the water systems? The latter may be especially important when dealing with non-standard, former commercial, industrial or trailer park areas.
These grey field sites were frequently severed from their natural surroundings. Use this opportunity to reconnect to existing natural and public systems.

Onion Flats
Rag Flats

Founded in 1997, the Philadelphia-based, developer-architect-builder office Onion Flats has completed several projects motivated by the goal of intensifying nature in the city, while building at a higher density than manifest in the existing neighborhood. In 2006, Onion Flats completed Rag Flats, comprised of eleven new dwelling units on the site of a former manufacturing plant located within a small-scale residential neighborhood in North Philadelphia. The previous owner had acquired a variance for the former industrial property, but only for single-family residential use. Onion Flats then engaged in an eight-month negotiation with the neighborhood to reach the current scheme. There was no parking variance required, however, since the project provides the standard one space per unit.

OPPOSITE
At Rag Flats, every unit has access to planted open space. The ground-floor patio of a Trinity row house.

BELOW LEFT
The site plan organizes eleven units around a shared open space. Five free-standing single-family houses are sited along Wilt Street. The attached units are located along Berks Street.

BELOW RIGHT
Aerial perspective of the project within the city.

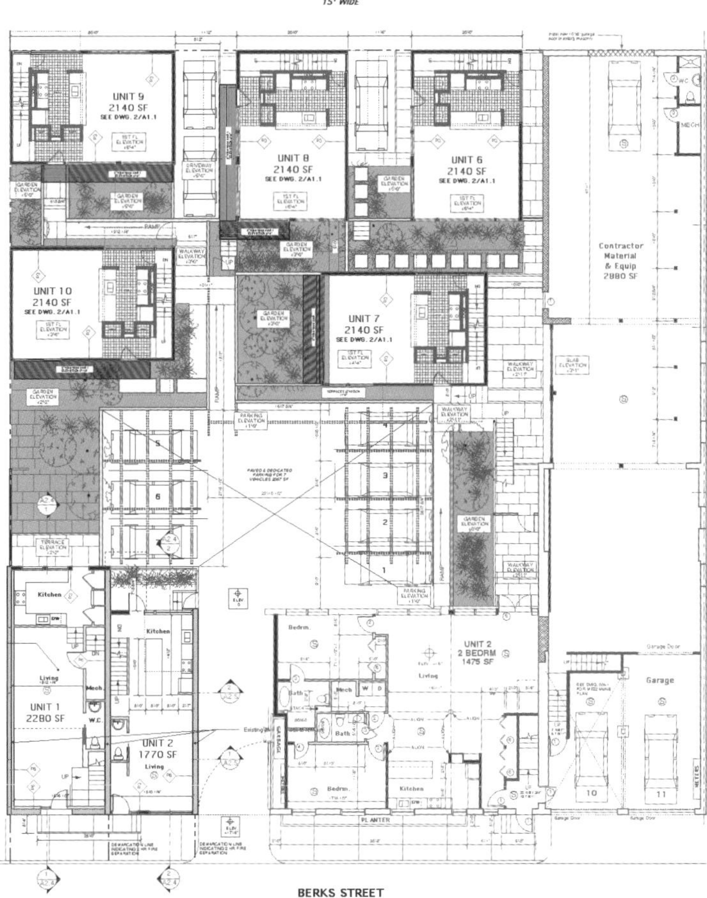

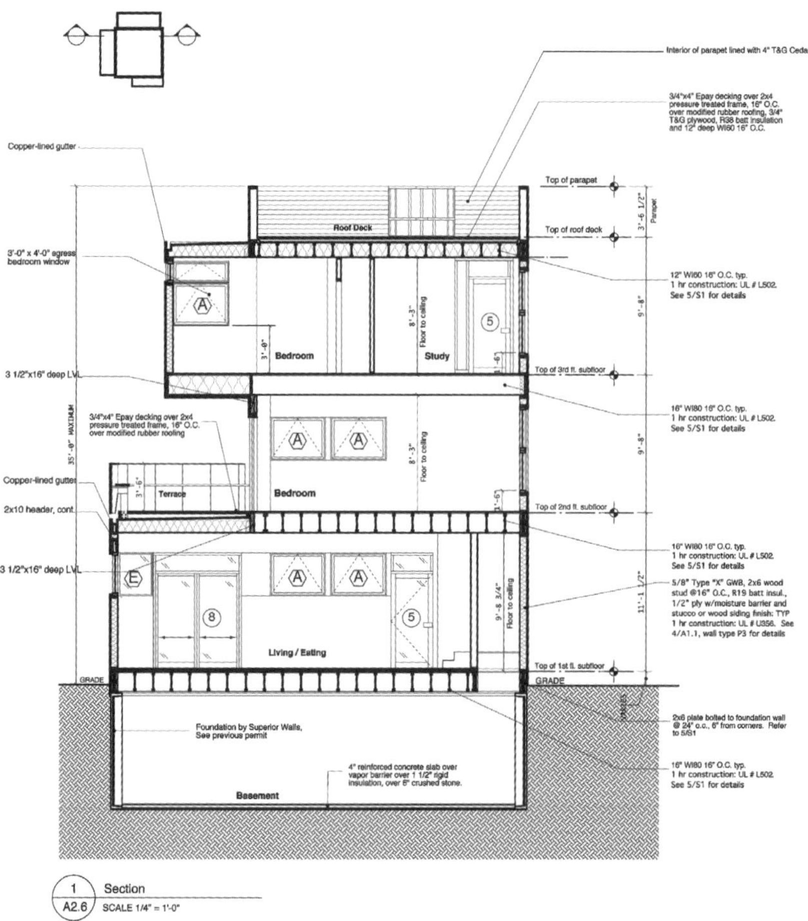

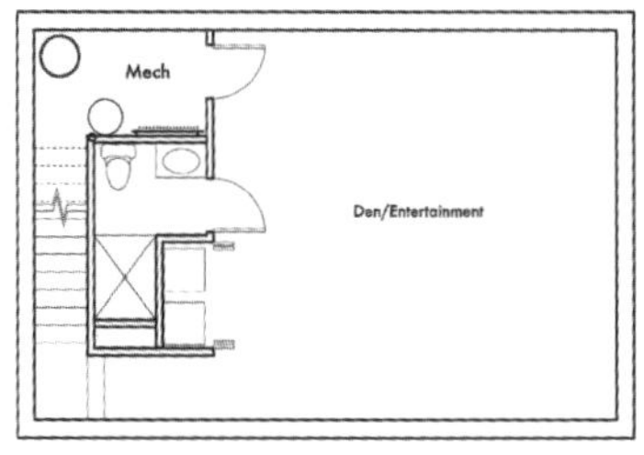

BASEMENT PLAN: Trinity

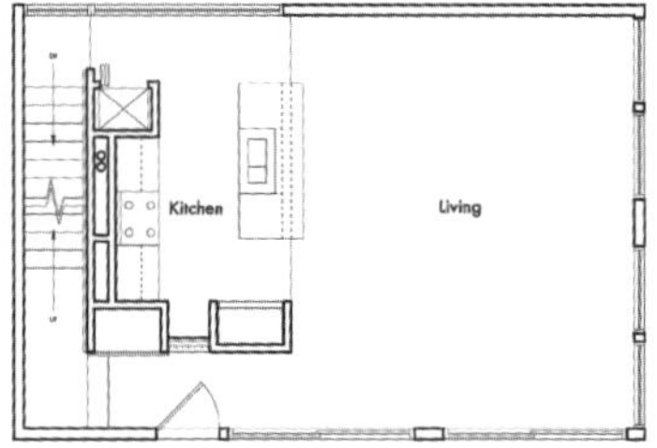

FIRST FLOOR PLAN: Trinity

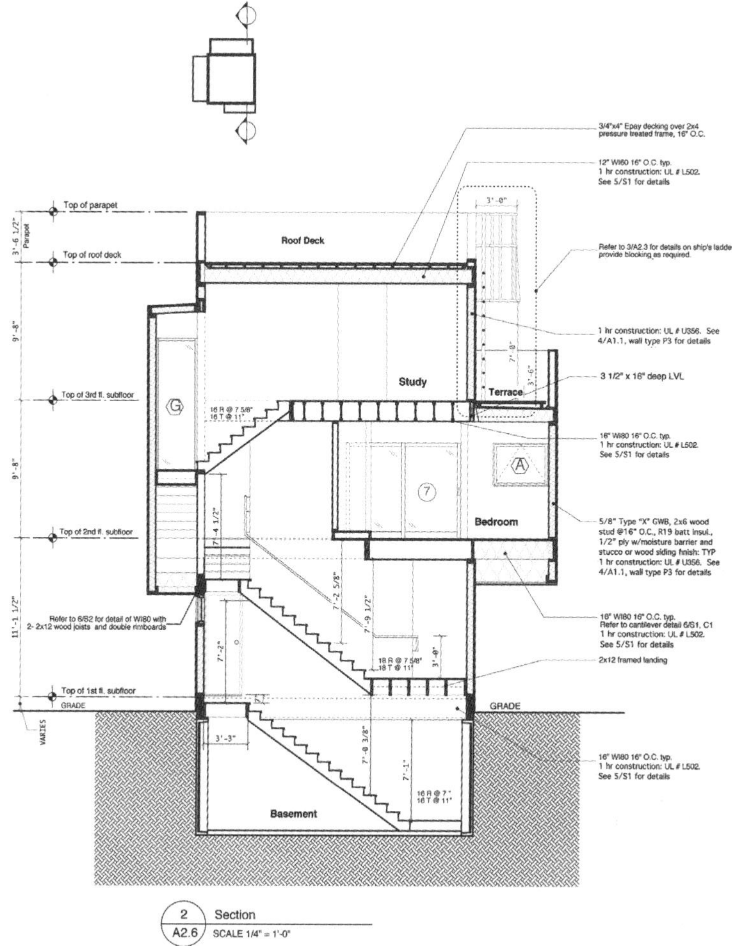

THIS SPREAD
Floor plans and sections of the free-standing, three-bedroom building, Onion Flats' interpretation of Philadelphia's smallest row house type, the Trinity.

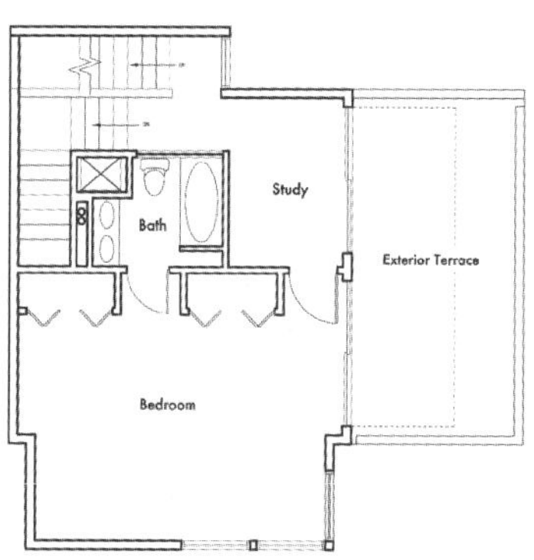

SECOND FLOOR PLAN: Trinity

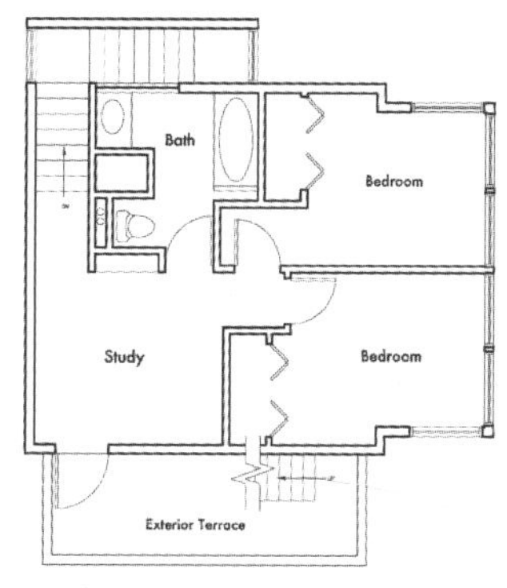

THIRD FLOOR PLAN: Trinity

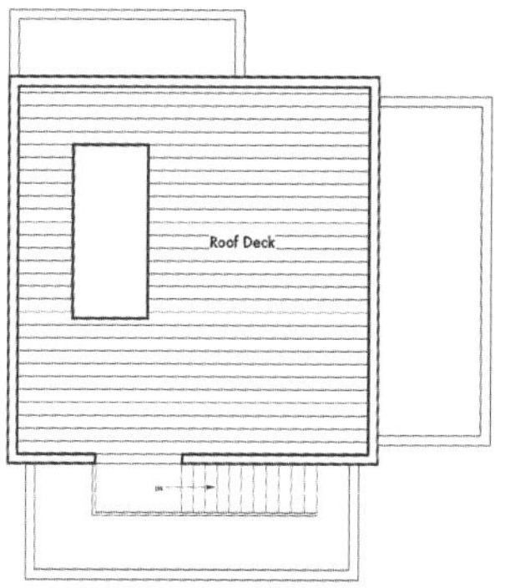

ROOF FLOOR PLAN: Trinity

The key to Rag Flats is the central, shared garden between the renovated factory building and the newly added iterations of traditional Philadelphia building types. The architects call this central courtyard, used for parking and access to the buildings, the "secret" space at the center of the block, or the "in between." While the edges are porous and anyone could theoretically walk across the property, the site is not officially public.

The buildings sit tight, but each dwelling unit has access to a private exterior space, positioned to maximize sun exposure and connect to the central, shared open space. Furthermore, the roofs of the individual buildings are accessible and their green roofs provide planted areas. In short, Rag Flats managed to intensify nature by increasing density.

OPPOSITE
View from an upper-level patio across the site.

BOTTOM LEFT
View from the central open space, which also accommodates parking.

BOTTOM RIGHT
The planted roof of a Trinity.

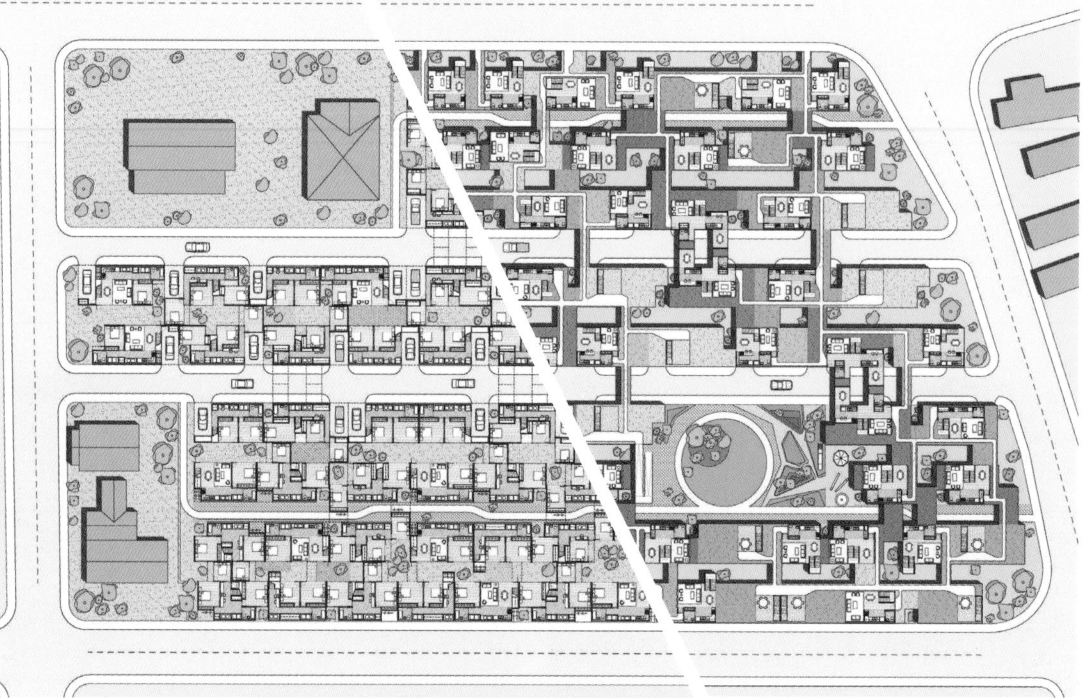

Abruzzo Bodziak
Charlottesville Green

In their Urban Habitats competition proposal, Charlottesville Green, Abruzzo Bodziak of New York takes a larger scale approach to intensifying nature: they slip the majority of the new development beneath a blanket of new landscape. As the project's name implies, the approach refers to the qualities of civic urban space in the American colonial tradition, while at the same time making the case for a type of development that is environmentally sustainable in the contemporary sense. The architects explain:

Our list of requirements for the project dictated that the residences would all have equal access to the outdoors, private gardens, and plenty of natural light. They would also meet stringent density requirements and share services through an economy of means. The subdivision would act as one large entity, but be experienced as discreet moments; green lawns, sidewalks and porches would replace long impersonal corridors.

The site is laid out as a collection of small, detached two story houses. As a whole, however, the mosaic of private homes and gardens adds up to a large, interconnected multi-family building. As the architects describe it,

From Carlton Avenue, the community appears as a field of small, distinct houses. Below and connected to each of those structures, however, is a spacious second level, housing the more private programs such as the bedrooms and full bath. The two-story houses nest to form a continuous green surface at the first level's roof height, creating an artificial ground upon which the second floors of the houses sit apart from one another.

The scheme takes advantage of the 25-foot drop from Carlton Avenue to Midland Street to gather and filter stormwater. Like Anderson Anderson *(see p. 212)*, Abruzzo Bodziak propose that a professional contractor complete the site work, while the individual houses are built by volunteer labor using traditional stick-built methods.

Charlottesville Green shows that high density need not mean less open space. Other projects elevate and shift gardens on roofs, but this scheme demonstrates that an urban project can act in a pastoral way.

OPPOSITE, TOP
Charlottesville Green links individual homes to create a communal whole. View from an upper-level garden to other homes.

OPPOSITE, BELOW
The site plan showing both the lower level (left) and upper level (right) of the development.

BELOW
An aerial perspective revealing the community's network of paths.

NEXT SPREAD
A matrix of housing types at Charlottesville Green.

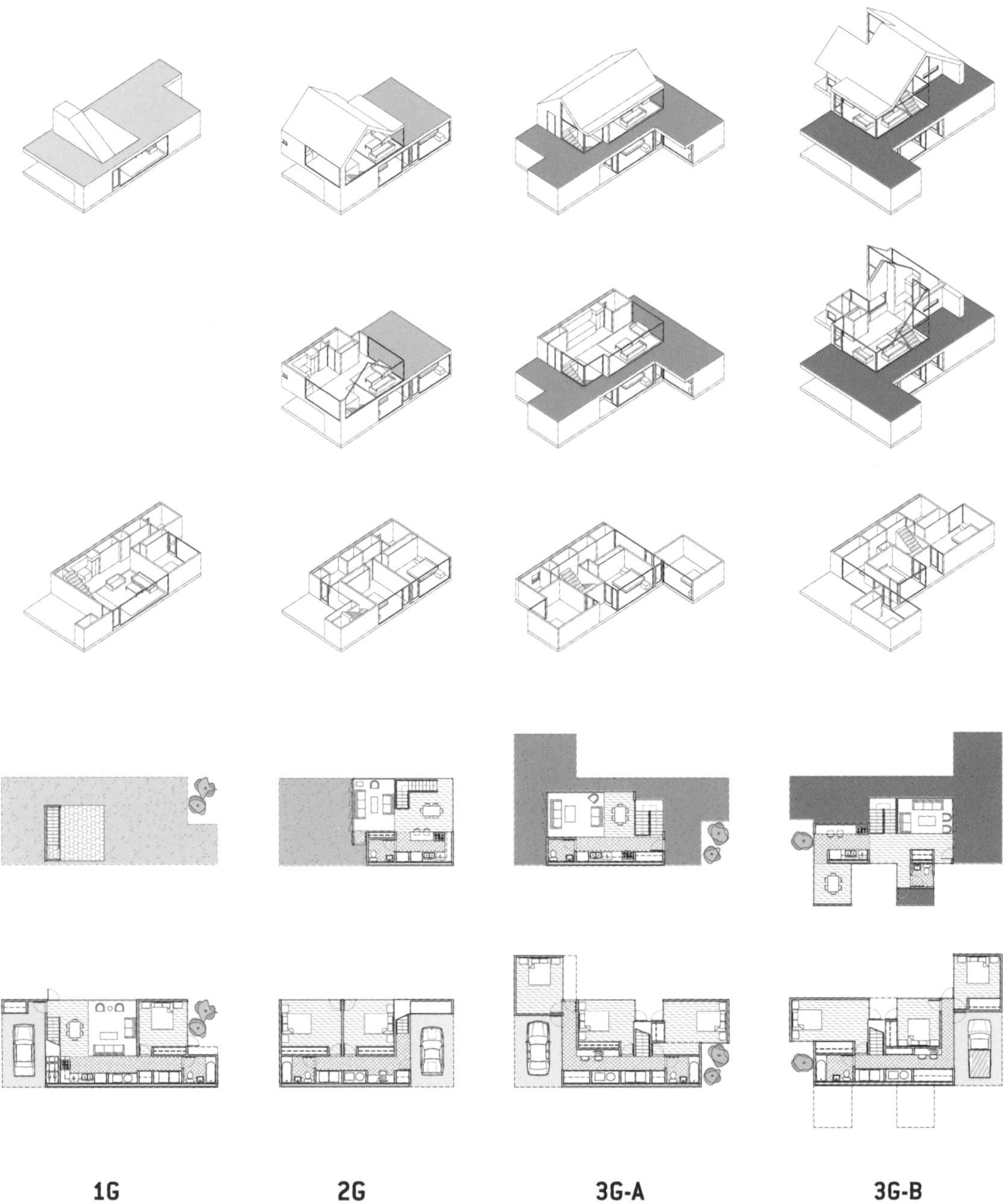
1G
2G
3G-A
3G-B

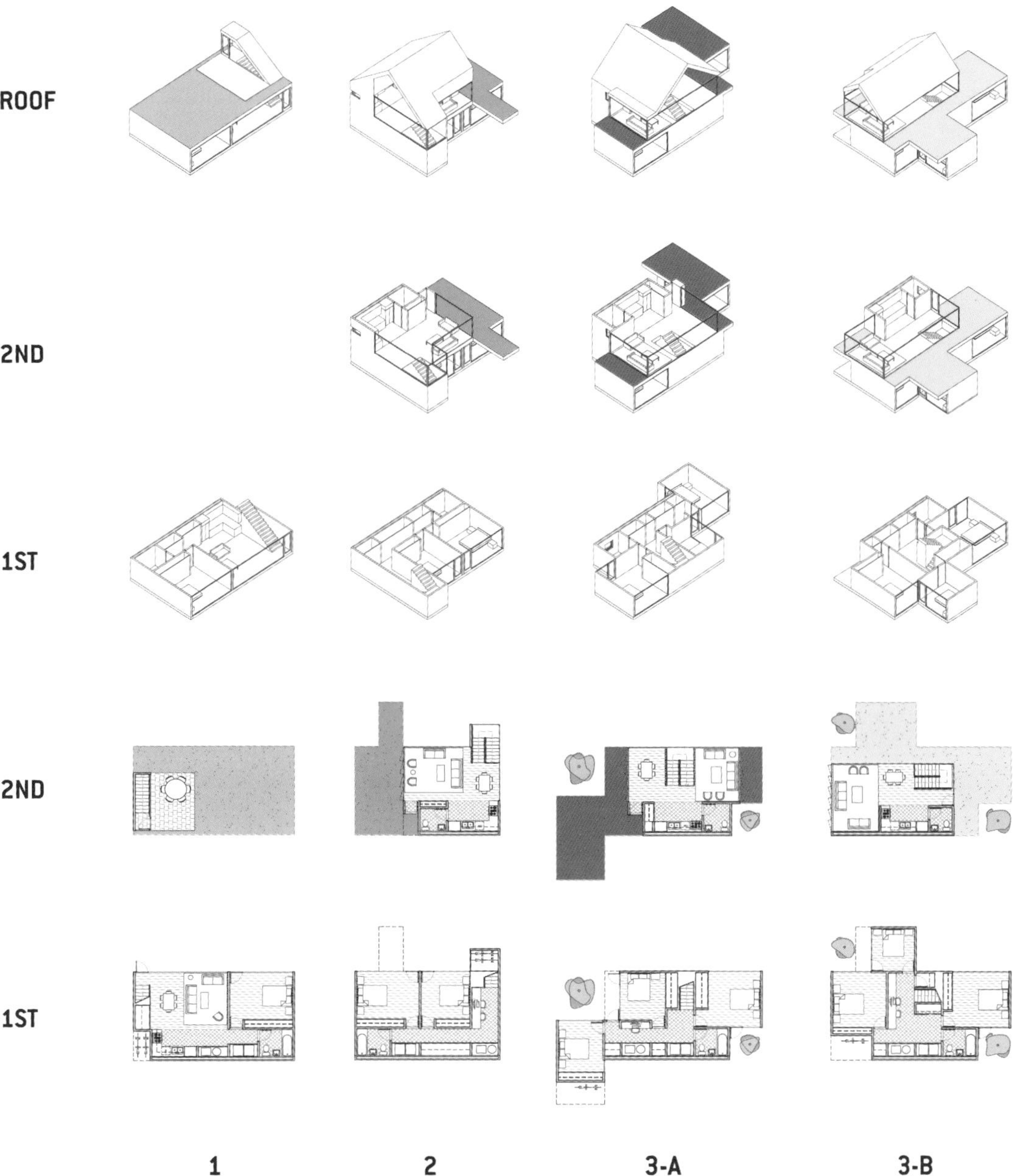
ROOF
2ND
1ST
2ND
1ST
1
2
3-A
3-B

BELOW
A diagram of the relationship between renewable energy sources and architecture.

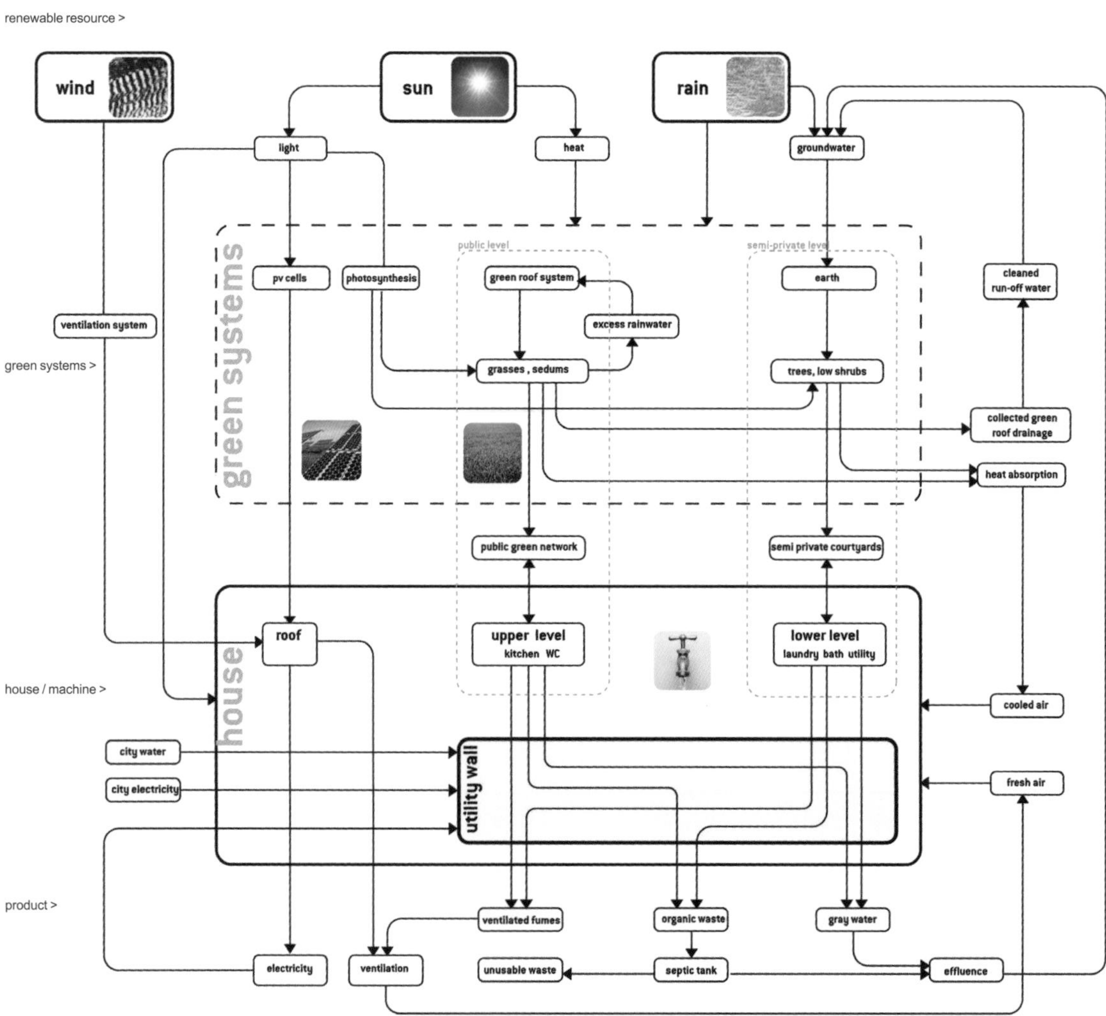

Extension
Abruzzo Bodziak

LEFT
The "Big Re-Dig", designed together with Jonathan Solomon, takes the idea of layering uses as proposed in Charlottesville Green to a larger scale.
Site axonometric.

Emily Abruzzo and Gerald Bodziak are architects working in New York. Their research and speculative work is focused on new ways of interpreting density and using renewable lifecycles in the design of buildings. Their most recent work on housing has taken the form of written works that address contemporary residential architecture in America. Gerald and Emily are both graduates of the Princeton University School of Architecture Master's program, and Emily is an editor of 306090 Books.

What role does / did the Urban Habitats competition play within your practice?

We used the Urban Habitats competition as a test for radically rethinking traditional strategies for suburban residential planning. Our goal, however, was to conceal this reorganization through the careful application of traditional low-density suburban vocabularies. Charlottesville Green was a complex algorithm that attempted to mesh architecture with landscape and blur the understanding of where private property begins and ends. Where we think it is most successful, however, is in the creation of a heterogeneous field of unique moments, within an arrangement of what are, essentially, repetitive modules.

Have you been able to further develop the concepts put forward in your entry?

We continue to refine our ideas though speculative design projects and writing. A critical part of such work is the identification of decorative and formal techniques that successfully marry the ecological and organizational goals that we aim to achieve. We have come to understand, for example, that Charlottesville Green's interest lies in its aesthetic qualities as much as its organizational ones. Referencing traditional pitched roof homes with the upper floors of our houses, the icon of the detached single-family dwelling is used as an effective tool for breaking the vastness of the large agglomerate building. Thwarting the image of the imposing megastructure, our project embraces the imagery of suburbia. By using familiar materials, forms, and common construction techniques, we think that it is possible to create architecture that is familiar yet wholly new.

Have you been able to realize any projects that are related to the Urban Habitats project, be it in scale, approach, client, philosophy?

Our proposal for a 45-acre post-industrial site situated along an obsolete elevated highway in the Brickbottom area of Somerville, Massachusetts, is a larger-scale attempt at similar concepts. Designed together with Jonathan Solomon, "The Big Re-Rig" won the Boston Society of Architects' 2006 "Edge As Center" competition. It is a project of sectionally varying densities that comprise an array of programs. Here, while a loose, low mat forms the majority of the site plan, larger scale buildings define its edges, containing the mat and effecting a change in scale as the project meets the more industrial neighborhood beyond. It is the transition between the project and its context which we find most interesting: in Charlottesville Green, we intended for our construction to meet the northern sidewalk seamlessly, disguising the nature of the project.
In Brickbottom, the mass is increased at the edges, and a presence reasserted.

In implementing these techniques at different scales and over different sites, we have understood that such approaches need a critical mass. A project the size of Charlottesville Green approaches the minimum area and number of units at which this agglomeration technique could work. For the relationships between the units to be fruitful—that is, for the array to allow semi-private courtyards, continuous pathways and anomalies like parks—there must be enough units interconnected over enough land. Residents become an ingredient in the system: without enough of them, the shared benefits cannot be achieved.

Build for Change
: Allow for Growth

Planning, or setting up change as your constant.

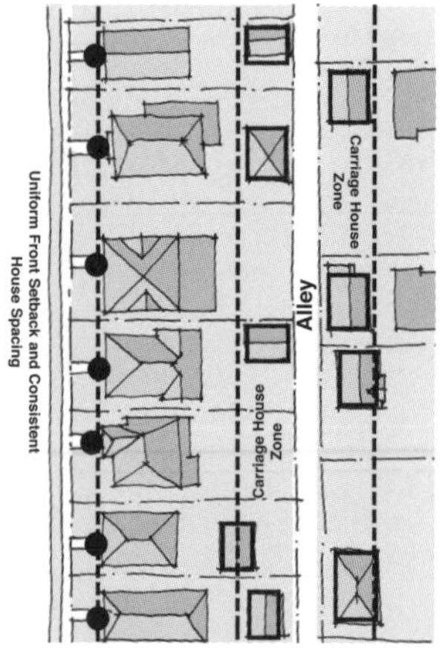

Traditional Neighborhood Blocks

Features:
- Shallow lots, with or without alley
- Carriage houses and garages at the back of the lot
- Original carriage houses small single bay buildings

ADU Sites:
- Place ADUs along alley frontage or rear property line

One of the most overlooked issues in planning a new development is how to accommodate unanticipated change. Thinking about project implementation and long-term phasing for different scenarios is critical when setting the design and development program criteria. How to plan a project in light of shrinkage or growth?

: Make it work for only one out of ten.

Imagine: You begin construction and the funding runs out. The economy stalls. The contractor goes broke. Consider your development plan with this scenario in mind. Would that one building you have been able to complete still be a place worth living in, or would it be an intolerable place to get to? Would you still have funding left for the next buildings, or would you have spent it all on infrastructure now idling away? Play through these worst-case, what-if scenarios and try to make your plan workable, no matter what.

: Make it work for fifteen.

Imagine you've actually completed all ten buildings on time and on budget. Congratulations! The residents are happy. Their families grow. They would like to have their relatives live closer to them. They would like to incorporate their business. They would like to start a daycare center. But they do not want to leave the neighborhood to find a suitable option. Consider your development with this scenario in mind. Can you make it work? Where would the daycare go? Where does the additional building go, what do you sacrifice for it?

: Make it work for ten again.

And now, suddenly, it's all about shrinking. Residents are moving. Down-scaling. Aging. What happens with the vacant apartments? Can they be added on to existing apartments and used by residents already there? What happens to the gardens, the landscape? Have they been planted to survive without intensive, full-time care?

City of Santa Cruz
Accessory Dwelling Unit Ordinance

Even when fully built-up, neighborhoods continue to change and face the pressure of growth. Santa Cruz, California provides an example of how municipalities are beginning to find innovative ways to address this issue. The town, priding itself on its coastal, small-town quality of life, realized that the rising cost of homes made its alternative lifestyles—think: surfing—virtually impossible. The City therefore initiated a process to create an Accessory Dwelling Unit Ordinance. More commonly known as in-law units, secondary apartments or granny flats, Accessory Dwelling Units (ADUs) are a mechanism for providing affordable housing within existing neighborhoods without dramatically altering their character. They frequently take the form of a garage conversion or a cottage-style structure behind the main building.

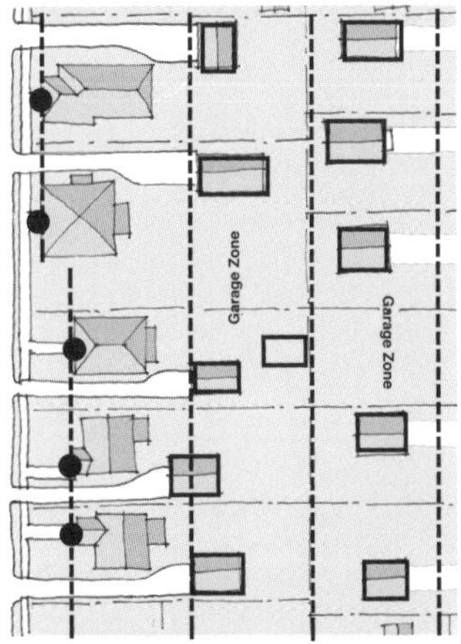

Transitional Neighborhood Blocks

Features:
- Pre-war grid blocks with pre- and post war housing
- Deep lots
- Garages located in rear yards

ADU Sites:
- Place ADUs within garage zone in rear yards

In a striking turnabout, new regulations were adopted in 2003 to encourage a practice that had previously required a zoning variance. By simply eliminating the requirement for covered parking, the new rule allowed the conversion of the typical secondary structure on a lot, the garage, into a second, independent dwelling unit. Furthermore, the ordinance allows the two parking spaces required for the main house and the one new parking space required for the ADU to all be accommodated in tandem on an existing driveway. Some additional rules were drawn up: the homeowner must live on site, door and window locations must be oriented away from the neighbors and the ADU must be similar in design to the main structure.

The City of Santa Cruz then engaged six architecture firms to develop prototypical plans as how-to guides for placing a second dwelling unit on a single-family parcel. These schematic plans are now available from the City to illustrate what is feasible on a site. In addition, various financial incentives were put in place to encourage the construction of ADUs as affordable housing. In order to obtain a low-interest construction loan from the city, for instance, the owner agrees to controlled rents of the ADU for 15 years. The target group are tenants with up to 80% Area Medium Income, a bracket that incorporates many nurses or teachers starting their career. With the new ordinance in place, the number of ADUs permitted annually has risen from an average of 10 to 40.

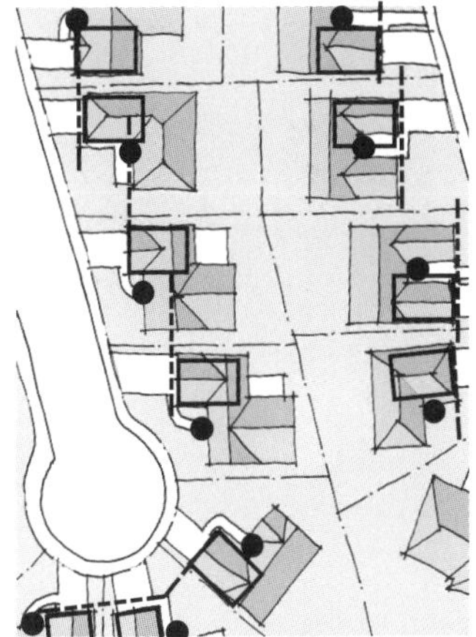

Suburban Neighborhood Blocks

Features:
- Cul-de-sac blocks
- Small yards
- Parking in front of lot with 20' driveway parking

ADU Sites:
- Garage conversions
- Place ADUs in rear lot areas on bigger lots

The city's first ADU loan recipient set a high standard for Santa Cruz: **David Foster**, born and raised in Santa Cruz, wanted to provide a home for his aging parents. He opted to build a straw bale house plastered in mud, and in so doing, engaged in a green building experiment. He was attracted by straw

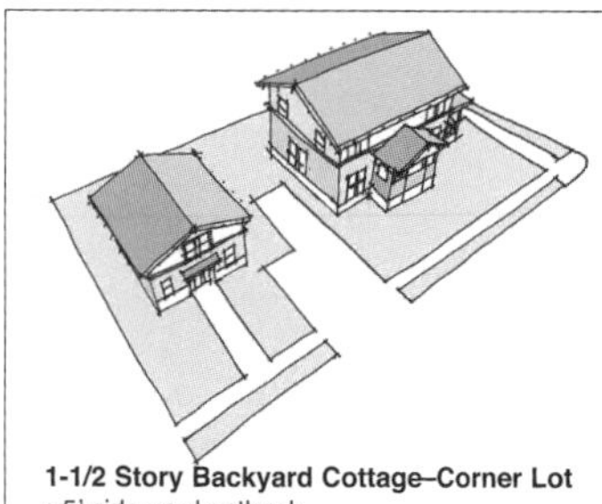

1-1/2 Story Backyard Cottage–Corner Lot
- 5' side yard setback
- 20' rear yard setback
- Uncovered parking in driveway

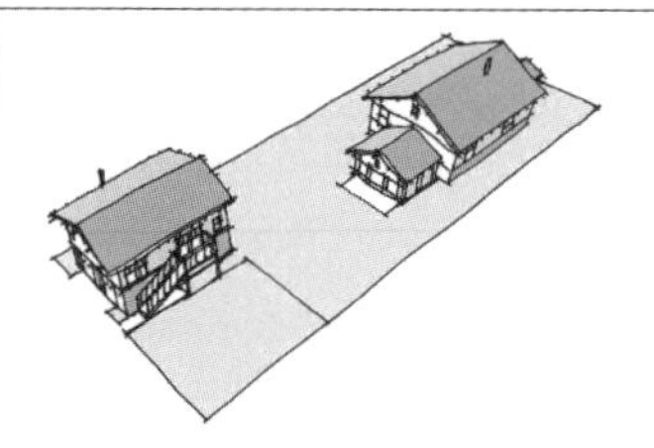

Two Story ADU over Garage–Alley
- 5' side yard setback
- Private ADU yard space
- Parking in alley garage and front driveway

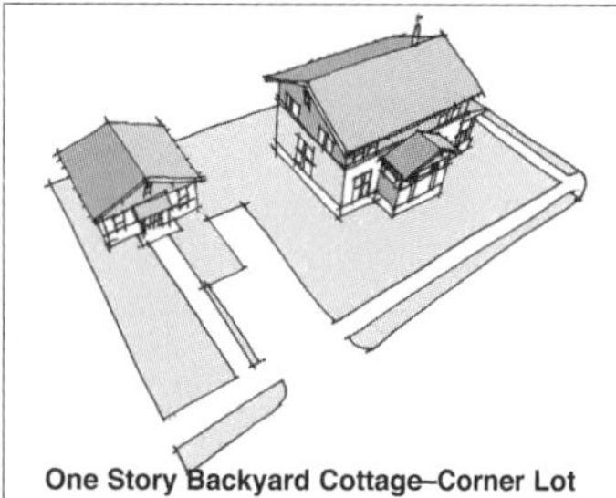

One Story Backyard Cottage–Corner Lot
- 5' side yard setbacks
- Uncovered parking in driveway

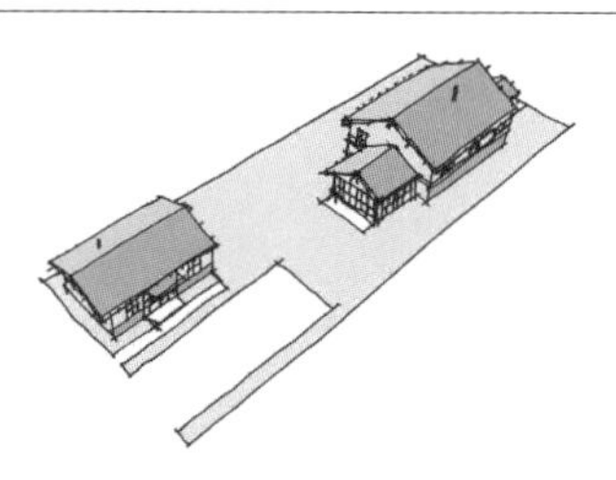

One Story Backyard Cottage–Alley
- 5' side yard setback
- Uncovered parking in driveway

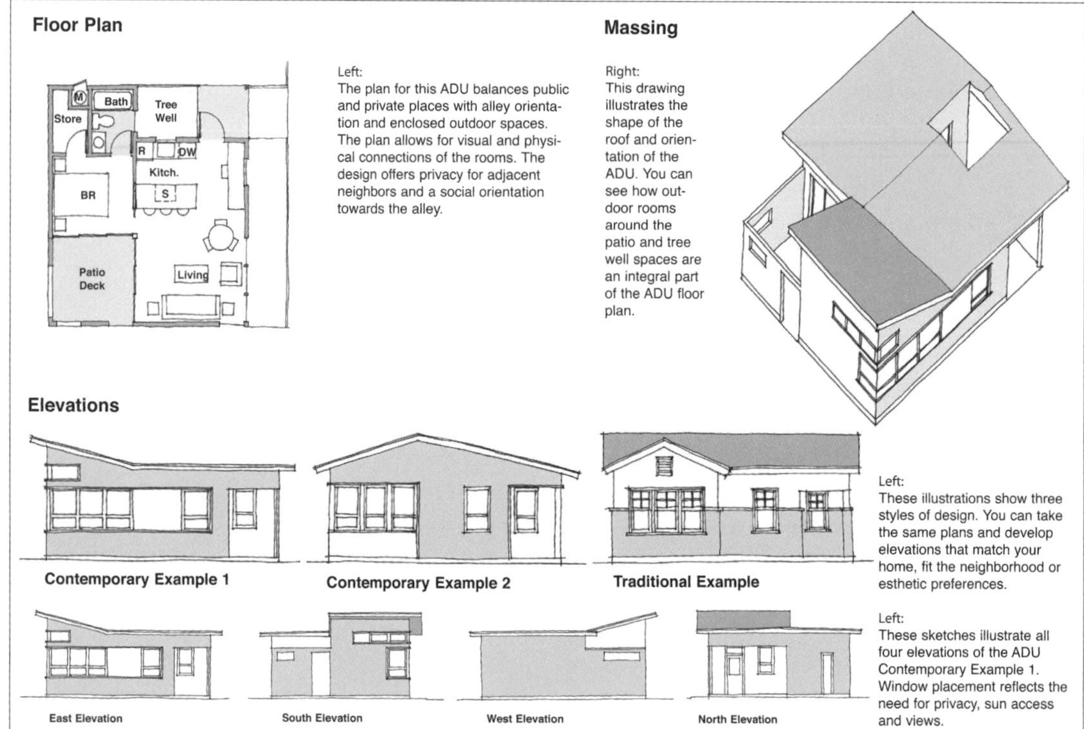

Floor Plan

Left:
The plan for this ADU balances public and private places with alley orientation and enclosed outdoor spaces. The plan allows for visual and physical connections of the rooms. The design offers privacy for adjacent neighbors and a social orientation towards the alley.

Massing

Right:
This drawing illustrates the shape of the roof and orientation of the ADU. You can see how outdoor rooms around the patio and tree well spaces are an integral part of the ADU floor plan.

Elevations

Contemporary Example 1

Contemporary Example 2

Traditional Example

Left:
These illustrations show three styles of design. You can take the same plans and develop elevations that match your home, fit the neighborhood or esthetic preferences.

East Elevation

South Elevation

West Elevation

North Elevation

Left:
These sketches illustrate all four elevations of the ADU Contemporary Example 1. Window placement reflects the need for privacy, sun access and views.

bale's breathable highly insulating qualities. Guided by an experienced general contractor, the actual construction involved the labor of countless volunteers, and building the detached ADU became a local community-building affair.

According to Carol Berg, Housing and Community Development Manager of the City of Santa Cruz, few homeowners had taken advantage of the city's financial incentives such as the fee waiver program or construction loans. With the crisis in the housing market and the difficulty in refinancing homes, however, she has started to see more interest in these programs. And the example set by Santa Cruz is catching on. Towns, but also states, are recognizing the benefits of this model of gradual growth within existing neighborhoods. California, Vermont and Florida have passed legislation encouraging or even mandating municipalities to allow for secondary buildings on single-family parcels.

PRECEDING SPREAD
The City of Santa Cruz provides a manual for developing accessory dwelling units. Illustrations explaining the three possible locations for ADUs.

OPPOSITE
Graphics from the manual showing options for backyard cottages, in contemporary or traditional style.

BELOW
The straw-bale, mud-plastered unit that David Foster designed and built for his parents.

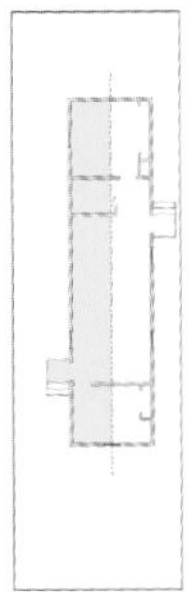
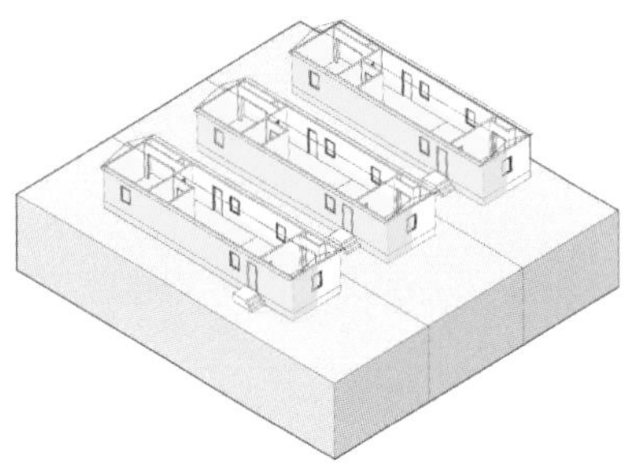

Typological consistency 01
Longitudinal sideness as a result of manufacturing process: Units are never mirrored

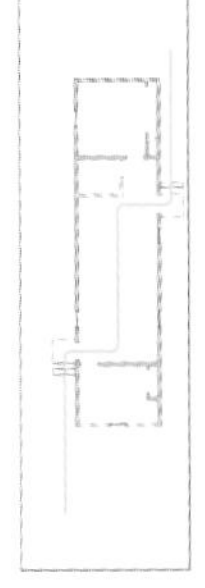
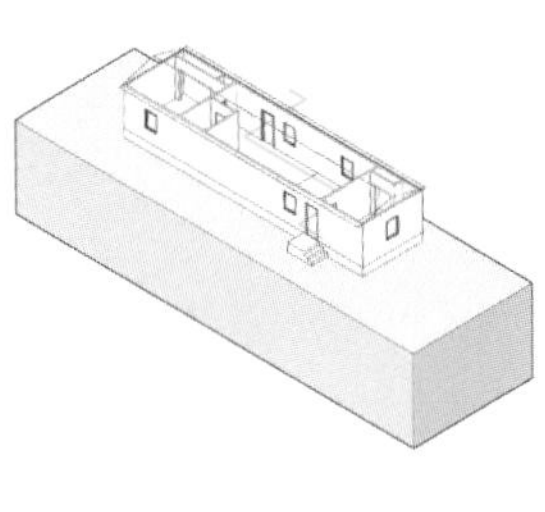

Typological consistency 04
Typical staggering of entry / egress locations

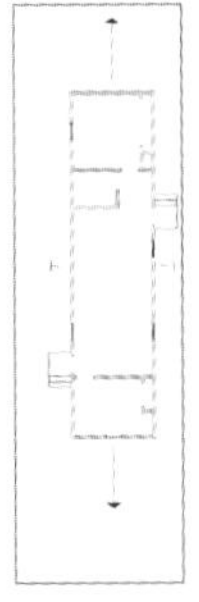
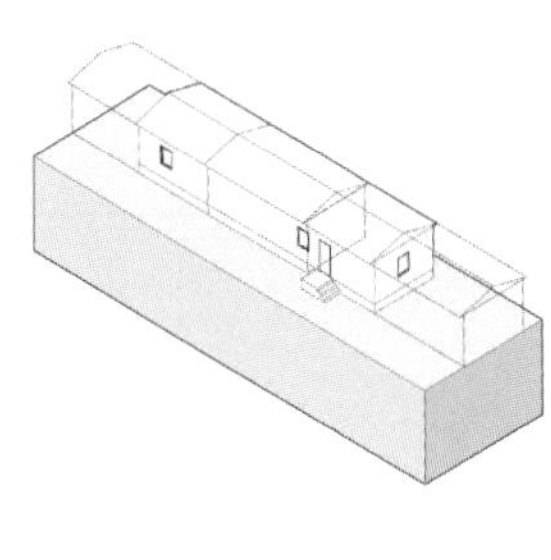

Typological consistency 02
Transverse sideness / directionality with respect to mobility

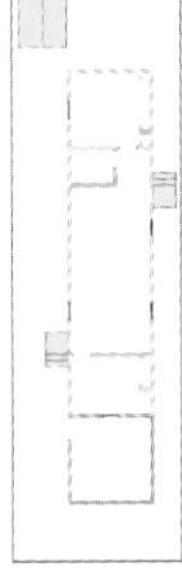
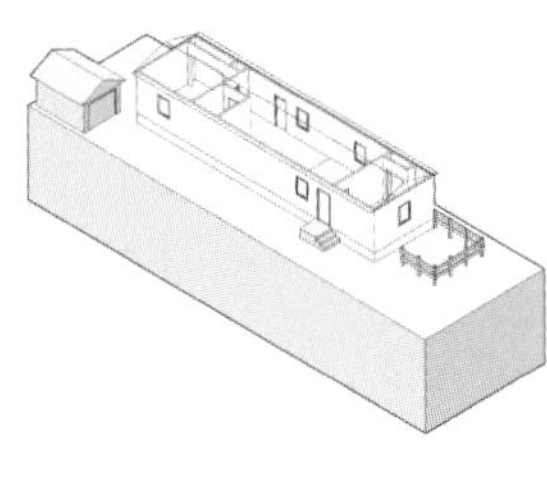

Typological consistency 05
Typical 'book-end' plan diagram which sandwiches bathroom, kitchen and living space between two bedrooms at either end of the long dimension

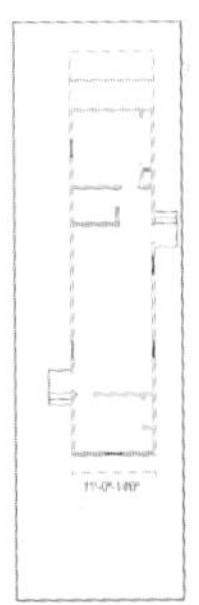
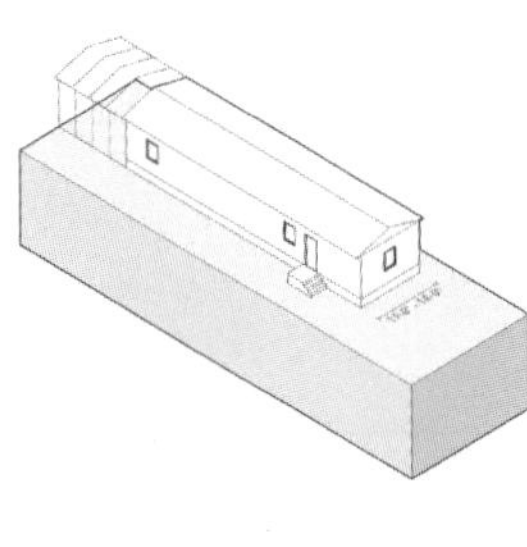

Typological consistency 03
Substantial variation in unit length with little-to-no variation in width due to the consistent dimension of a traffic lane

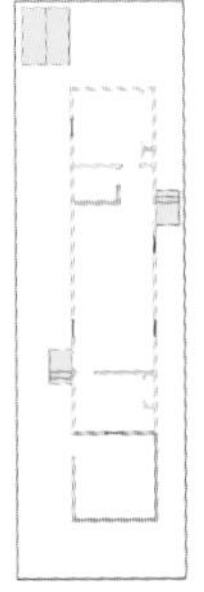
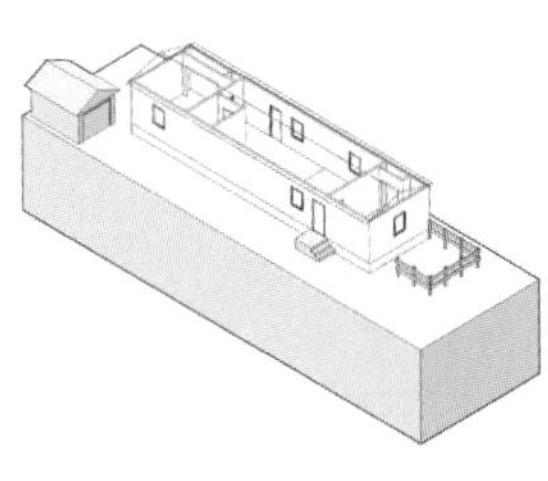

Typological consistency 06
All items external to the unit are strictly superficial, prefabricated additions

Paul Tebben
Tit-for-Tat

The Urban Habitats competition proposal Tit-for-Tat by Paul Tebben of Cambridge, Massachusetts, is based on another approach to allowing for growth and the inevitable change associated with it. Tebben proposes a prefabricated, standardized element be added to existing structures to allow for the gradual transformation of Sunrise Trailer Court. Tebben's approach to Sunrise is based on the premise that the existing trailers and the social network of their residents needs to be maintained and built upon. He therefore proposes a process of incremental change that would be "mutually beneficial" to both the current residents of Sunrise, interested in staying there, and to a for-profit developer of the site, driven by the interest in generating profit.

Tebben declares that the existing trailers are the "cornerstone upon which permanent development may occur" and proposes a modular "Add-On" as a catalyst of change. This new, prefabricated element includes stairs, a porch and a utility room. Adding it to an existing trailer upgrades that trailer and creates access to an upper level for new development. In this way, the transition of Sunrise to an integrated, affordable and market-rate neighborhood occurs unit-by-unit, as residents and developer demand.

Using a standardized product toward the goal of customizing homes can, of course, be seen as a contradiction in terms. In addition, practice has shown that one element, manufactured by one producer, rarely provides the flexibility to be able to respond adequately to actual situations encountered in the field.

However, Tebben addresses the fundamental issue of "Time and Architecture," of what can be planned and what cannot be planned. Tebben summarizes:

This proposal seeks a development strategy based on open-ended indeterminacy. The final building configuration is not restricted to the will of the designer but is instead a result of the behavior of the existing residents within an architectural rule structure predetermined by the designer. That is, the designer prescribes the framework within which the residents must operate under their own agendas.

Tit-for-Tat maps out a striking approach to orchestrate the unpredictable individual interventions that will transform the community as a whole.

OPPOSITE
Tit-for-Tat builds on a thorough analysis of manufactured homes. Plans and axonometric views of trailers.

BELOW
Views of the proposed Add-On.

NEXT PAGE
The proposed step-by-step transformation of a conventional, low-income trailer park into a two-story, mixed-income community.

1—existing, fully occupied trailer park with standardized lot configurations, setbacks, utilities locations and unit spacing.

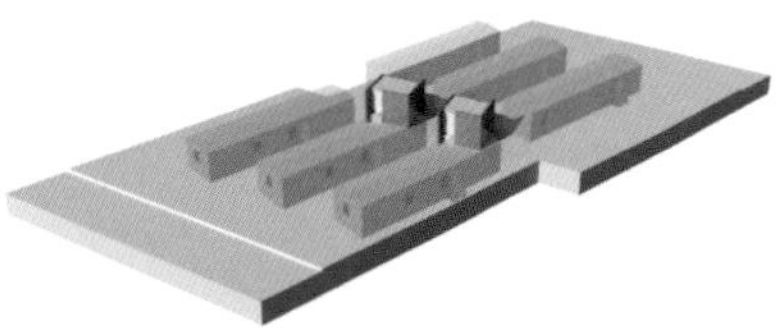

2— construction of shed-like modules along shared rear lot line by volunteer laborers, for use by current tenants with anticipated role of structural / infrastructural support for future upper-level units.

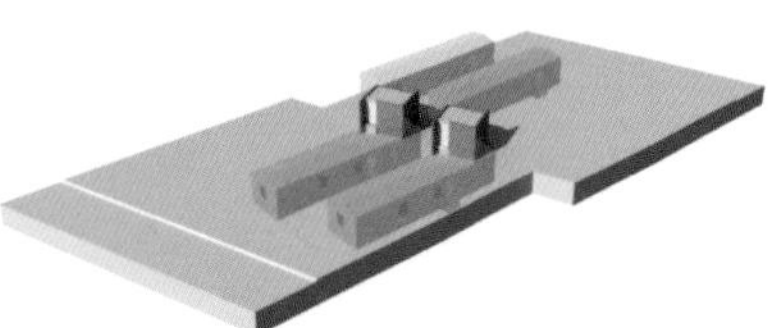

3—evacuation of one or more lots by previous tenants wishing to move their trailer unit(s) off-site. this is viewed as an inevitability based on an average national evacuation rate of 6-8% per year.

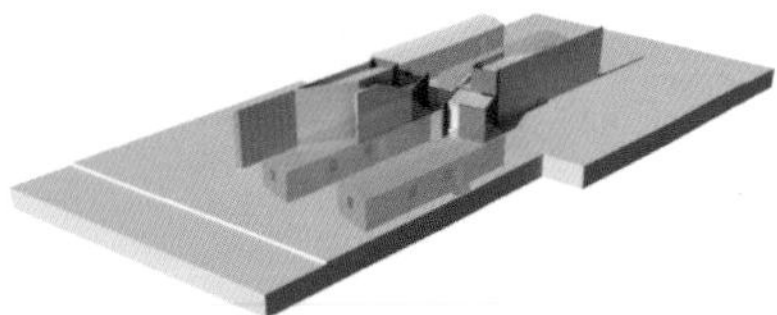

4— developer enticement = preparation of empty lot(s). this includes new slab / footings and construction of new amenity module on lot. amenity module provides storage, 1/2 bath, dining room and mezzanine level.

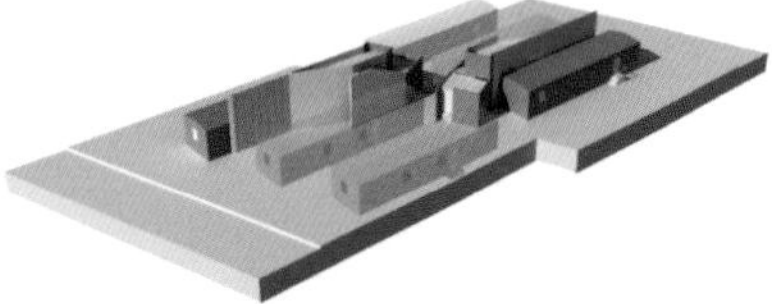

5—occupant cooperation = movement by any existing tenant(s) into newly-prepared lot(s). trailer unit plugs into amenity module via existing trailer egress opening.

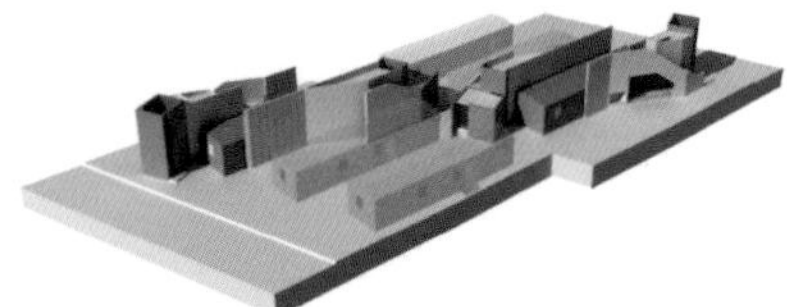

6—developer reward = provision of second amenity module. second amenity module provides entry sequence, porch and utility room.

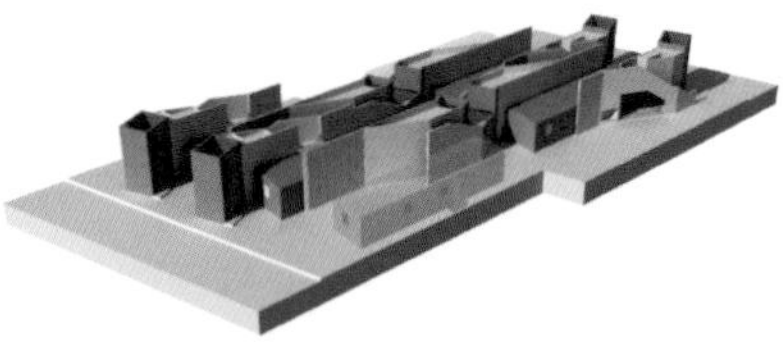

7—two adjacent lots have been successfully reinhabited under the rules of the new configuration providing the necessary structure for upper-level rental units to be constructed above.

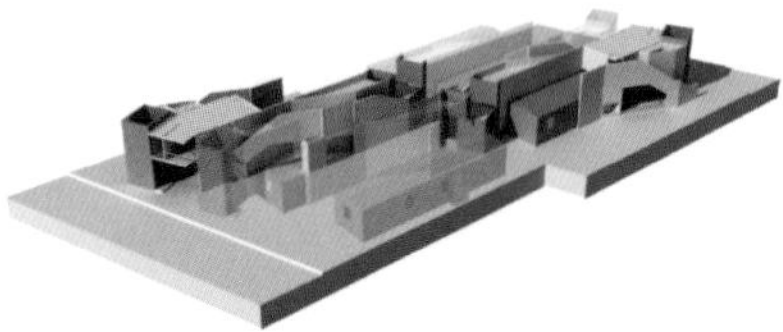

8—vertical construction commences above existing trailers and continues in these locations until another area of the site becomes ready for vertical construction.

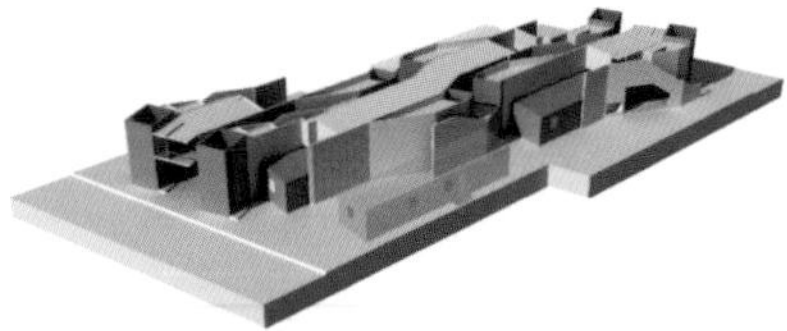

9—new upper-level affordable unit is able to be constructed following the re-habitation of two back-to-back lots under the rules of the new configuration.

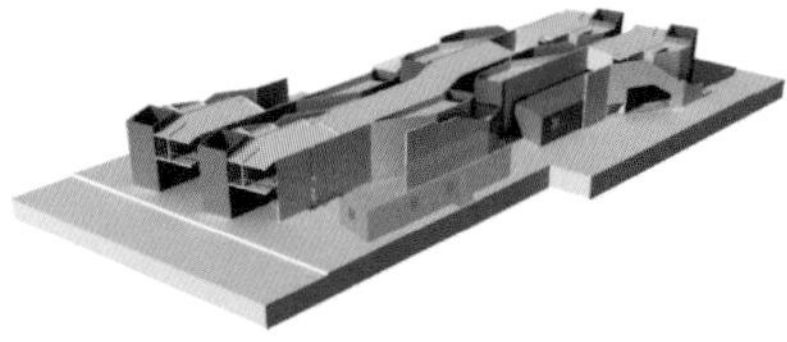

10—upper-level rental units are constructed as conditions permit and / or real estate demand in the area increases.

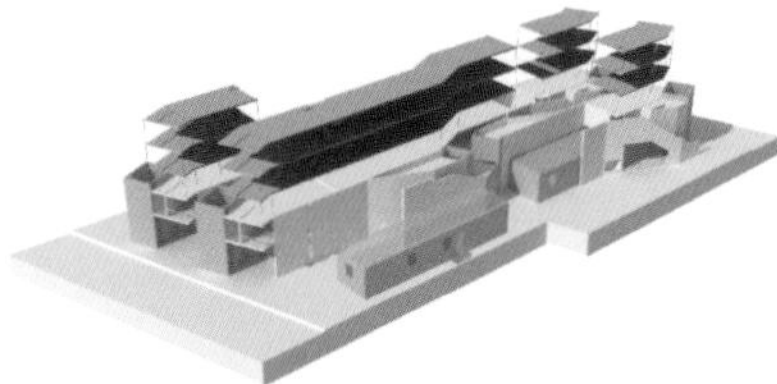

11—vertical construction takes place where conditions permit and continues upward in those locations until conditions elsewhere on the site are ready for vertical construction.

Extension
Paul Tebben

Paul Tebben earned his bachelor's degree in architecture from the University of Michigan and completed graduate studies in architecture at Harvard University. His professional background includes work with WW Architects, Office dA, and Krueck and Sexton Architects. He is a founding partner in the Chicago based design / build practice, STUDIO IDE, along with its tandem development company, ellipsis.

What role does / did the Urban Habitats competition play within your practice?

Because the timing of the competition found me in school as opposed to practice, its impact began as the basis for an academic pursuit and has managed to carry through to my current professional life. The trailer court dilemma was, initially, the center point around which the majority of my graduate thesis research revolved. Among other topics, my research focused on suburban housing and ways to increase density in suburban areas. Many of the existing proposals I found fell short in terms of practical application due to the fact that suburban lots are privately owned. The trailer court, on the other hand, allows more global strategies to be used because multiple "lots" are owned by one owner. Though much of my professional work since then has focused more on non-profit, institutional clients than it has residential, I've recently come full circle with the establishment of a new design / build firm, STUDIO IDE. The firm will focus largely on residential design and pre-fab, low-cost construction. The intent is to use small-scale residential projects as testing grounds for new ideas in design and construction that can be honed over time and applied universally to a wide range of conditions, not unlike Sunrise Trailer Court and other Habitat for Humanity initiatives.

Have you been able to further develop the concepts put forward in your entry?

The concepts pursued in developing my proposal have and will continue to influence my work. The clash between community needs and the financial pressures of the Real Estate and Development Industry extend far beyond Charlottesville. These two forces have historically been at odds, demanding the establishment of a framework that defends an individual's right to a sense of home and community while allowing the natural progression of urban development to unfold. It's a dilemma that permeates the built environment, irrespective of scale. Reconciling this dilemma will continue to weigh heavily on my mind.

Have you been able to realize any projects that are related to the Urban Habitats project, be it in scale, approach, client, philosophy?

As of yet, no. I'm optimistic, however, that this theme will have a compounded influence on my career.

Chapter 3—

Compact Dimensional Diversity

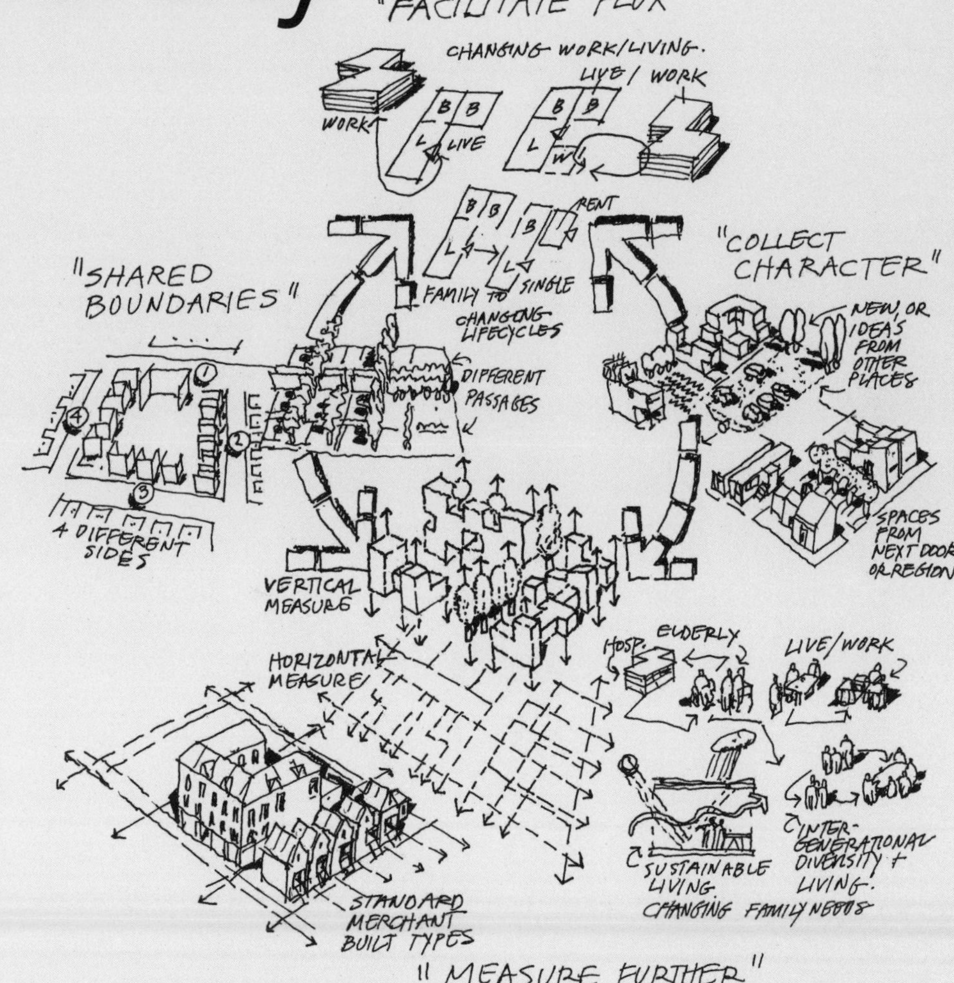

1—Karrie Jacobs, The Perfect $100,000 House, Viking Press, New York 2006, p. 10.
2—Laurie Volk, Todd Zimmerman, "Mass Markets, Housing, and the Illusion of Choice", On the Ground, Volume 2, Number 1, 1996

Affordable housing has the same rules as market rate if you to talk to the architect. You make everything an opportunity. It's about personal space, it's about sustainability, it's about cross ventilating. The disabled access becomes a place for the children; how you organize your landscape gets trees in the ground and parking below.

Julie Eizenberg, Koning Eizenberg Architects, Santa Monica, Growing Urban Habitats Symposium, September 2005

For years, "bigger is better" has been the mantra in housing production. Builders and buyers alike have been subscribing to the notion that a bigger house produces higher profits for the seller and better resale value for the buyer. Most of these ever-bigger homes have been built further and further from existing infrastructure, generate high operating costs due to their size, and are rarely laid out to accommodate possible change. These aspects were simply not an issue, since, in the short term, the numbers seemed to work. Rather than producing housing options, the building boom seems only to have solidified homogeneity.

The issue is pointedly illustrated by writer Karrie Jacobs, who set out in the summer of 2003 on a journey across the United States to find "a place to call home" for $100,000. She visited with architects, developers, builders and housing organizations from Vermont to Seattle and Texas to North Carolina, but could not find a house to satisfy her needs. The problem was only indirectly related to cost and taste. Jacobs simply could not find a home that fit. She writes:

The average American home today is 2,200 square feet (up from 1,400 in 1970), and the median home price (as of late 2005) is about $220,000, so my perfect house actually would cost the same per square foot as a typical American house. The complication, of course, is that I have no interest in the typical American house. In truth, the single most radical thing about my ideal house is not the price tag but the square footage. [...] I don't really understand what most people do with 3,000- or 4,000-square-foot homes. It's not as if the American family itself has gotten bigger. The average number of people per household was 3.14 in 1970 and had declined to 2.59 by the 2000 census.[1]

Jacobs was not able to find what she was looking for because the market was not responding to her demand. That real estate developers should be attempting to create homes for a diversity of households, however, has long been shown. Because neighborhoods change over time, the variety of its housing stock is central to their long-term well being. This was summed up well by real estate market researchers Volk and Zimmerman:

Housing's initial success requires detailed knowledge of probable first occupants; long-term community health requires flexibility of design at both the dwelling and the neighborhood level. This recognition is a contrast to the typical reliance on niche markets to create highly-targeted housing types that lack the flexibility to respond to changing social and economic conditions.[2]

The recent dramatic collapse of the housing market has shown that bigger is no longer better and that having the same thing that your neighbor has, may actually not be a good thing for your neighborhood. What we need, in growing urban habitats, is dimensional diversity. The housing options in a development need to be able to accommodate diverse members of society who will be able to support each other.

This chapter outlines some of the design opportunities related to dimensional diversity.

Without turning the lights on

Aging residents, digital live / work patterns and a wider range of lifestyles demand a greater variety and flexibility of housing options. At the same time, spatial conventions in multi-family housing—like an eight-foot ceiling height resulting from sheetrock and plywood dimensions—have become obsolete in the face of the need for better-lit and ventilated units. Growing urban habitats means capturing the potential of these changing lifestyle preferences as well as the changing notions of efficiency. The following two examples show how doing so can generate surprising results—social, economic, architectural—for all parties concerned.

The San Francisco-based firm of **David Baker + Partners Architects** has taken on the issue of dimensional diversity in numerous projects. One of its clients is the Citizens Housing Corporation (CHC), whose mission is to increase and preserve affordable housing opportunities for low-income Californians, especially seniors, people with special needs and families. Completed in 2005, CHC's **Folsom + Dore Apartments** is a 98-unit, mixed-income building located in San Francisco's South of Market neighborhood and built around existing commercial buildings. Fifty of the apartments are allocated for residents who earn 60% AMI (area median income) and 46 units serve those earning only 27.5% AMI. Residents range from technology workers earning $65,000 a year to formerly homeless individuals living on subsidies.

BELOW LEFT
View of the Folsom + Dore Apartments from the south. The building incorporates several older, rehabilitated commercial structures.

BELOW RIGHT
View of the same corner before the construction of the new housing.

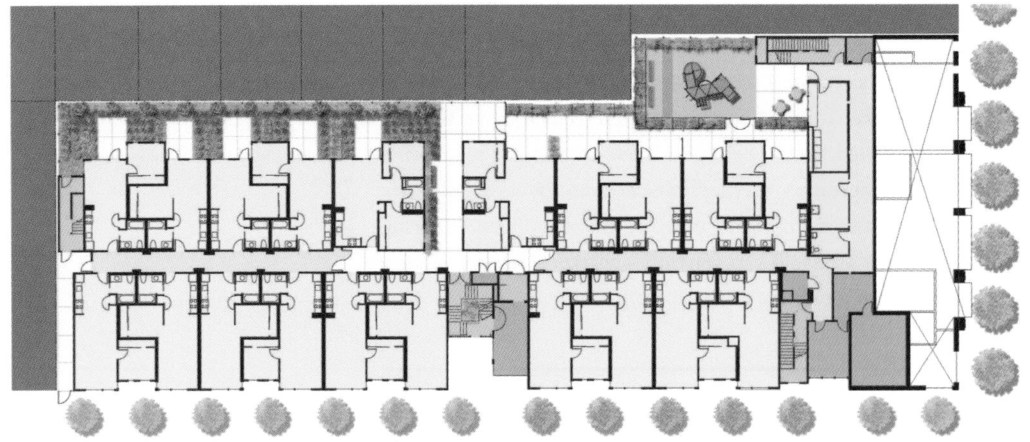

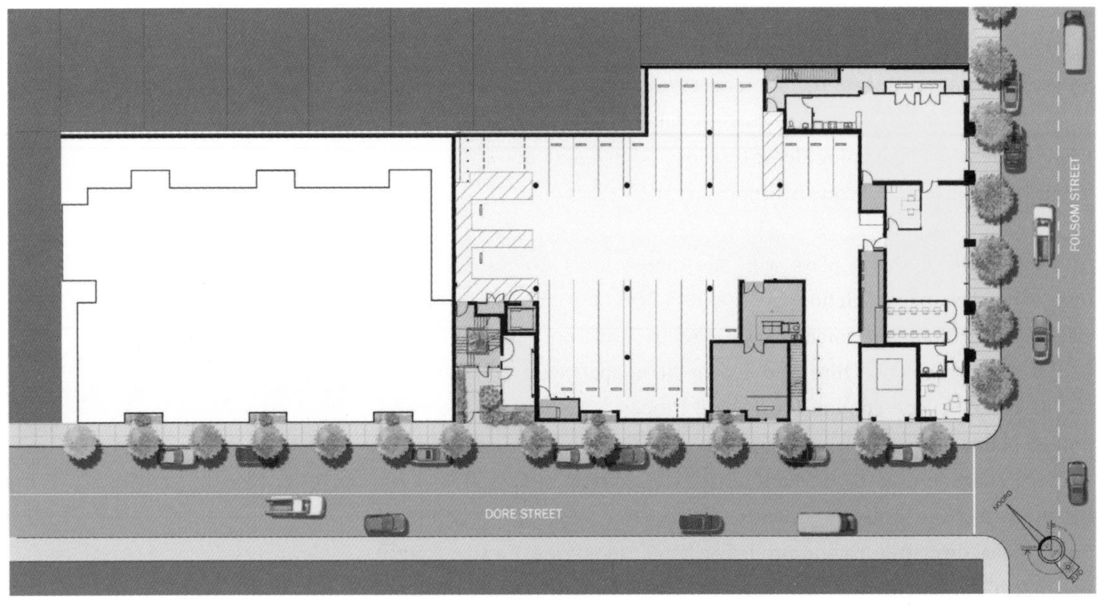
FOLSOM STREET
DORE STREET

Fine tuning the building's dimensions began at the ground floor. Commercial spaces enliven Folsom Street and create a scrim hiding the parking behind, which is accessed, like the building's main entrance, from Dore Street. The need for parking spaces was reduced by mixing mobility options. Thirty compact parking spaces, 28 bike stalls and one space for a car sharing program are accommodated on the ground floor, eliminating the need for the costly construction of a larger parking structure, and offering the residents options tailored to their budget. The parking, in turn, creates the platform for residents' gardens above.

The building's floor plan appears at first pass to be a standard, double-loaded corridor serving apartments on either side. In fact, the building operates quite differently. The corridors are minimized and incorporate outside areas, promoting both social interaction and passive cooling and heating. Within the units, the combination of high ceilings, placement of clerestory side windows, overlapping bedroom arrangements and balcony openings support through-unit air flow and improve daylighting. The need for a standard mechanical heating and cooling system was eliminated, reducing residents' monthly utility bills. The ingenious interlocking of one-bedroom and studio units maximizes the number of units that can be accommodated along the exterior wall by having two units share three windows. This works because the studio's sleeping alcove has no window and therefore can be set behind the bedroom of its one-bedroom apartment pair.

In section, the building plays with the dimensional diversity resulting from vertical change. Each floor opens out to the rear courtyard in different ways. Second floor apartments have garden patios on the planted roof of the parking below. Third and fourth floor apartments benefit from large balconies wide enough for a small dinner table and room to grow potted plants. The fourth and top floor is composed of double-height, loft-type apartments with mezzanines, which open onto small balconies. In summary, the Folsom + Dore Apartments show how addressing dimensional diversity for a non-profit developer can result in an architecture that doesn't just benefit the residents, but the entire neighborhood.

OPPOSITE ABOVE
Typical floor plan. The common courtyard located on the roof of the parking below brings light and views into the double-loaded corridor.

OPPOSITE BELOW
Ground floor plan. The double-height commercial space (yellow) conceals parking behind.

BELOW
Perspective view looking down into a pair of interlocked studio and one-bedroom units. The studio's sleeping niche is tucked behind its neighbor's bedroom.

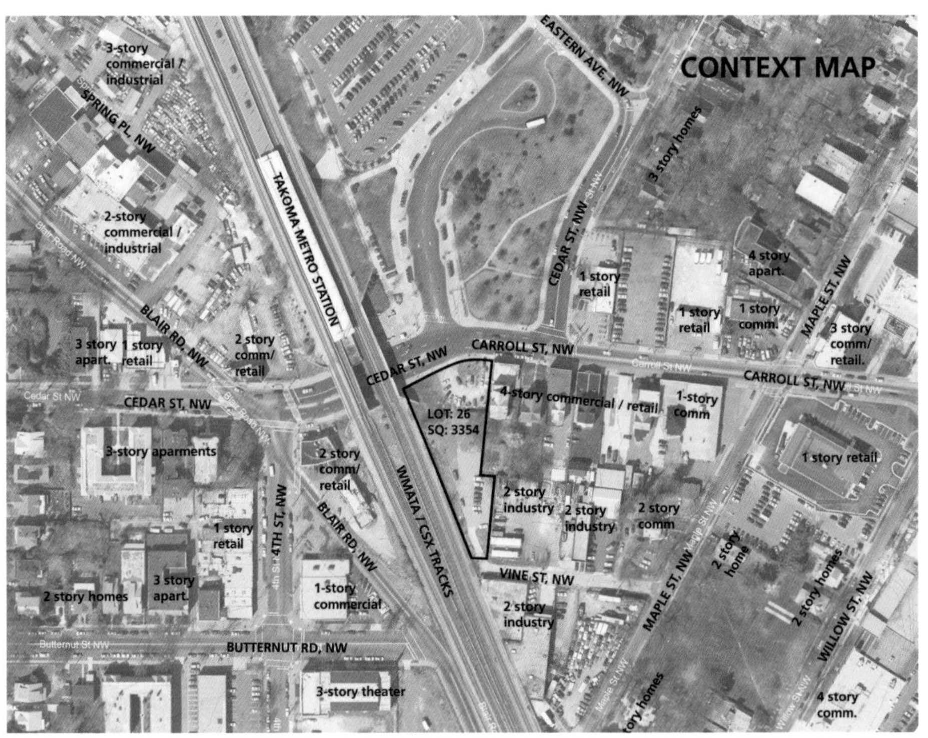
CONTEXT MAP
3-story commercial / industrial
SPRING PL, NW
EASTERN AVE, NW
TAKOMA METRO STATION
3 story homes
2-story commercial / industrial
CEDAR ST, NW
1 story retail
4 story apart.
MAPLE ST, NW
1 story retail
1 story comm.
3 story comm/ retail.
BLAIR RD, NW
3 story apart.
1 story retail
2 story comm/ retail
CEDAR ST, NW
CARROLL ST, NW
CARROLL ST, NW
LOT: 26
SQ: 3354
4-story commercial / retail
1-story comm
CEDAR ST, NW
3-story aparments
2 story comm/ retail
WMATA / CSX TRACKS
1 story retail
1 story retail
2 story industry
2 story industry
2 story comm
4TH ST, NW
BLAIR RD, NW
2 story home
2 story homes
3 story apart.
1-story commercial
VINE ST, NW
MAPLE ST, NW
2 story homes
WILLOW ST, NW
2 story industry
BUTTERNUT RD, NW
3-story theater
4 story comm.

Elevation 314, a 52-unit apartment building in the Takoma Park neighborhood of Washington, D.C., achieves similar benefits for residents and neighbors, but was designed and developed for profit. Completed in August 2004, its dimensional diversity originated in the bizarrely shaped, three-quarter-acre site next to Washington's Metro that sat empty for 20 years, and tracks all the way to the 26 different apartment floor plans provided in the building.

OPPOSITE, ABOVE
Context map showing the neighborhood's heterogeneous, low-scale buildings and the site's irregular geometry.

OPPOSITE, BELOW
Collage combining photographs of the existing street front with an image of Elevation 314.

At the Growing Urban Habitats Symposium, Elevation 314's architect and developer **Russell Katz** recalled the design process that led to the courtyard solution of the 68,000-square-foot project. Not only did the site's triangular geometry require a non-standard approach, but the trains running along the site on an elevated rail line had an enormous acoustical impact. A courtyard building scheme allowed most units to front onto a sheltered outside space, turning their backs to the tracks.

BELOW
Street view of Elevation 314.

While this seems like the obvious solution in hindsight, Katz had a hard time communicating the rationale:

The comment I got from the bankers was, "You've taken the best part of the site, and there's no building there." So you have to explain what exactly you are doing: capturing the quiet space that didn't exist before, which in turn gives value to everything else.

Adverse conditions may have led to the courtyard configuration. Ultimately, however, the courtyard became the unifying space that gives the building its identity. The stairwells open out to the courtyard so all residents enter the building by passing through this interior open space.

The building's units aren't large. One-bedroom units measure around 650 square feet in size, and two-bedroom units are around 975 square feet, but courtyard views and a private deck for every unit creates the perception of spaciousness nonetheless. Due to the constrained dimensions of the site, Katz conducted extensive lighting studies of each unit so that all residents could "read at the back of [their] apartment without turning the lights on." Common features of all apartments include a generous 12- by-25-foot living space and ten-foot-high ceilings. Katz has found that the social result of the mixture of apartment types is an equally healthy mix of households:

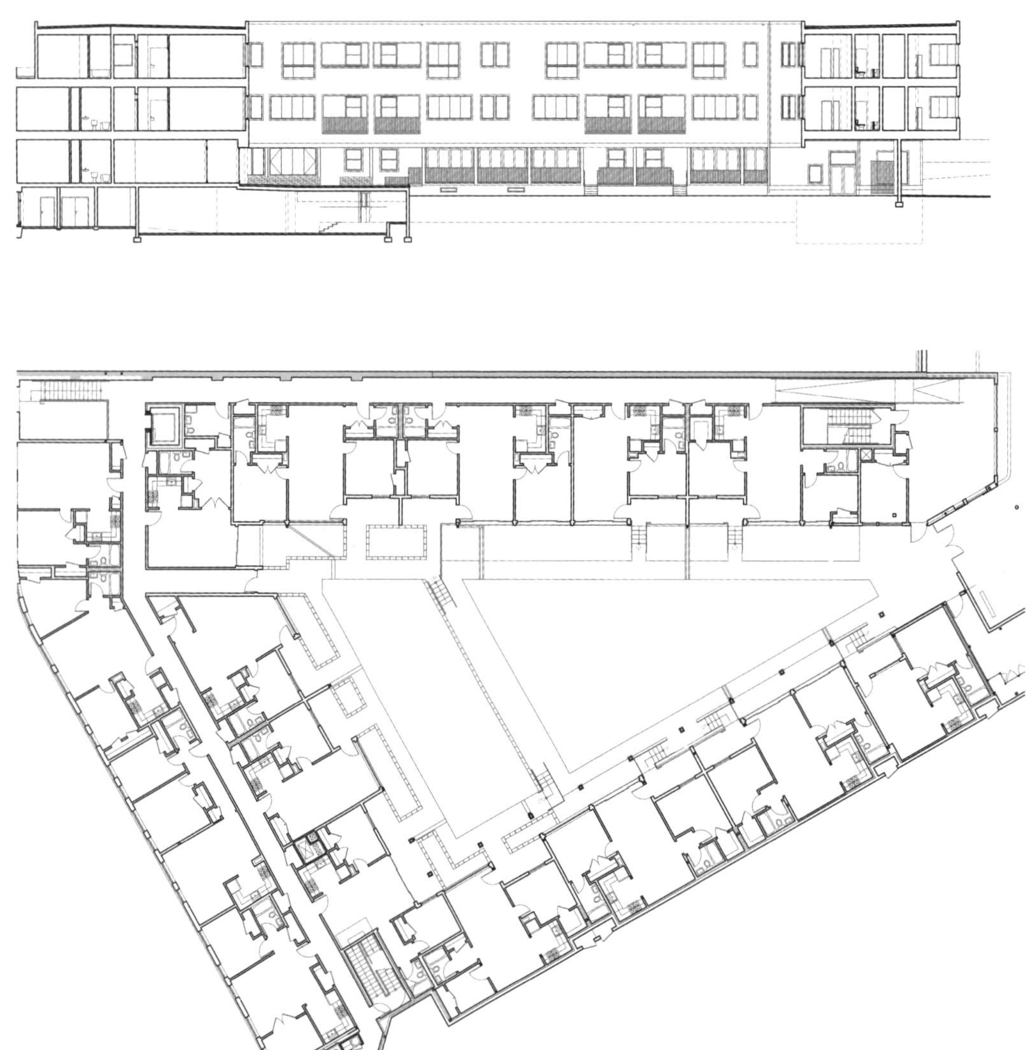

The diversity of the plans led to a diversity of users. Most of the new buildings in Washington are renting up 90% with the 20-, 30-year-old professionals. We've got a woman who's 80-something years old, a number of retirees, empty nesters, down to young families with kids from all sorts of backgrounds.

The residents like the building community and many choose to stay even when their personal situation changes. The diversity of unit sizes enabled a couple that had their first child to move from a one- to a two-bedroom without leaving the building. Conversely, a family that has separated considered renting two smaller units. Ultimately, the diversity of residents also provides the developer with a broader footing in the market.

The building's economic and environmental strengths support its social sustainability. From the start, Katz was driven by the vision that a well-designed, environmentally conscious project can achieve financial success. He described how three project goals were clear from the outset of the project and guided all subsequent decisions:

First: How do we maintain a sustainable, environmental attitude, because that's our purpose? Second: How do we do this with architecture? And third: How do we make this a market-driven project, one that will support itself and get a return on the investment? We used these criteria every time we had to evaluate something. The best solutions were the ones where all three were satisfied and you couldn't take away one or another and not drop the other two.

Just as the different unit types cannot be dislodged from one another in the building, its sustainable features cannot be removed from it. The storm water retention system nestled in the landscaped courtyard, a geothermal heating and cooling system and a green roof—the first ever to be approved in Washington, D.C.—have substantially lowered utility bills for residents and were seen as long-term investments by Katz. In a rental property such as Elevation 314, the immediate benefits of all of these aspects of dimensional diversity go to the residents; the long-term payback is to the owner.

OPPOSITE, ABOVE
Long section through building.

OPPOSITE, BELOW
Courtyard level plan.

BELOW
View of the courtyard. A storm water retention system is nestled in the landscaped area.

Count Again
:Measure More

Quality and Quantity, or why all square feet aren't created equal.

You may only have limited space. Or perhaps you have too much space. Either way, it's not the amount of space you have; it's how you dimension it that matters. To create supremely liveable spaces, measure more.

:Try it on.

Location matters. A ground-floor unit is different than the unit above. Views are shorter, light is darker, noise is closer. Why then should all the units be the same? Perhaps the ground-floor unit needs higher ceilings, extra privacy. The penthouse unit on the other hand, with its ample views, might only require half the area to feel generous. Gauge the spectrum and calibrate accordingly.

:Shrink to fit.

Once you've determined the particularities of location, start measuring. It's not just to save space and materials, and therefore cost, that dimensioning is critical. It's fundamental to make your spaces liveable.

How large is the bed, how big is the dresser, how much closet space do you need? These are the basics. Then: How does the door open, what can you put behind the door, next to the door when it's open? Can you get from the door to your bed? What do you see when you wake up in the morning? Where is the window, where is the source of heat? Move on to alternate scenarios. Perhaps you don't need a king size bed. Whatever happened to the desk? Where will the trophy collection go? Perhaps this room wants to be more than a bedroom. What do you need to use it as an office?

:Stretch for comfort.

Dimensioning isn't just about the plan. It's very much about the section, the vertical cut through the building.

Consider the floor-to-floor dimensions. Higher ceilings might be more expensive to build in the short term. In the long term, however, a ten-foot-high ceiling, compared to the standard eight feet, will save you money. It provides better ventilation conditions since hot air rises, and guarantees better lighting conditions, since light can enter further into your spaces. A higher ceiling will also make your space feel more generous, even if you can't accommodate a larger footprint.

Take it further. A double-height space can visually connect spaces that would otherwise be separate. A mezzanine level, carefully dimensioned, can provide living space that may not count toward the floor area tally of the zoning permit.

Smith and Others / Lloyd Russell
The Merrimac Building

The Merrimac Building was developed, designed and built by Lloyd Russell and Ted Smith of Smith and Others in 1997 in San Diego, as an alternative to the dominant model of developer housing. They were troubled by buildings organized around dark, double-loaded corridors, accessed by an elevator, that impose their ground-floor parking garage on the surrounding streetscape. The steel-framed Merrimac, in contrast, was able to forgo an elevator, because according to zoning categories, it includes only three stories plus a mezzanine; parking was accommodated behind the building. The building contains a total of nine small suites, dimensioned to accommodate both living and working, and a commercial space. The suites are arranged so that they can also be easily combined to create four larger units. By measuring more, the architects thus created an intelligent strategy for affordable living: small units when finances are tight, more sumptuous living when money and available space allow it.

The building's masonry base accommodates five suites, or two units, depending on how they are combined. Each unit consists of a narrow,

OPPOSITE
Limited in footprint, generous in height, the Merrimac's ground-floor suites are dimensioned to allow for living and working.

BELOW
The architects of the LIND block challenged the practice of building double-loaded elevator buildings atop parking plinths. They developed building types where people occupy the street level and units maximize day lighting and cross-ventilation.

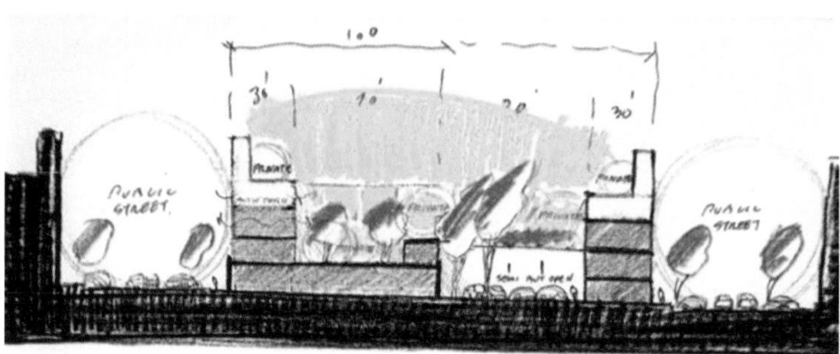

The Perimeter Block

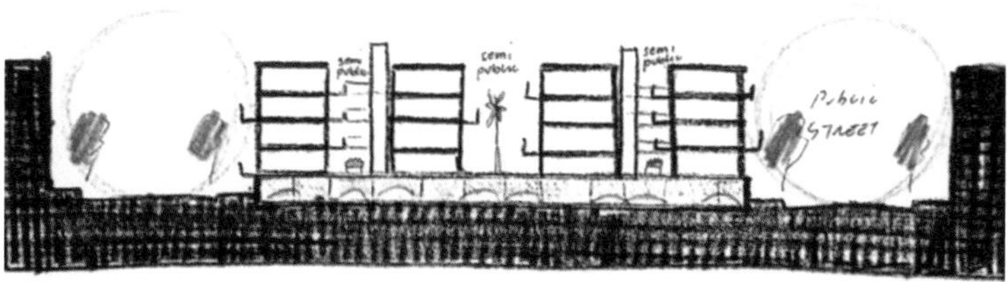

Four Story Over Parking

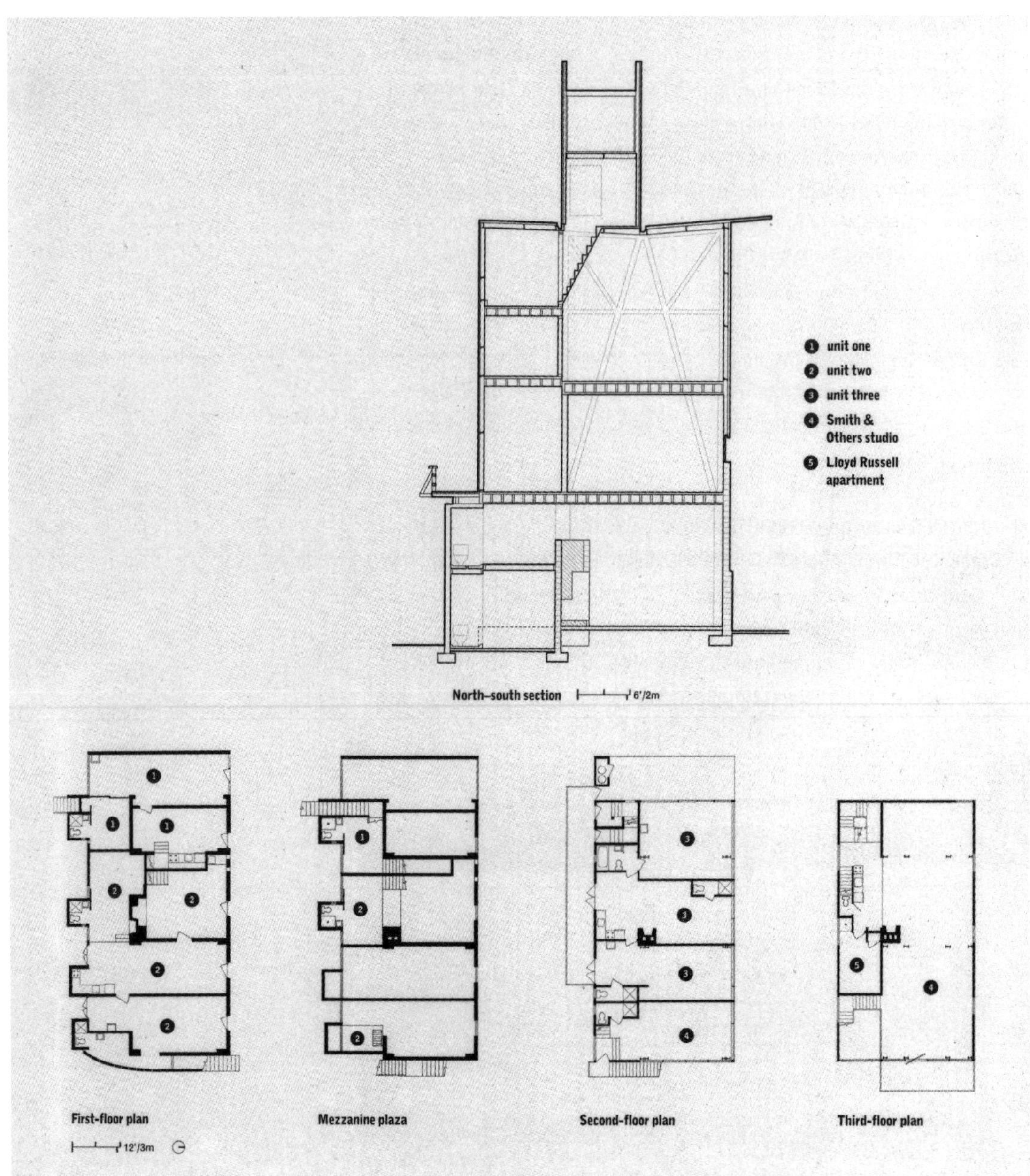

1 unit one
2 unit two
3 unit three
4 Smith & Others studio
5 Lloyd Russell apartment
North–south section
6'/2m
First-floor plan
12'/3m
Mezzanine plaza
Second-floor plan
Third-floor plan

undivided, double-height space. Stairs lead either to a mezzanine level above or a room a few steps below grade. The units are accessed directly from the street, enlivening the street. The upper part of the building is accessed by two external stairs. One, located along the eastern end of the building, leads to the office of Smith and Others, currently used to teach the Masters in Real Estate Development Program developed by Russell and Smith for Woodbury University. The office space, which takes up a small part of the second floor and the entire double-height third floor, is connected by an internal stair. The other external stair, located to the west, leads to an open gallery at the third floor level and access to one apartment (or three suites, again depending how they are combined), and an open deck. A final, very small apartment is located on a mezzanine of the third floor along the south side of the studio, and is accessible both through the studio and the extension of the western external stair.

Lloyd Russell sums up the Merrimac experience like this: "The basic belief was that since individuals are different, the spaces should be different as well. Over time, the spaces have proved to be the perfect size and price for independent yet affordable living. In addition, the Merrimac always feels like a community of people. I don't know if it is the number of people, the outdoor spaces, or the architecture. It is a hard thing to put your finger on."

OPPOSITE
The Merrimac, floor plans and section.

BELOW
The double-height office space of Smith & Others.

BOTTOM LEFT
The generous living space of a second-floor unit.

BOTTOM RIGHT
Ground-floor suites have direct access to the street.

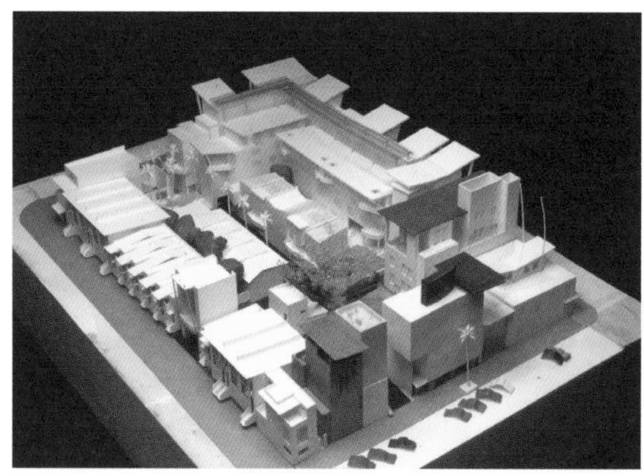

It is important to note that the Merrimac is part of a design exercise at the scale of an entire block. Located in a once run-down area of San Diego, it was redeveloped by the Little Italy Neighborhood Development (LIND), a group of architects turned developers that included Smith and Others. The team sought to achieve "authentic diversity" by dividing up the site and giving each architect/developer the freedom to define the architecture within their distinct part of the block. As a result, the block's buildings include row houses, lofts and apartments over shops.

OPPOSITE, ABOVE
Model view of the LIND Block with a Merrimac at center front.

OPPOSITE, BELOW
View south across the third-floor deck with San Diego beyond.

BELOW
Street view of the Merrimac at dusk.

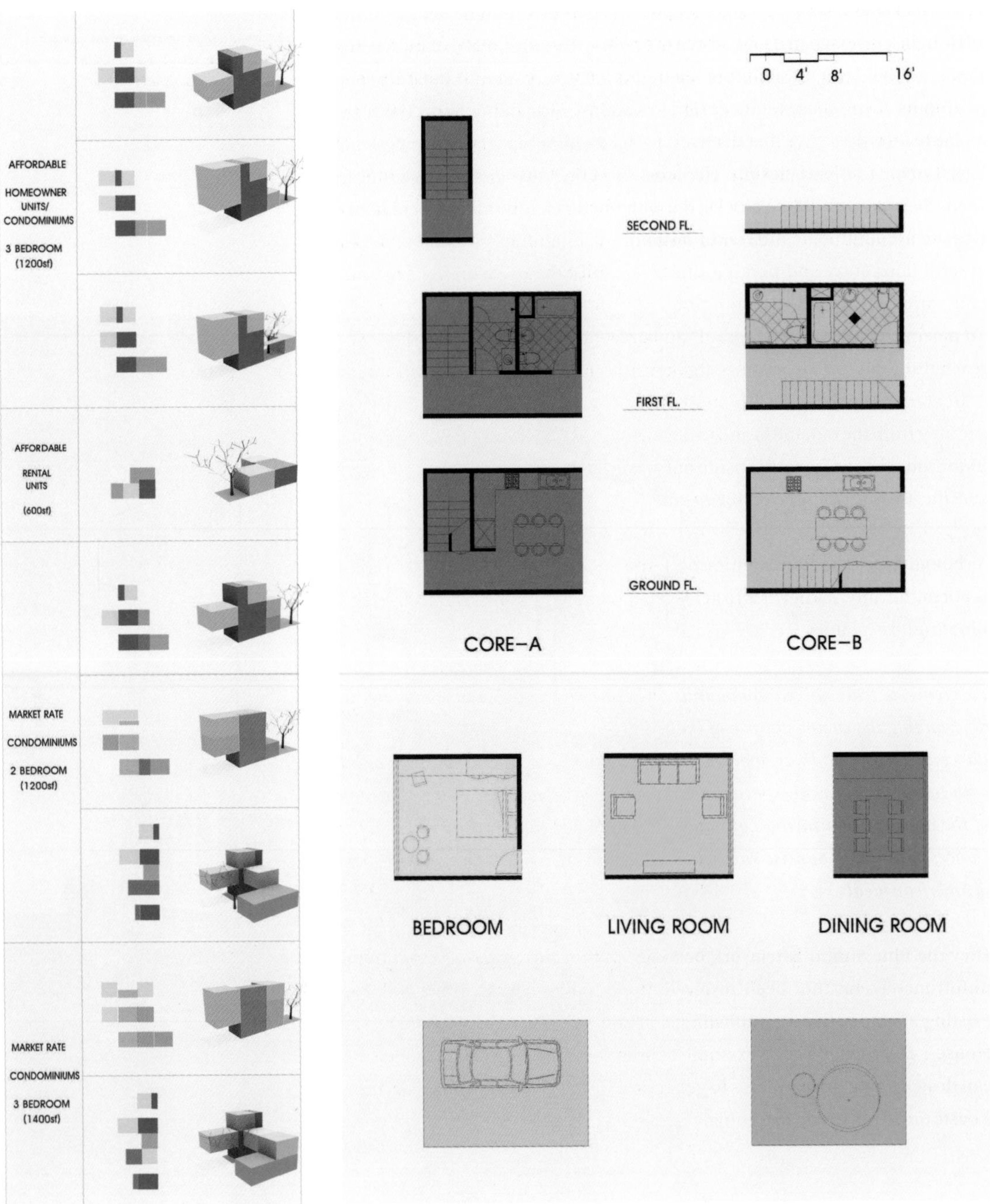
AFFORDABLE
HOMEOWNER UNITS/ CONDOMINIUMS
3 BEDROOM (1200sf)
AFFORDABLE
RENTAL UNITS
(600sf)
MARKET RATE
CONDOMINIUMS
2 BEDROOM (1200sf)
MARKET RATE
CONDOMINIUMS
3 BEDROOM (1400sf)
0 4' 8' 16'
SECOND FL.
FIRST FL.
GROUND FL.
CORE–A
CORE–B
BEDROOM
LIVING ROOM
DINING ROOM

Blue Studio
1 House + 1 Garden

The Urban Habitats competition proposal 1 House + 1 Garden by Blue Studio of Hongik University in Seoul, Korea is premised on the notion of measuring more at the level of building elements. These elements—bathrooms, bedrooms, living spaces—are designed according to minimum dimensions. As the team writes, "We first determined the most compact module possible based upon the least flexible elements of stair, kitchen, and bathroom." From these basic building blocks, the team then assembles a variety of house types to accommodate different household sizes and needs. "All units have ground floor entry and parking under a cantilevered second-floor module and various possible configurations of garden and roof garden spaces. To maximize the garden areas, all units except for the 600-square-foot type reach three floors." These units are then arranged on the site. This approach is in stark contrast to Smith and Others' Merrimac Building; rather than working from the outside in and fitting hybrid spaces within a given envelope, Blue Studio works from the inside out according to idealized dimensions for specific uses and then assembles a building.

Although the elements are uniformly dimensioned, the goal of the operation is not uniformity. Rather, it is to achieve the greatest possible overall diversity. Blue Studio explains:

To create a truly mixed community, where every member has options in determining the composite size of their shared gardens and roof terraces, and the configuration of their home modules, we gave each unit an individual lot with garden and parking space that could be grouped together. [...] A reflection of the democratic principles of Jefferson, it is hoped that by offering as many choices as possible, Sunrise Park will be a patchwork quilt that reflects the best of American ideals.

How the Blue Studio patchwork becomes part of the larger Belmont quilt, unfortunately, has not been resolved; the building edges collide with the existing streets without establishing a spatial relationship. Nevertheless, 1 House + 1 Garden is a good example of how, by measuring what we need, we can design an iterative process to generate a variety of housing options, from a basic unit to an expansive home.

OPPOSITE
The kit of parts. The basic room types are shown in plan, how they can be combined into different dwelling types is shown in axonometric.

BELOW
View of an apartment interior.

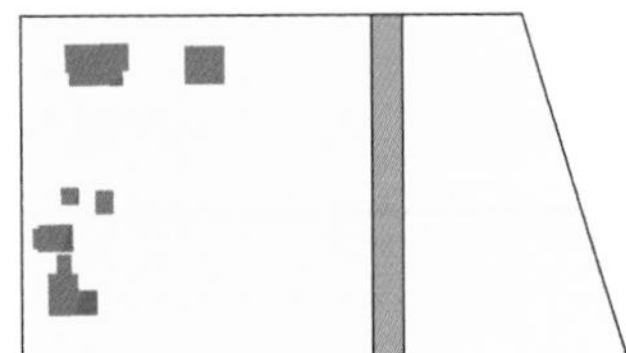

EXISTING SITE

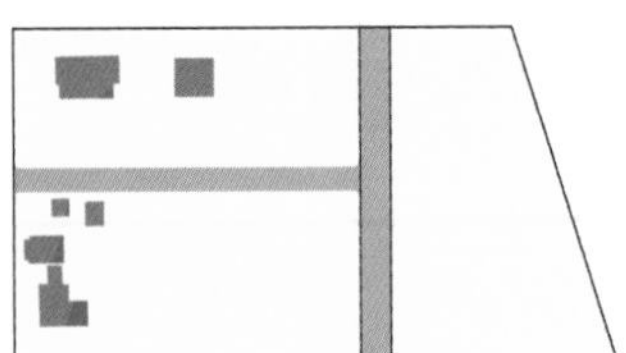

INTERNAL ROADS

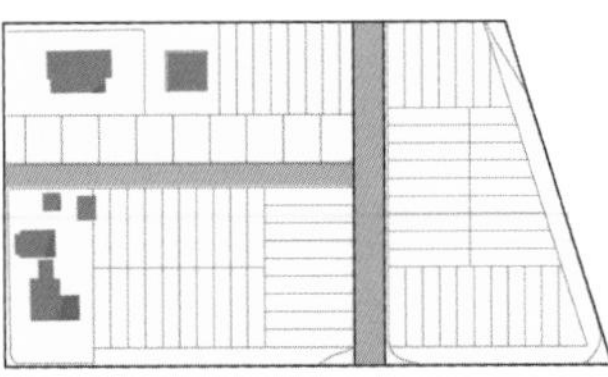

UNIT LOT DIVISIONS

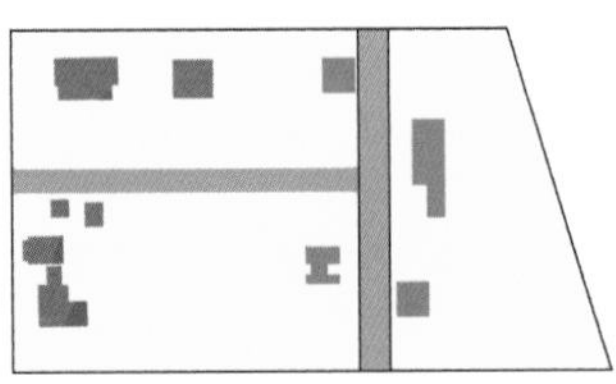

COMMERCIAL BUILDINGS ALONG MAIN STREET

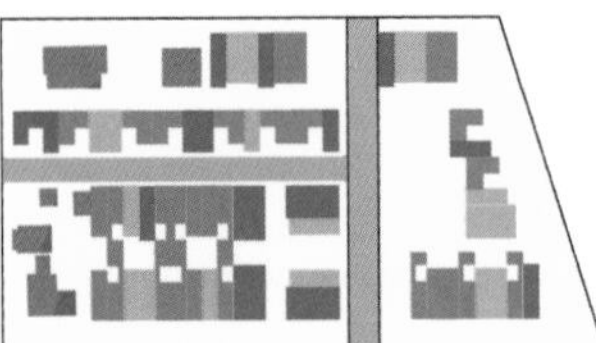

6 UNIT TYPES

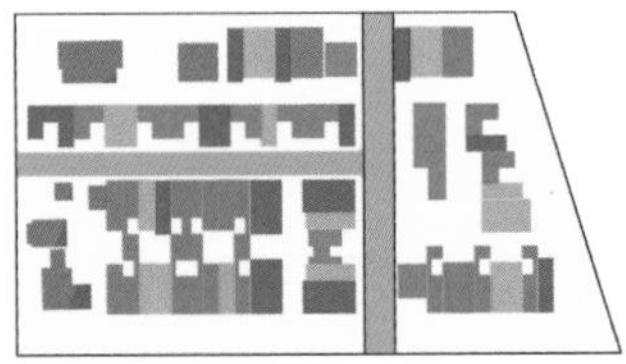

NEW SUNRISE PARK

TOP, FROM LEFT TO RIGHT
Views of a roof garden, a courtyard, and the street level, tuck-under parking.

OPPOSITE, BOTTOM
The elements of the site plan.

BELOW
The site plan showing the ground level.

Mix It Up
:Collect Character

Unity and Diversity, or how to deal with difference.

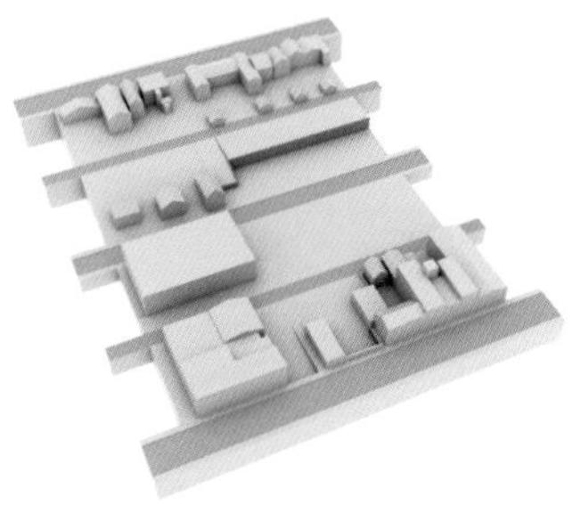

You want to provide a panoply of living options. How do you translate this diversity into a coherent building, a liveable neighborhood? Do you express the uniqueness of each household or do you aim for a single identity that unifies them as one? To ensure both unity and diversity, collect character.

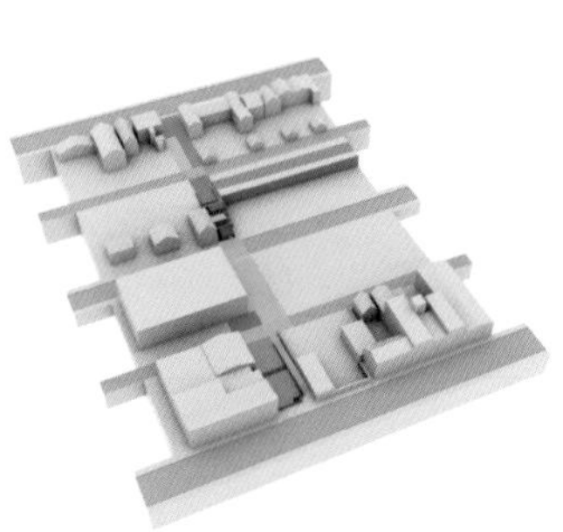

:Exploit the site.

A balance of unity and diversity will invariably result if you work with the site. Read its character, embrace its flaws. Each angle, each irregularity, each constraint is an opportunity for design. Don't try to iron out these folds; work with them. As a result, both the overall development and the individual buildings will become unique and yet connected to where they are. This has little to do with copying your neighbors. It's about tickling out your parcel's potential.

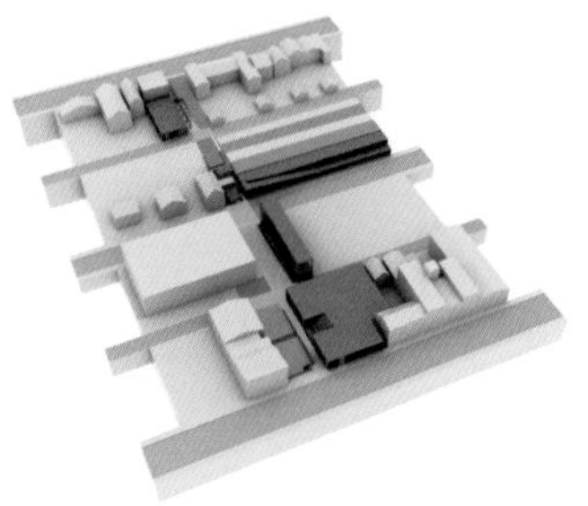

:Mind the gap.

Buildings are backdrop. Focus on the in-between. Character builds through interaction with others. How do you interact with your neighbors? Who do you meet when you get your mail? Who do you hear when you sit on your porch? Who do you see when you park your car?

:Calibrate collisions.

Again, buildings are backdrop. Character results from how residents live. Invest, up-front, in setting up how people with diverging household incomes, biological clocks and musical tastes negotiate their interests. Who cuts the grass, and how it is paid for? Do you decide on the color of awnings and the types of flowers, or do you leave that up to chance?

*Estudio Teddy Cruz / The PARC Foundation—**Hudson 2 + 4***

OPPOSITE AND BELOW, FROM TOP TO BOTTOM
A sequence of models showing how a new spine of open space will reconnect Hudson's residents by creating mixed-income housing, businesses and community facilities.

In 1790, Hudson, New York was the eighth largest city in United States and a global port for whalers who hunted their prey in the Pacific Ocean off the southern coasts of California and Mexico. Today, it is a city of around 7,000 residents struggling to overcome the major economic and demographic downturn that began in the 1980s. Meanwhile, there are new demands for housing coming from two radically different immigrant populations. On the one hand, wealthy couples are seeking weekend and retirement homes just two hours north of New York City. On the other, Hispanic and Bangladeshi families, attracted by jobs in the agriculture and construction industries, are settling in Hudson. These new immigrants are competing with the local elderly and African-American residents for housing.

In 2006, David Deutsch, a local artist and director of the non-profit PARC Foundation (Planning + Art Resources for Communities) called the San Diego architect Teddy Cruz, principal of Estudio Cruz who works with situations of comparable economic and cultural polarization in the American-Mexican border community of San Ysidro, California. *(See p. 48 for more information on the San Ysidro project.)* Together with local residents and civic leaders, Deutsch and Cruz generated a design and development proposal for 60 new mixed-income housing units on a total of 2.3 acres in Hudson. The units are to be built on six city-owned vacant parcels, including abandoned structures, spread across a large city block. A public passageway lined with social services will connect the individual projects to each other and the city's bustling downtown. The project's title—Hudson 2+4—reflects an approach to bridging differences by collecting character, and aggregating numerous small assets into a cohesive community.

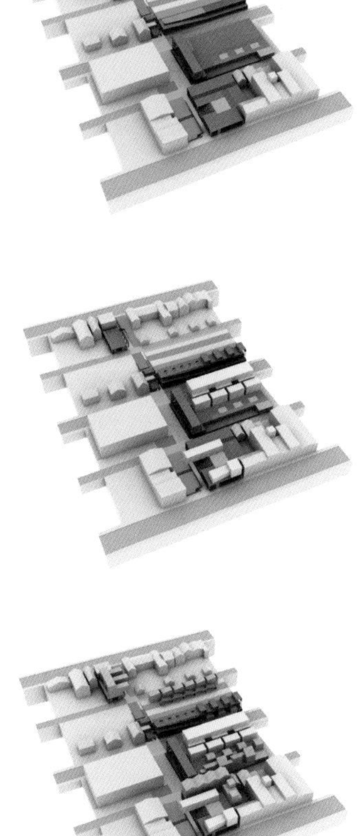

The collecting of character began in a series of community workshops where all interested citizens were asked to draw out, in images and narratives, the spaces and places of their daily lives. This process began with two key questions. The first: What are the things that draw you to live in this place? The second: What amenities are missing? Cruz and Deutsch then took the problems, needs and characteristics they found and responded to them with a multi-layered site plan.

The plan offers a variety of housing types to support diverse ethnic and social family formations, incorporating high-end weekend residences and live / work housing as well as subsidized housing. Many of the units have an open

arts and culture
multi-use instruction / performance space - 6
two screen theater - 5
community art studio - 4
community dark room - 1
commerce
food co-op - 57
micro-retail / business incubator - 3
community green space / park - 129
community pool - 19
farmers market - 3
green power - 6
winter garden / solarium - 12
covered bus stops - 5
parking garage / surface parking - 10
police / court building - 11
primary care clinic - 5
infrastructure
multi-income housing - 7
housing
social services
community center / meeting space - 17
educational / vocational center - 14
hands-on science center - 4
intergenerational center - 23
basketball courts - 18
bicycle paths and lanes -12
bowling alley - 7
ping pong table area - 4
recreation
ymca health center - 26

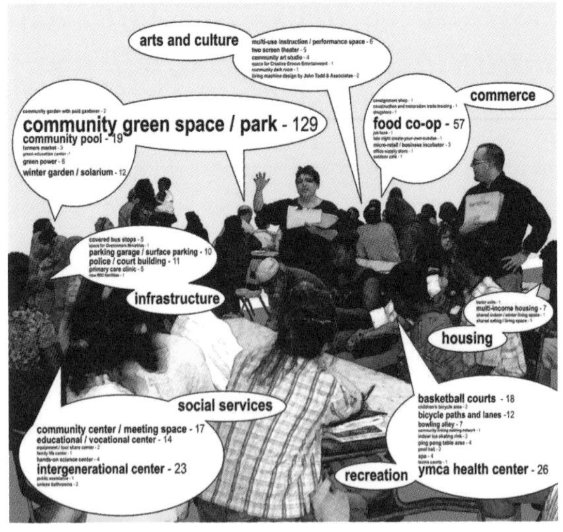

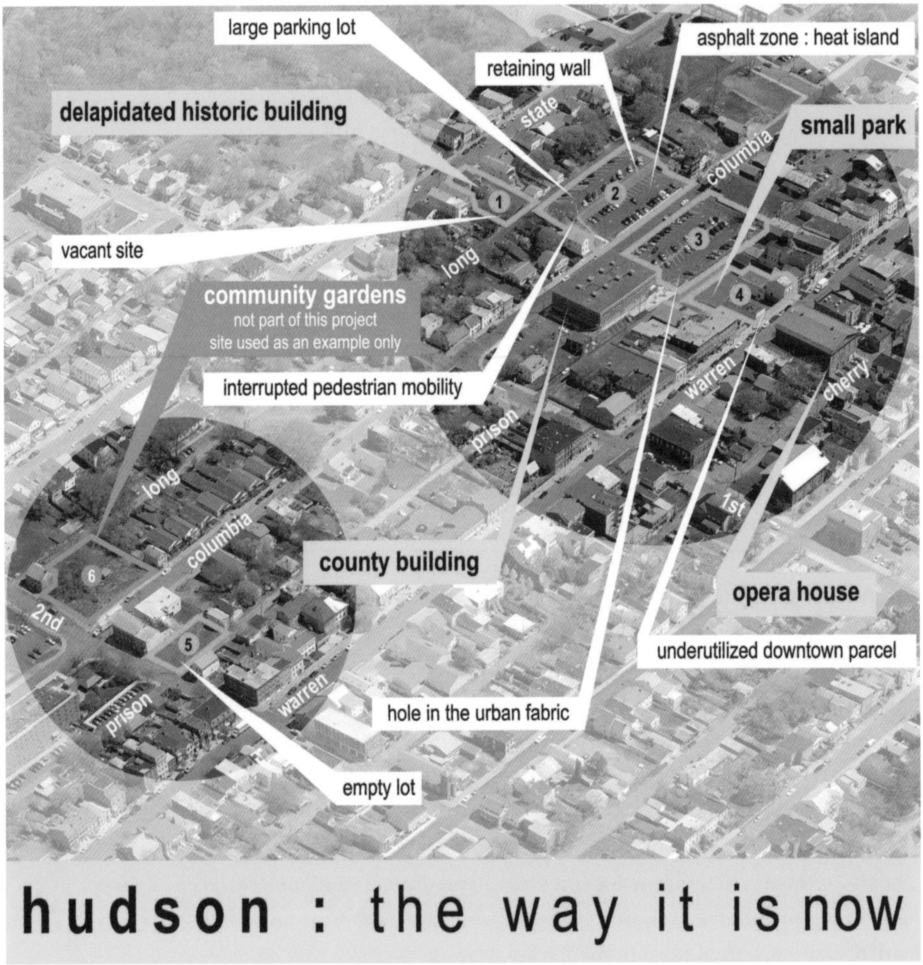
large parking lot
asphalt zone : heat island
retaining wall
delapidated historic building
small park
state
columbia
1
2
3
4
vacant site
long
community gardens
not part of this project
site used as an example only
interrupted pedestrian mobility
warren
cherry
prison
long
columbia
1st
6
county building
opera house
2nd
5
underutilized downtown parcel
prison
warren
hole in the urban fabric
empty lot
hudson : the way it is now

OPPOSITE, ABOVE
Intense consultation with residents of Hudson generated the basis for the proposal.

OPPOSITE, BELOW
The annotated aerial photograph gives an overview of the six vacant sites in Hudson's downtown.

BELOW
The same photograph shows the potential for action.

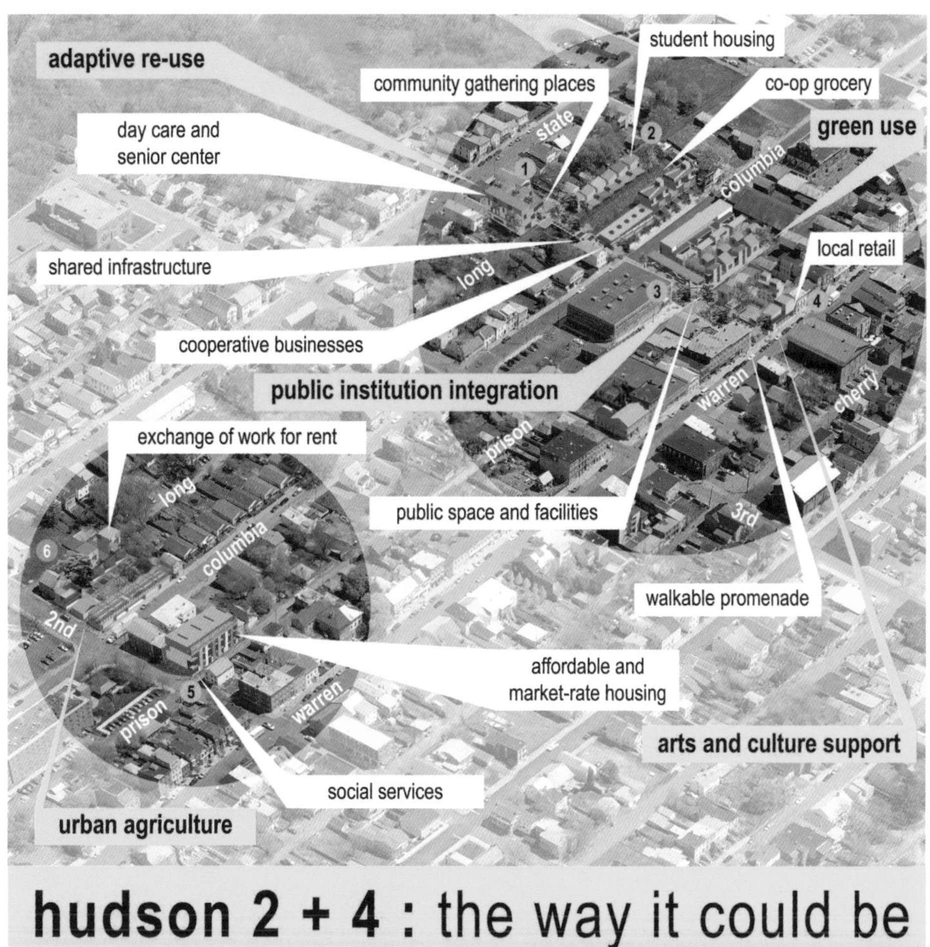

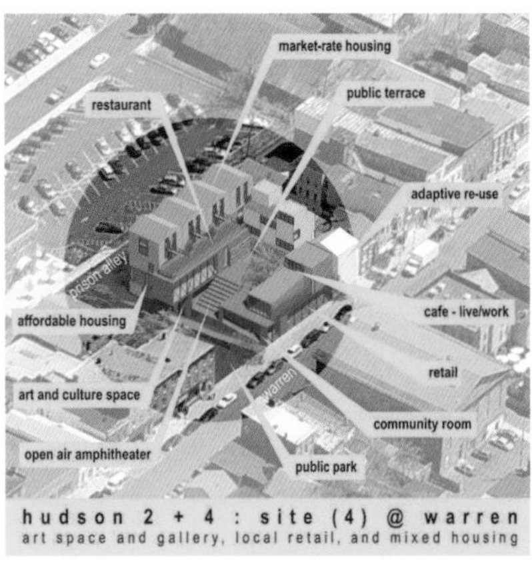
market-rate housing
public terrace
restaurant
adaptive re-use
cafe - live/work
affordable housing
retail
art and culture space
community room
open air amphitheater
public park
warren
hudson 2 + 4 : site (4) @ warren
art space and gallery, local retail, and mixed housing

floor plan with only basic kitchen and bathroom services, to allow a family to add and subdivide over time as needed. Many of the stacked unit types draw their building dimensions and material vocabulary from Hudson's historic architecture, itself a hybrid of local traditions and ideas imported from distant places by Hudson merchants and whalers. The new architecture mixes these cues and responds to residents' needs, providing space for Bangladeshi women to teach sewing workshops or an industrial kitchen to be used for large events or to operate a catering business. The plan's spine or central organizing feature, the "collective front yard," expresses the project's core philosophy that public and private open space can reinforce each other. Private patios and balconies overhang the shared open spaces, while storage rooms accommodate work tools, facilities provide work spaces, and a guest house allows residents to host family and friends.

OPPOSITE
Model views and an annotated aerial photograph of the proposed project for a partial city block at Warren Street. A plinth combines retail, art, community uses and affordable housing, with market-rate housing and a café on the upper level. Together, the new uses frame a public, open air amphitheater.

In 2008, the City approved the plan and signed a land disposition with the PARC Foundation giving it the right to develop the six parcels. The team is now moving ahead with a three-track effort to implement the proposal. One track is to convince cultural and social service organizations, such as a food cooperative and an elder care provider, to relocate to the site and act as the social glue of the public spaces. The second track is to assess the site's environmental characteristics and existing infrastructure in order to decide what uses can be supported where. The third track is to unite governmental, for-profit and non-profit housing providers to identify a mix of household incomes and a financing strategy for the new homes.

Third Floor Plan
Color Legend
Habitat 3bdrm
1225 sq. ft
Habitat Rental Units
600 sq. ft
Habitat Condominium
1200 sq. ft
Market Rate 2 bdrm
1200 sq. ft
Market Rate 3 bdrm
1400 sq. ft
Retail
Second Floor Plan
Room Legend
1 – Foyer / Dining
2 – Dining
3 – Kitchen
4a – ADA washcloset
4b – ADA bathroom
5a – Master Bedroom
5b – Bedroom
6 – Terrace / deck
7 – Lightwell
9 – Washer / Dryer
10 – ADA hoist and pulley
elevator (optional)
or additional storage
Ground Floor Plan

The Three ***Unity Lots***

With their Urban Habitats competition entry Unity Lots, Alexander Levi, Amanda Schachter and Simeon Seigel of The Three, based in Brooklyn, New York, propose a single, unifying building type to bring together the different constituents at Sunrise, creating both unity and diversity. The building's T-shaped plan combines the street frontage of a three-story house with the side yard-focused living typical of trailers sitting perpendicular to the street. Each T incorporates nine units, gathering all the various unit types required, from the accessible one-bedroom Habitat rental to the three-bedroom market-rate condominium, in one building. The team explains:

We increase the density of the archetypal Belmont block by subtly transforming the proportions of the traditional home into a multifamily unit oriented about two sides of a yard. [...] The stand-alone, market-rate home joins with the trailer, creating a hybrid and dynamic multifamily dwelling of both one-time trailer-park residents and home-owning newcomers, each resident with his or her own porch or terrace set around a courtyard along a linear green access space.

As a result, who lives where becomes indistinguishable and residents meet in the shared linear yards. Within each building, the designers have staggered the unit types to the advantage of all. For instance, the two-story condominium units have large terraces located on top of the one-story Habitat units below. These ground-floor units in turn benefit from skylights punched through the terraces above.

A disadvantage of the single building type approach is the rigidity of the resulting site plan. Although the plan responds to Nassau Street with retail at the ends of the blocks, no other distinction is otherwise articulated. In contrast, the proposal by Metropolitan Planning Collaborative *(see p. 88)*, also based on making residents' income level a non-issue, does so by mixing the constituents throughout a wide array of building types.

OPPOSITE
First, second and third floor plans of the new, unifying building type.

BELOW
Axonometric diagrams showing how the different dwelling types are organized into one building type placed across the site.

NEXT PAGE, TOP
Section through the building's side wing, showing the terrace of a market-rate condominium over an accessible Habitat unit below.

NEXT PAGE, BOTTOM
Site plan showing the ground level.

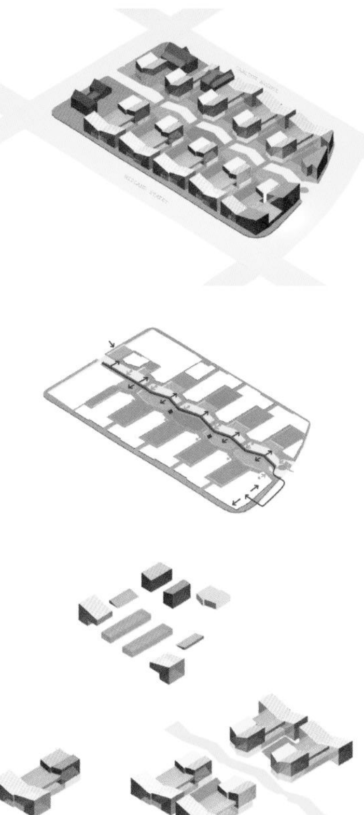

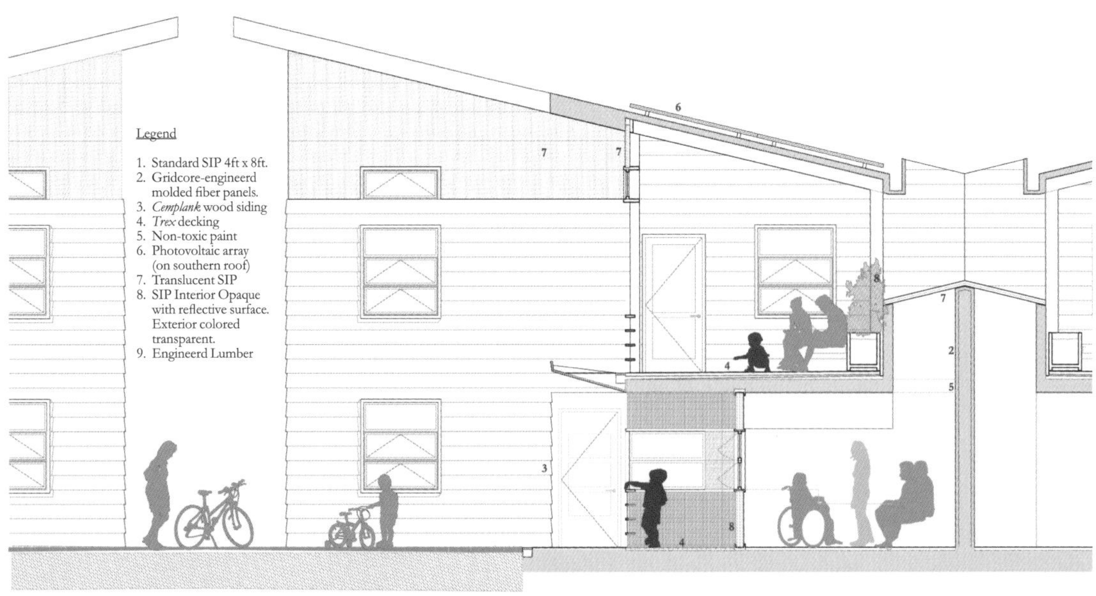

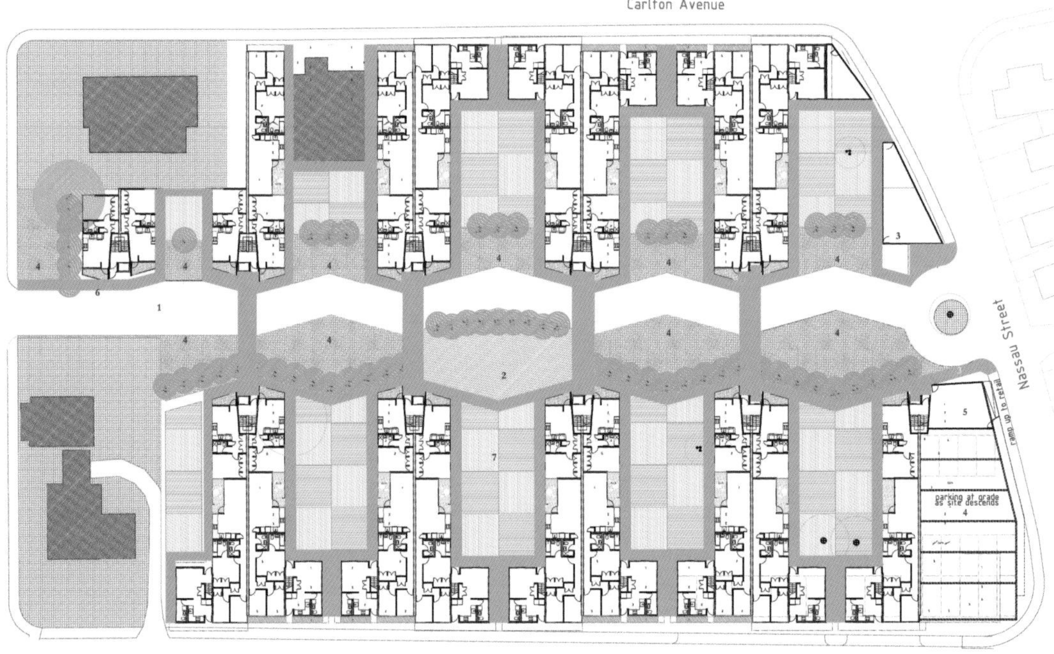

Site Legend 1. Interior Street / 2. Playground / 3. Community Center / 4. Parking / 5. Retail / 6. Pedestrian walks / 7. Gardens

Extension

The Three

Alexander Levi, Amanda Schachter and Simeon Seigel are architects practicing in New York.

What role does / did the Urban Habitats competition play within your practice?

We entered the Urban Habitats competition not long after being named a winner in the 2003 Home House Project competition initiated by the Southeastern Center for Contemporary Art in North Carolina. In Home House, we were asked to reconsider the low-cost single-family home. While many entrants chose to discard the typical Habitat for Humanity housing unit, we elevated its construction by equipping it with a new front facade to enliven both the streetscape and the living room. Our project, "Hand-Insulated Pop," proposed a quilted facade determined by the home-owning family and inserted between translucent shingles and interior wall panels, providing insulation to the house and luminous color to both street and living area.

The Urban Habitats competition interested us because it involved Habitat for Humanity at the level of an entire city block, not only as builder of stand-alone single-family units. We wanted to explore the possibilities for the positive tension occurring between street, sidewalk and yard, to produce a new hybrid model of low-cost American small-city urbanity embracing wide socio-economic prospects within a single neighborhood.

We entered both competitions from Spain, where we had been practicing architecture since 1998, as a way to tie our Spanish professional outlook to our American upbringing and sensibilities. While Spain trusts young architects to contribute to innovation by realizing some of the country's key new design projects, there is still little or no community design as an alternative form of practice, this role having been traditionally fulfilled by the State.

For the Urban Habitats competition, we teamed up with Simeon Seigel, a New York architect with experience in East Coast residential architecture. Seigel's graduate studies focused on housing types designed and built without the help of formally trained professionals. He began searching for methods which would benefit from the contribution of trained professionals while maximizing the contributions of homeowners and untrained labor: "self-built" homes, endowed with sufficient reserves of structure and technical systems to allow for ease of maintenance and later expansion. His designs ranged from a prototype for FEMA emergency housing to community playgrounds.

Have you been able to further develop the concepts you put forward in your entry?

Community design continues to influence, and emerge from, our practice. In 2004, Schachter initiated the Master of International Cooperation in Architecture degree program at the Escola Tècnica Superior d'Arquitectura in Barcelona (ESARQ), also becoming the director of the Department of Cooperation in Architecture at the school. Through these hands-on academic programs, we embarked on a series of cooperative architecture projects, from designing migrant farm worker housing in Lerida, an inland province of Catalonia (inspired by American architect Bryan Bell's non-profit initiative, Design Corps) to working in marginalized Barcelona neighborhoods to enable local residents and students to guide the transformation of their environment.

We have recently moved our practice to New York City to address local design projects requiring the expertise we built in Spain. Among other projects, we were awarded the 2009 Van Alen Institute New York Prize Fellowship in Public Architecture, to investigate, envision and realize interventions along the Bronx River in conjunction with middle school and university students, teachers, experts, and local residents and activists—and we hope to bring our Barcelona architecture students into the transformative design activity as well.

BELOW

"Barri Gotic as Relief" was a fourth-year cooperation studio at the ESARQ with youths from four local schools and community centers in 2006.

The project included ten weeks of workshops in Barcelona's Gothic Quarter to unite children in precarious situations through building three large-scale relief models of their neighborhood. The model's sectors are made from found materials, ranging from after school snacks to bottle caps.

An architecture student and one of the youths hang a finished model from the ceiling.

BOTTOM

Another finished model is hung on an orange wall.

Expand Options
:Share Boundaries

Neighbors, or embracing proximity

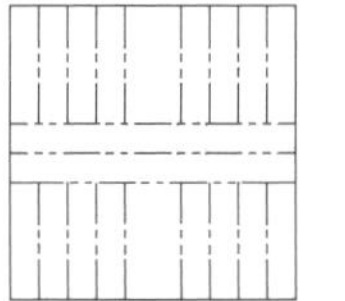
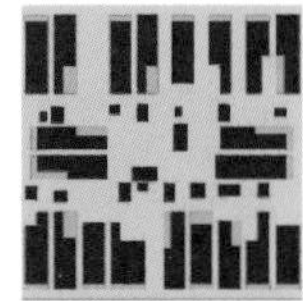

COMPARATIVE ANALYSIS - NEIGHBORHOOD BLOCK

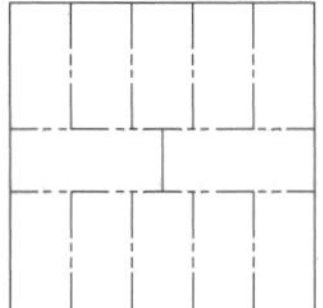
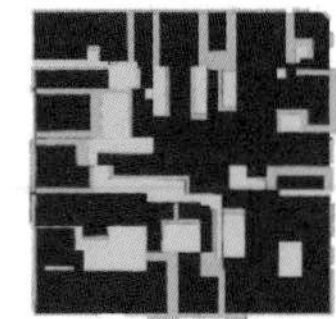

COMPARATIVE ANALYSIS - FRENCH QUARTER BLOCK

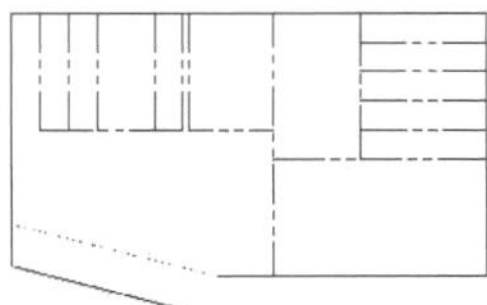
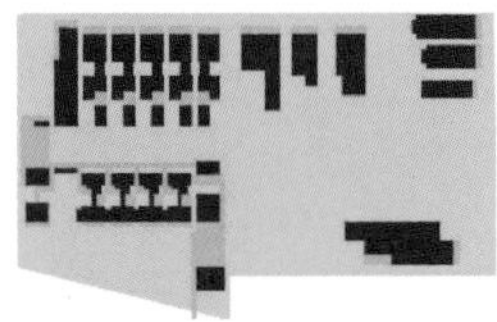

COMPARATIVE ANALYSIS - BREATHE

You like the idea of compact living, but you don't know if you can deal with your neighbors. Instead of withdrawing, step out. Living inside and out may be one of the best ways to expand your living options. Sharing boundaries is the way to go about it.

:Draw boundaries, create space.

Boundaries can be good: a small, enclosed exterior space can provide a stronger sense of privacy than a wide, unenclosed space. In a clearly defined open space, you are likely to make use of all the space you have, all the way up to the edge. A fence, a wall, a tree, a six-inch step—they all can create boundaries between different spaces. Instead of locating your building in the middle of the site with equally dimensioned "buffers" all around, consider challenging existing zoning to situate the building right on the property's edge, creating a "zero-lot line" house. In this way, you can reclaim space right up to your neighbor's house.

:Shift boundaries, create rooms.

The boundaries between the interior of your home and its exterior merit the same attention as your property line.

Think of exterior spaces as rooms: imagine what goes on in them, and how they relate to the rooms on the inside.

Try "folding" the boundary between inside and out. A patio bordered on two or three sides by living spaces is more private than one that is entirely exposed. A courtyard, open only to the sky, may be even more of an amenity, both as a place to spend time in, and a way of letting light into the unit. Balconies, decks and porches are equally important. Properly dimensioned, they allow for outdoor dining, study, work.

:Trace boundaries, create paths.

Given shared boundaries, testing the size, location and operation of your windows is key. When your staircase is next to your neighbor's patio, a high window with a view only to the sky is more appropriate than a lower one. Consider which windows you need for ventilation, and which ones only need to provide light.

The issue of visual and acoustic privacy extends to how you get to your home. Where do you park your car and how do you get home from there? How do you get to your home when you don't use a car? How do your friends arrive when they visit?

Eskew + Dumez + Ripple
Breathe

OPPOSITE
Figure-ground plans show how Breathe unites the advantages of two New Orleans housing types, the free-standing shot gun (top) and the attached courtyard house (below).

LEFT
Model view.

BELOW
Perspective view from the ground level of the apartment building up to its access gallery.

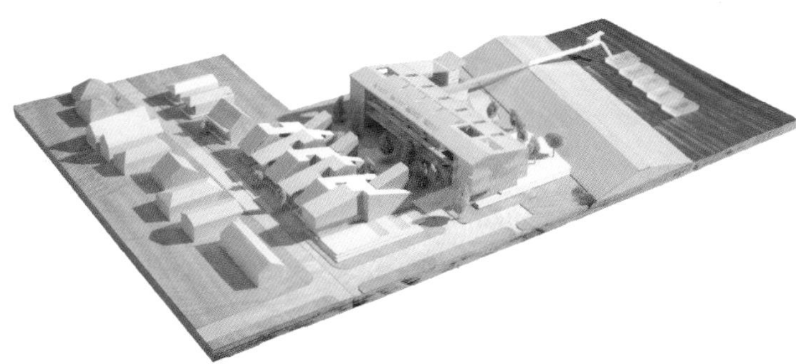

In 2006, the environmental organization Global Green staged an open competition for a site in New Orleans' Holy Cross neighborhood, an area of small homes devastated by Hurricane Katrina. The brief asked for sustainable and affordable housing, combing five single-family homes with 12 multifamily dwellings, as well as community amenities. The finalist scheme Breathe by New Orleans-based Eskew+Dumez+Ripple is an excellent example of how sharing boundaries can become a key asset, not only for living side-by-side, but also for living "on top" of one another. The courtyard, or cut-out, does the trick.

The single-family homes along the existing neighborhood street combine the benefits of an attached courtyard house, inspired by the traditional houses of the French Quarter, with the dimensions of the freestanding shotgun houses typical of the Holy Cross area. The courtyard introduces an exterior space of usable dimensions into the center of the house, allowing for cross ventilation and natural light throughout the building. It also creates a visual and acoustic buffer between the more public parts of the house toward the street and more private, bedroom areas toward the back.

Each dwelling in the three-story building facing the levees also enjoys the benefits of a courtyard. The two-bedroom units are accessed from secured, open galleries which connect to a unit's private courtyard deck. Entry to the unit is from this deck. Cut-outs in the decks are strategically placed to allow light to pass to lower units and cool breezes to flow to the units above. Cut outs also create a buffer between the bedrooms and the access gallery.

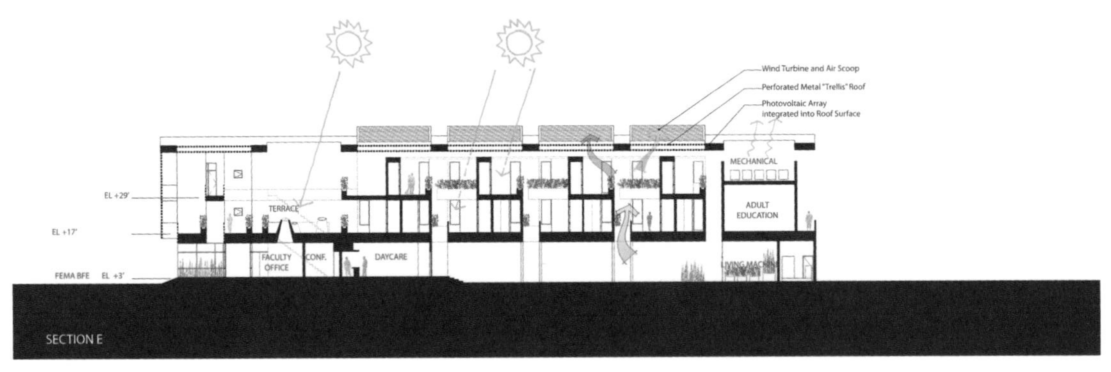

Wind Turbine and Air Scoop
Perforated Metal "Trellis" Roof
Photovoltaic Array integrated into Roof Surface
MECHANICAL
ADULT EDUCATION
TERRACE
EL +29'
EL +17'
FEMA BFE EL +3'
FACULTY OFFICE
CONF.
DAYCARE
SECTION E

OPEN TO BELOW
OPEN TO BELOW
TERRACE
ADULT LEARNING
COVERED WORK AREA
VOCATIONAL/ JOB TRAINING
BRIDGE TO LEVEE

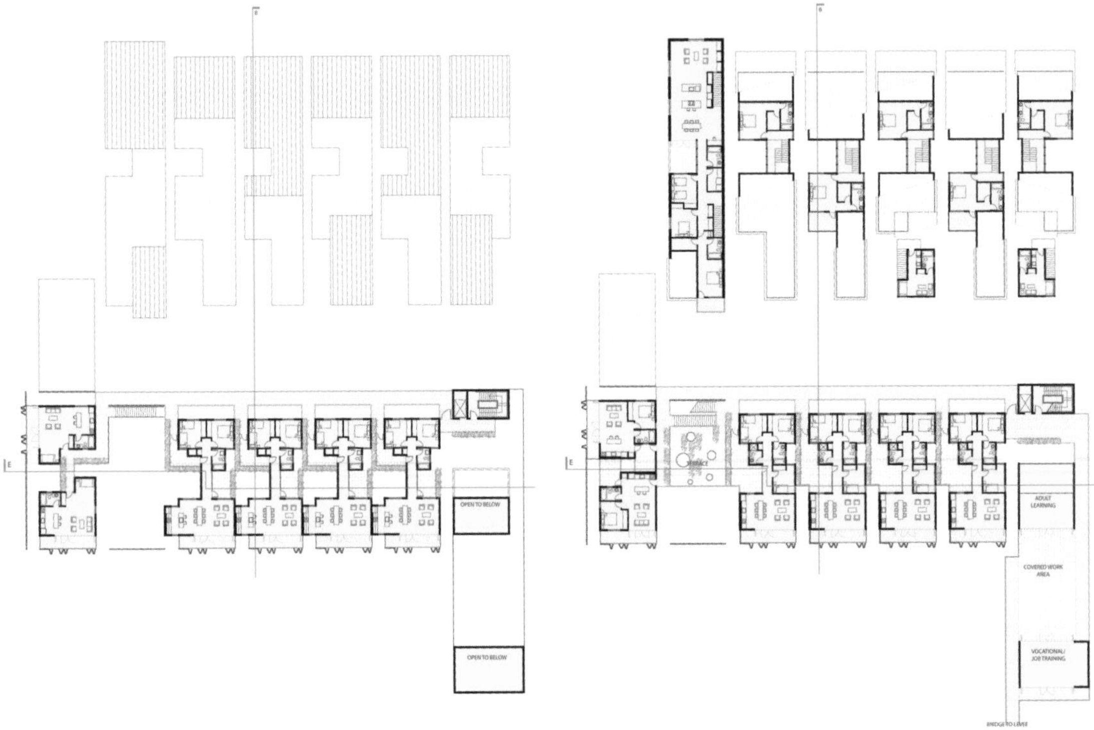

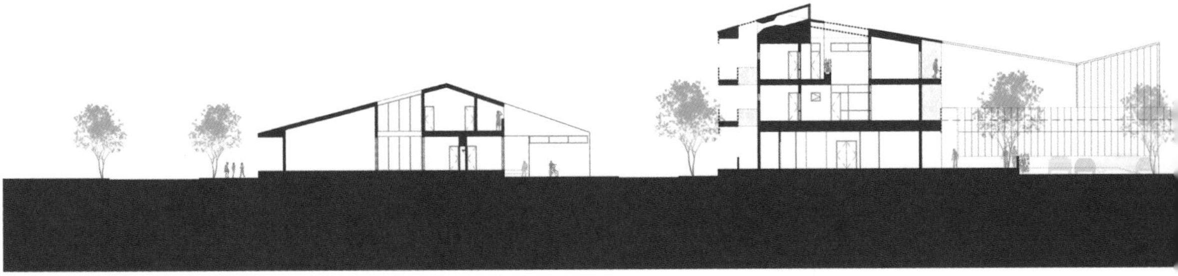

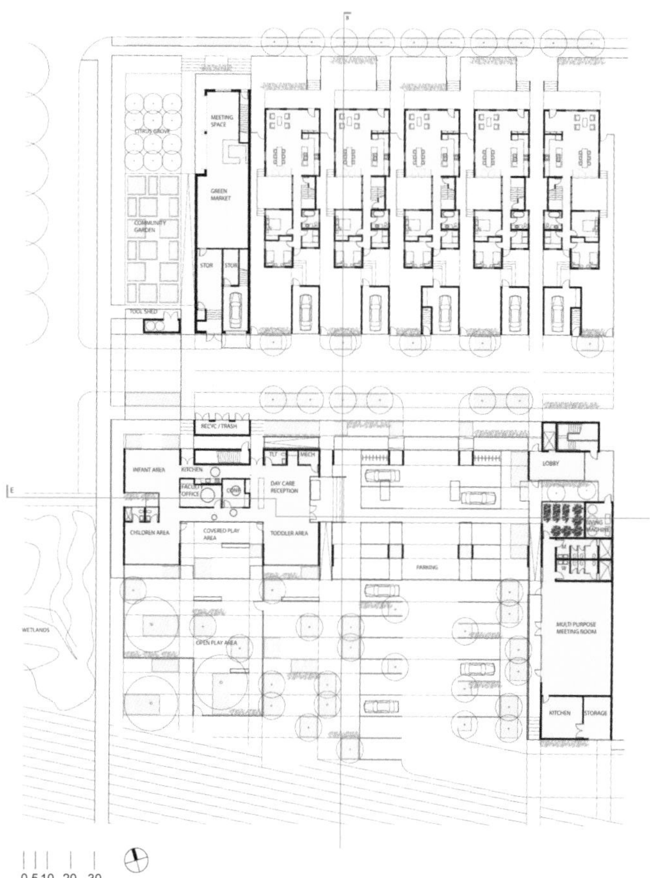

OPPOSITE, TOP

Cross section through the apartment building, showing the cut-outs in the decks and the private courtyards.

CENTER, FROM RIGHT TO LEFT

First, second and third floor plans.

BELOW

Site section looking east, showing the single-family home courtyards as well as the access galleries and courtyards of the apartment building.

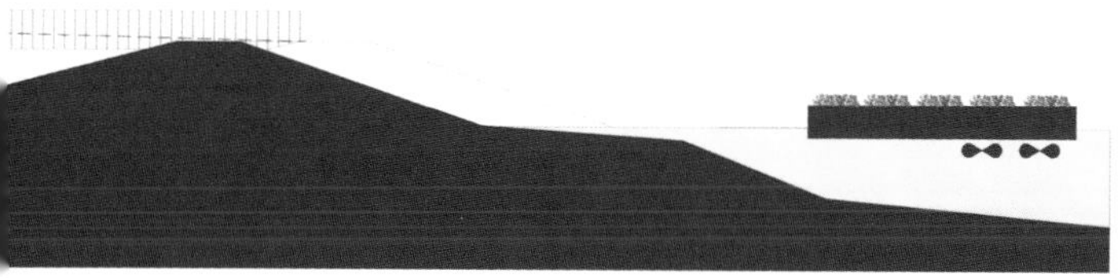

BELOW
Axonometric of site and building types.

OPPOSITE, FROM LEFT TO RIGHT
Views of the new street; the walkway from the community garden to the new street; the eastern community garden.

NEXT SPREAD
Site plan showing the first floor.

Each condo building, or Double Wide, comprises seven condominiums organized around a central scissor stair ❶. Residents park under the building along the street ❷. From here, they arrive to their building entrance located on a walkway connecting to the community gardens beyond ❸. Each floor has a different porch | deck configuration based on its vertical position in the building ❹ and incorporate green roofs ❺. With at least two exposures, all units can be cross ventilated. The material is CMU.

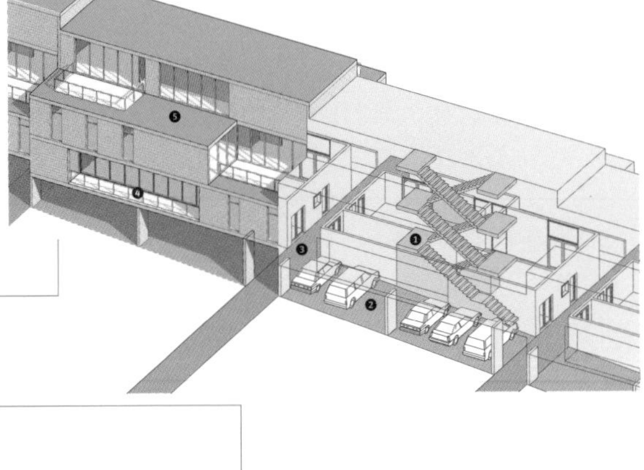

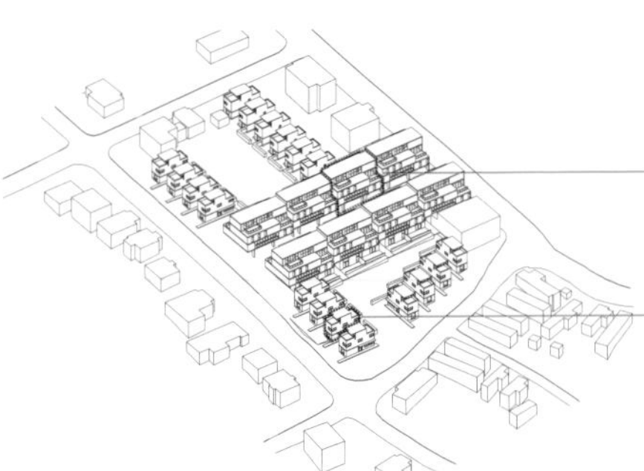

In the Habitat House, or Triple High, residents also arrive with a view to the community gardens: they park in their side yard ❻ which connects to the open space beyond. When the car is away, this structured grass surface becomes a play area. In addition, by reducing the number of cars, residents can increase the size of their yard. The building's central stair ❼ draws hot air up and out of the house and culminates in a porch ❽ and green roof ❾. The house is stick built and wood clad.

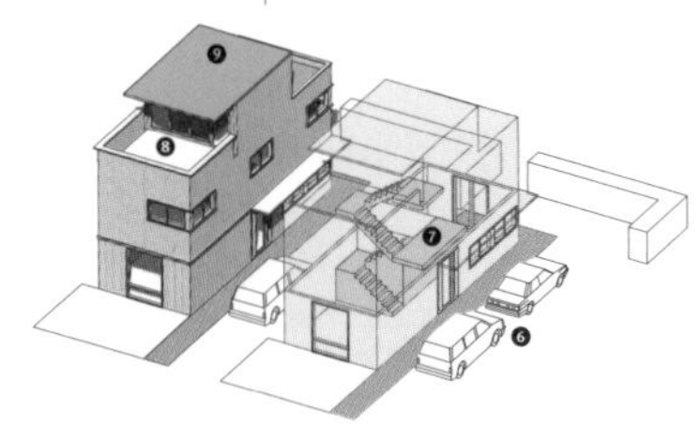

Genter Schindler
Double Wide, Triple High

The Urban Habitats competition entry Double Wide, Triple High by Genter Schindler relies heavily on drawing clear boundaries between units to create private outdoor spaces. The spaciousness of the units is enhanced with private yards that are visually connected to the common areas beyond.

First Place Finalist

Team Members
Christopher Genter, Susanne Schindler

In the Triple High, or Habitat house, the side yard is porch, yard and parking area in one. The side yard fronts directly onto the common green space, bordered on two sides by other Habitat houses. In this way, the yards seem bigger than they are, and the common space is monitored at all times. The houses also have a roof deck as an additional open space.

In addition to this visual extension, outdoor space is doubled by superimposing space for leisure and space for parking, two uses typically found incompatible. The side yard of the Habitat house is dimensioned to accommodate two cars. In owning two cars, however, the resident foregoes the pleasure of having a yard. The design invites the residents to manage their own open space by providing an area that can be used for parking or leisure. Ideally, the number of cars is reduced, and the space saved immediately made useful to the resident.

The four-story Double Wide, or condominium building, is based on the idea that the location of a unit determines the type of private open space it incorporates. While the ground-floor efficiency units front onto the common garden, the second-floor unit benefits from a narrow balcony running the full length of the unit, the third-floor unit works around a deeper patio, and the penthouse condominium opens on to perches in the sky.

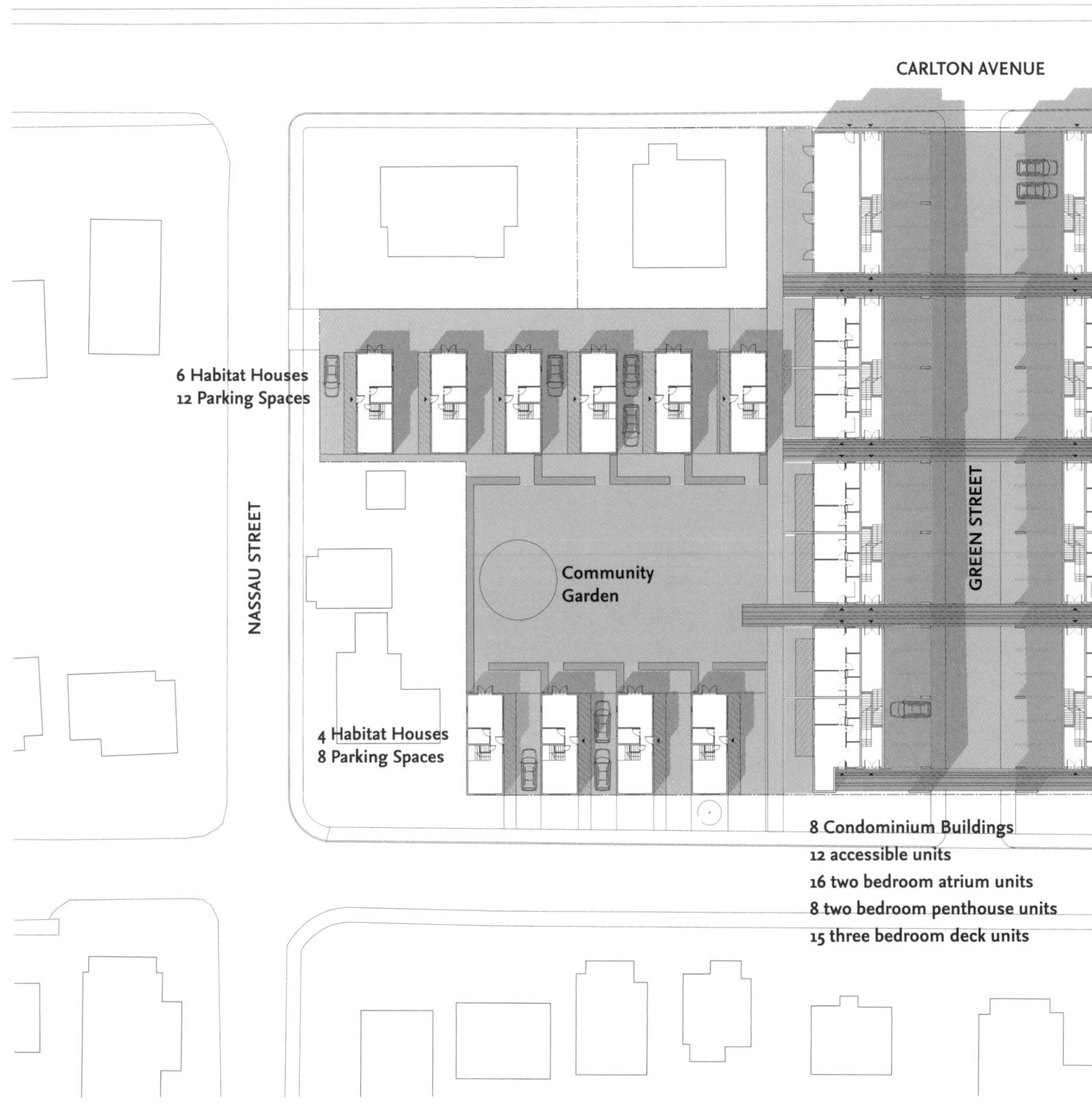
CARLTON AVENUE
6 Habitat Houses
12 Parking Spaces
NASSAU STREET
Community
Garden
GREEN STREET
4 Habitat Houses
8 Parking Spaces
8 Condominium Buildings
12 accessible units
16 two bedroom atrium units
8 two bedroom penthouse units
15 three bedroom deck units

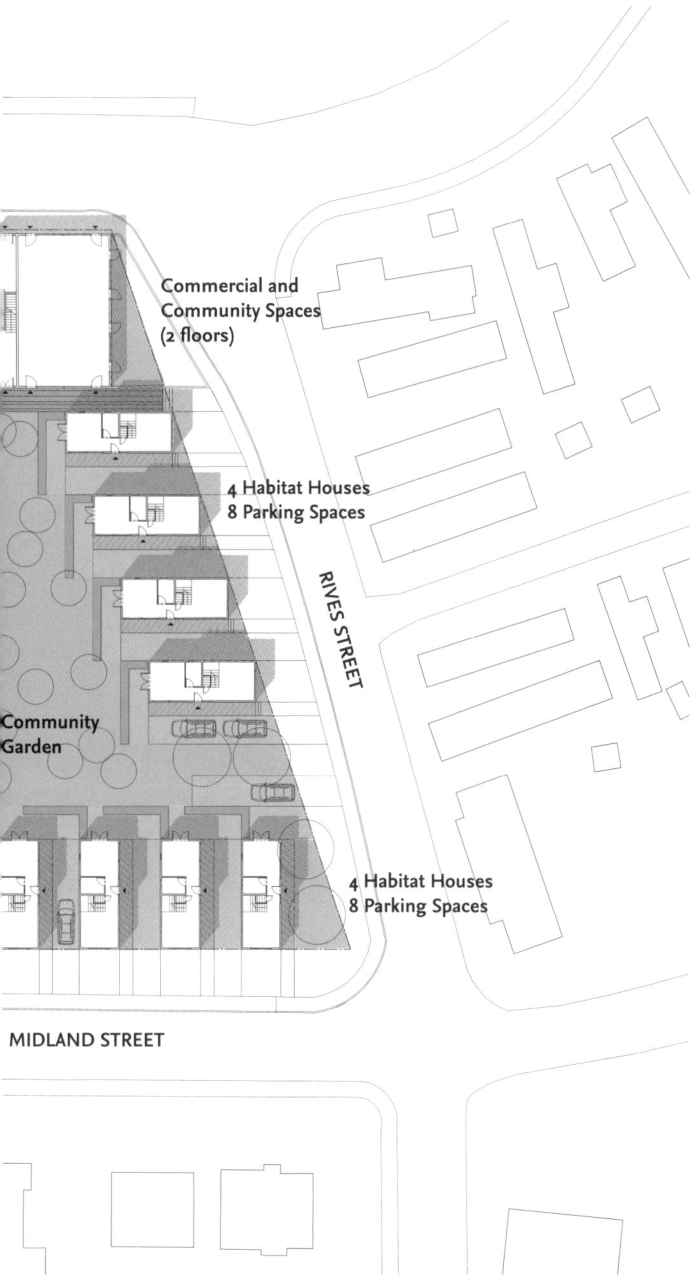

Statement

Laying out a single new street allows all new units to be sited directly on a public street. The new street is fronted by condominium buildings, while Habitat single-family houses are sited along existing streets. Community gardens, framed by both condominium buildings and Habitat houses, serve the residents of both.

Each condominium building, or Double Wide, comprises seven units organized around a central scissor stair. Residents park under the building along the street. From here, they arrive at their building entrance located on a walkway connecting to the community gardens beyond. Each floor has a different porch / deck configuration based on its vertical position in the building. With at least two exposures, all units can be cross-ventilated. The buildings are constructed of concrete masonry units and are to be constructed professionally.

In the Habitat House, or Triple High, residents also arrive with a view to the community gardens: they park in their side yard which connects to the open space beyond. When the car is away, this structured grass surface becomes a play area. By reducing the number of cars, residents can increase the size of their yard. The material is wood frame with wood cladding. The buildings are to be constructed using volunteer labor.

Jury Comments

Not only does this design most closely recognize and incorporate the existing orientation of the site, it does so while addressing, with generosity, the residents' desire for open communal spaces where they may gather and garden. Jurors were also impressed by the way the design anticipates different types of encounters and different types of spaces, the way it organizes the site through attention to spatial detail and circulation between the private and semi-private spaces of the courtyards. The street is at a scale appropriate to the neighborhood context. In the words of juror Marion Dudley, who currently resides at Sunrise Trailer Court, “This one said ‘home’ to me. It's more like our own home that we have now than any of the other entries.”

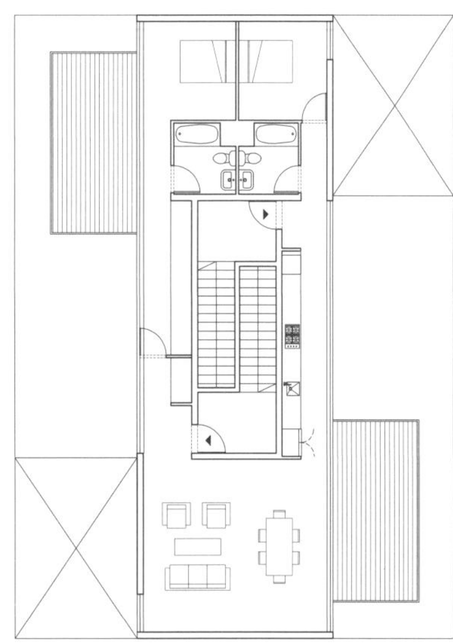

two bedroom penthouse

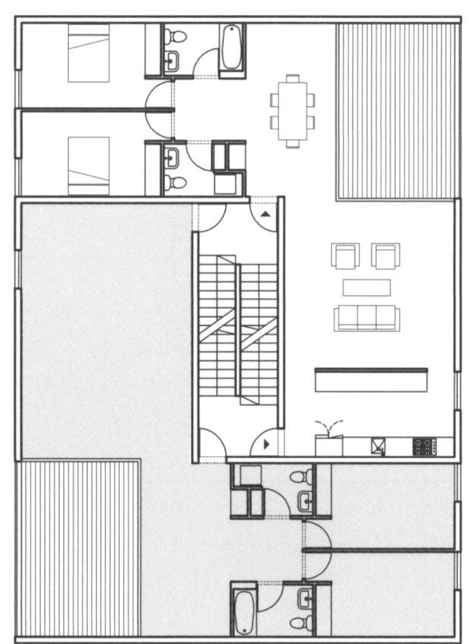

two bedroom atrium unit

3

OPPOSITE

View from a condominium penthouse at sunset.

LEFT

View from a first floor condominium across the western community garden.

BELOW

Double Wide floor plans.

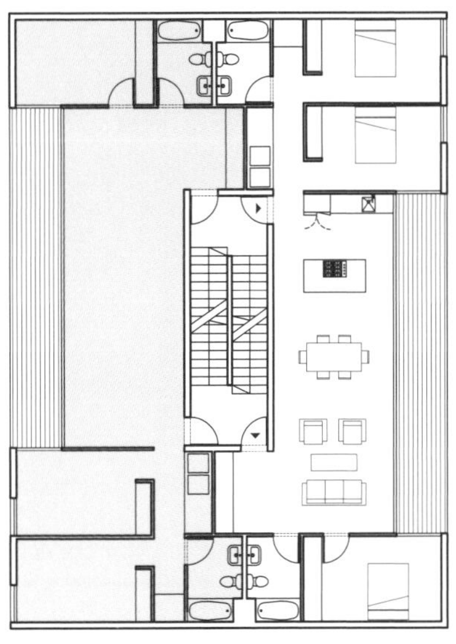

three bedroom deck unit

2

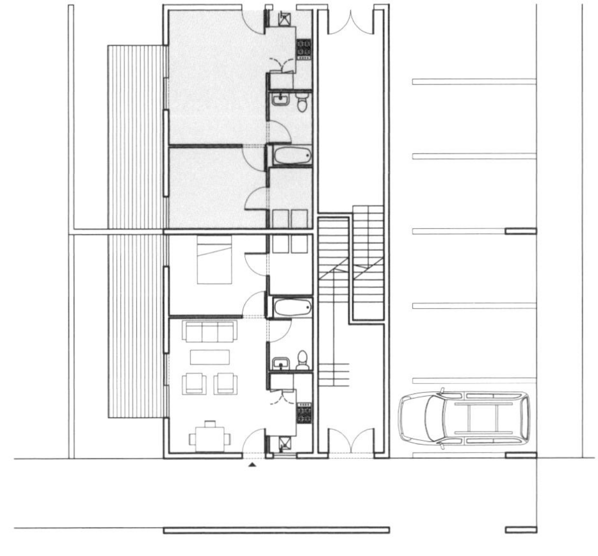

one bedroom accessible unit

1

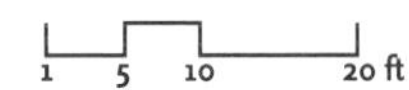

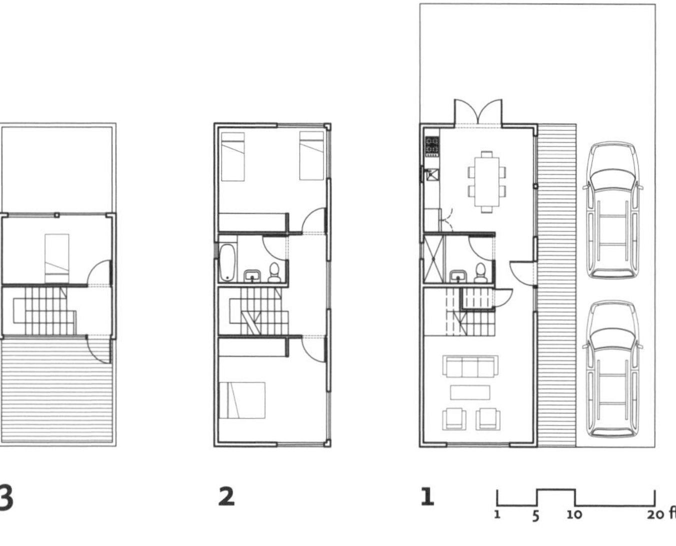

LEFT
Triple High floor plans.

BELOW
View from the side yard toward the community garden.

Extension
Genter Schindler

Genter Schindler is Chris Genter and Susanne Schinder, a design collaborative that began in 2005. It continues to operate as a fluid design partnership; not so much an office but an identity under which to work collaboratively. Chris is based in Boston; Susanne in Rotterdam.

What role does / did the Urban Habitats competition play within your practice?

The competition was our first project together; we were attracted to the call for entries by its clear goals, consistent brief and the idea of redeveloping a trailer park—a challenge since we are aware of the qualities that can develop through halfway informal, semi-nomadic living which are very hard to generate through a traditional master planning effort.

At the time, we were both working at Utile, a new architecture practice in Boston. Boston was in the midst of a housing development boom, so we were designing quite a lot of housing with smaller developer / builders and community development corporations willing to take a chance on a young office. These projects tended to be for infill sites either too small for established developers or in slightly riskier neighborhoods. Prior to working with Utile, housing had been an integral part of Chris' love for buildings and designing them, not a research agenda per se. For Susanne, housing had been a longstanding focus, including research in the Gaza Strip, Uruguay and Germany.

Because Charlottesville has a strong culture of porches and gardens, our agenda was to develop a set of straightforward, easily buildable housing types whose rules of aggregation would shape defined public and private landscape spaces. This work with the landscape and the complex sets of relationships between indoors and out, public and private, was by nature of scale, culture and climate something quite distinct in our work.

Have you been able to further develop the concepts put forward in your entry?

Shortly after the competition London Calling LLC, a small development partnership, commissioned us to design a multifamily project on two adjacent single-family lots in Fifeville, a neighborhood of Charlottesville within walking distance of the growing UVA hospital and downtown. Rather than being subsidized or financed through volunteer labor, these units were to be affordable by virtue of their size and density—we proposed six compact houses on sites previously occupied by two. Urbanistically, the project is an iteration of our Urban Habitats proposal. Each house is accessed directly from one of the three streets, assuring each a distinct address and identity. Toward the inside of the block, however, the units' gardens all front on a densely planted, shared open space which acts as a visual extension of the private open spaces and as a visual and acoustical buffer between them.

Have you been able to realize any projects that are related to the Urban Habitats project, be it in scale, approach, client, philosophy?

We continue to work with Habitat for Humanity on Sunrise in collaboration with MPC. While the site plan and housing types have both radically changed from our competition proposal, the logic of the initial scheme—particularly in the flexibility of types, and the use and shaping of outdoor spaces for each unit—remains consistent. *(See Epilogue for the revised Sunrise plan.)*

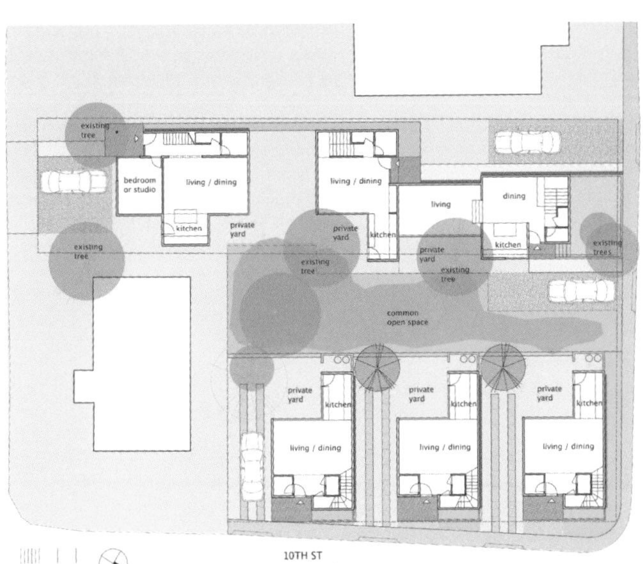

Site plan.

Site axonometric.

Build for Change
:Facilitate Flux

Flexibility, or accommodating lifecycles

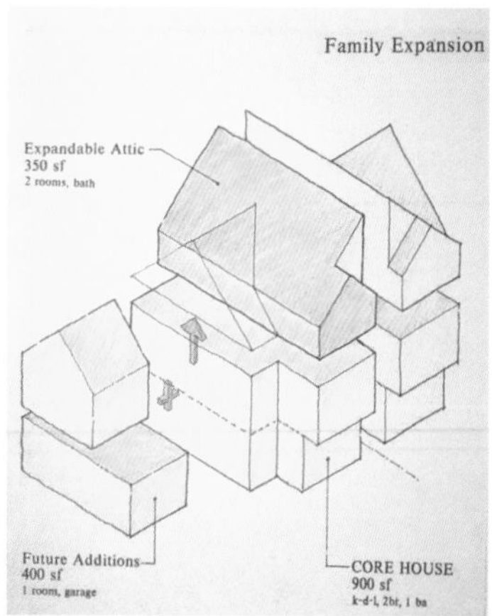

All of a sudden you find yourself working from home. You can no longer climb stairs, need to sublet a room to make ends meet, are expecting another baby. How can a dwelling accommodate such flexibility? As a designer or developer, how do you anticipate the vagaries of life and facilitate its cycles?

:De-designate.

The simplest way to facilitate flux is to create rooms that can be used for any number of purposes. Forget "bedroom" or "living room"—design rooms that can do both, either alone or in combination. Rather than resorting to one large living space and many small bedrooms, is there a way to create neutral rooms? Think about how rooms can be connected and separated, as the situation requires. Closed French doors between two spaces can give you a living room and a bedroom. Opening them will create a generous space.

:Demand both-and.

Some spaces seem inflexible no matter what. A staircase, for instance, or a corridor. It doesn't have to be that way. In designing, think about how they can be used for more than just climbing or just gaining access to rooms. The stair becomes a play area if the landing is wide enough; the corridor serves as a home office if it's lined with a desk.

Demand both-and. Don't settle for either-or. Achieving this flexibility is frequently just a matter of inches, of smartly located openings and of working through scenarios.

:Don't touch the drains.

In order to allow for more substantial change within the house, the building's load bearing elements and its mechanical systems—water, waste, heating, cooling—need to be located so that they can remain in place when everything else in the house changes. Why? Structural and mechanical changes are the messiest and the most expensive. Therefore, as a rule of thumb, wet rooms should be stacked, kitchens and bathrooms located next to each other, and interior partitions made non-load bearing so that they can be moved. For future adaptability, allocate space and plumbing on the accessible floor for the build-out of an accessible bedroom and bath.

Pyatok Architects Jingletown Homes

OPPOSITE
Axonometric showing how a Jingletown home was designed to expand. On the interior, the attic can be converted to living space. On the exterior, there is space for a garage or living space with a second room above.

LEFT
View of Jingletown Homes from the main access road.

The Oakland, California-based practice of Michael Pyatok has realized several residential developments that facilitate flux, both as purely residential and as live / work arrangements. The 53 different units of Jingletown Homes in Oakland, completed in 1996, anticipate both internal and external adaptations. The project was developed by the non-profit Oakland Community Housing after residents opposed the plan for a trucking terminal on a former industrial site. In several community meetings, the neighbors, interested in acquiring a future residence for themselves, articulated that they wanted to stay in the neighborhood even if their families expand. Designing homes that could respond to such changes became a central project goal.

The smaller homes were designed with attics that allowed for the addition of one bedroom and one bath. The larger homes offer a space adjacent to the house reserved for a future garage and a potential bedroom above. An accessible bedroom and bath on the ground floor supplement the three upstairs bedrooms. This “grandparent suite”, with its own entrance from the yard, allows generations to share space with dignity. Other houses have living rooms located on the second floor, so that a flexible room on the ground floor can be used for a home-based business. An addition in the carport area could serve a growing business rather than a parked car.

Since the residents moved into their homes, about one-third have converted the reserved attic space into living space. Only two households have added a garage. According to Jingletown Homes’ property management, current residents are satisfied with their homes, but many would in fact have preferred a “finished” product including a garage, rather than having to build the addition themselves.

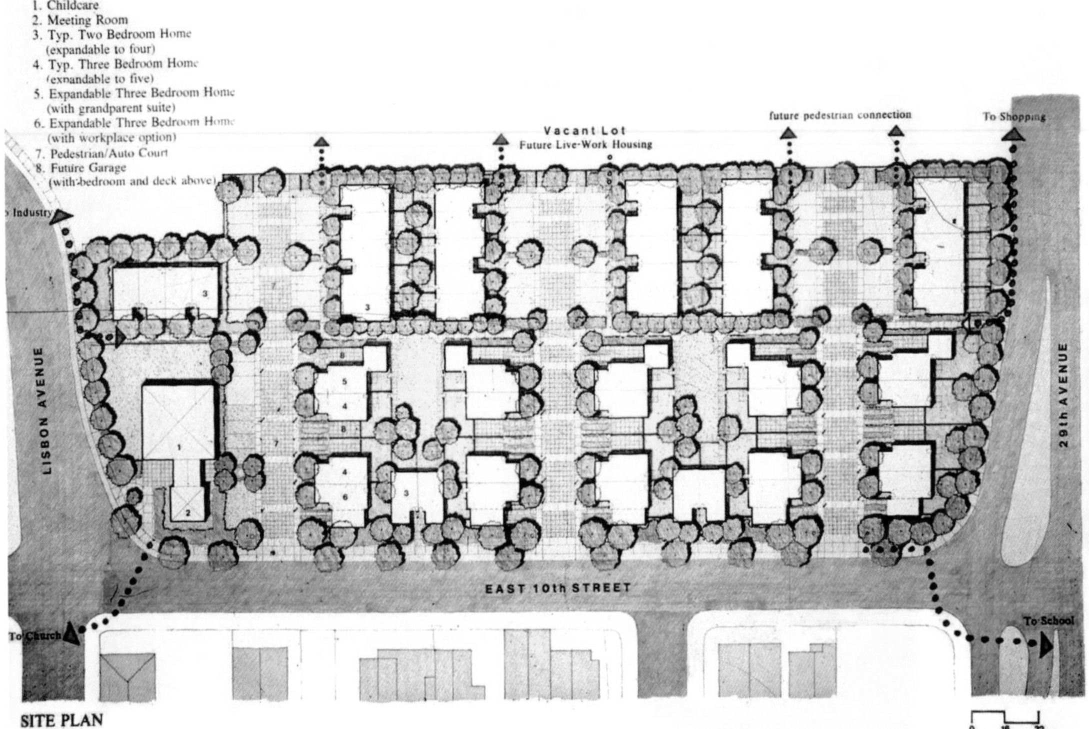
1. Childcare
2. Meeting Room
3. Typ. Two Bedroom Home (expandable to four)
4. Typ. Three Bedroom Home (expandable to five)
5. Expandable Three Bedroom Home (with grandparent suite)
6. Expandable Three Bedroom Home (with workplace option)
7. Pedestrian/Auto Court
8. Future Garage (with bedroom and deck above)
Vacant Lot
Future Live-Work Housing
future pedestrian connection
To Shopping
Industry
LISBON AVENUE
29th AVENUE
EAST 10th STREET
To Church
To School
SITE PLAN
0 16 32

OPPOSITE, ABOVE
Aerial photograph.

OPPOSITE, BELOW
Site plan.

LEFT
View of side-by-side houses along one of the internal streets.

BELOW
Floor plans of an expandable house with a home business at the first level.

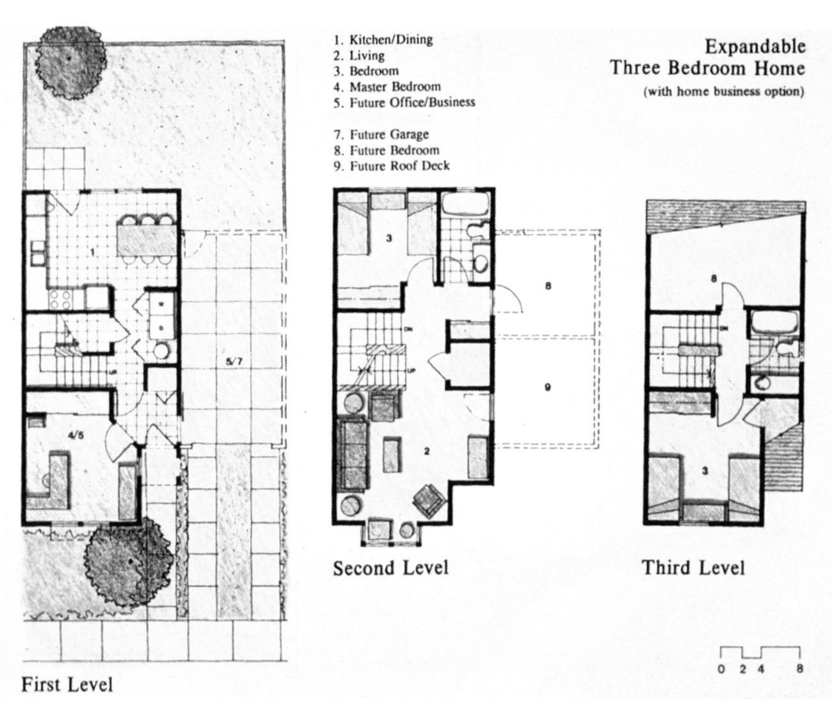

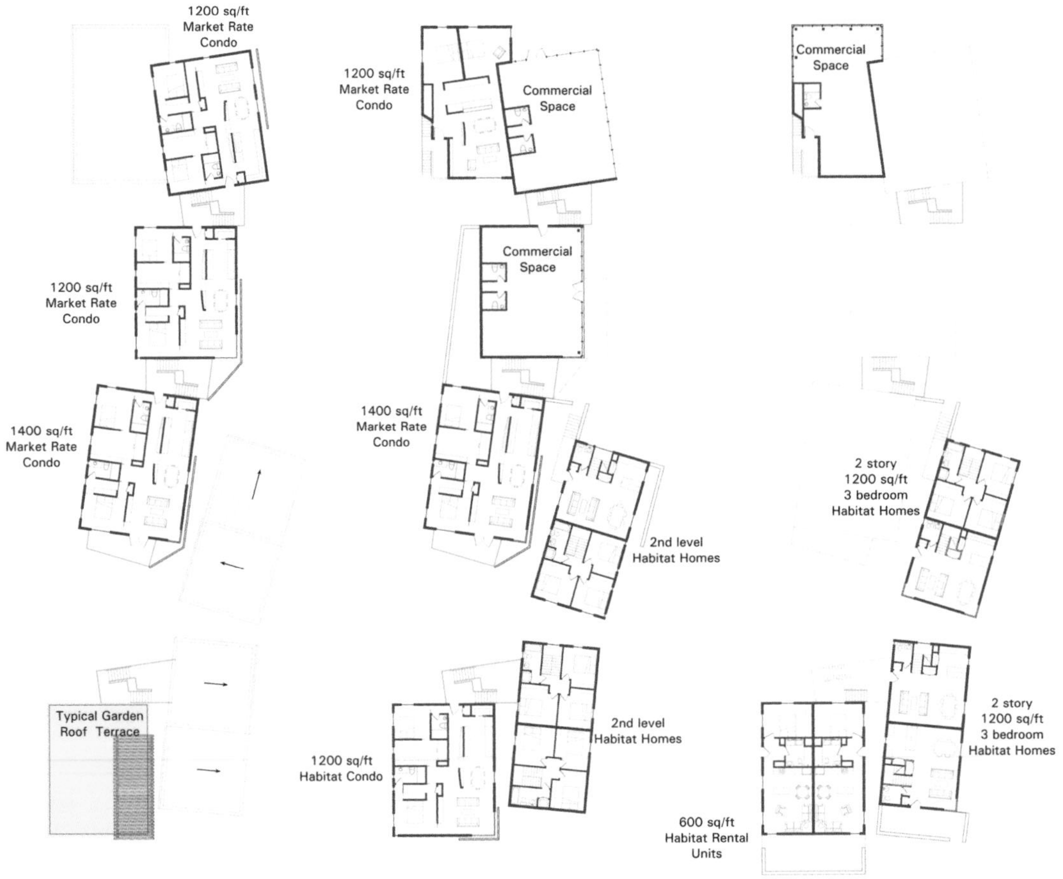

1200 sq/ft
Market Rate
Condo
1200 sq/ft
Market Rate
Condo
Commercial
Space
Commercial
Space
1200 sq/ft
Market Rate
Condo
Commercial
Space
1400 sq/ft
Market Rate
Condo
1400 sq/ft
Market Rate
Condo
2nd level
Habitat Homes
2 story
1200 sq/ft
3 bedroom
Habitat Homes
Typical Garden
Roof Terrace
1200 sq/ft
Habitat Condo
2nd level
Habitat Homes
600 sq/ft
Habitat Rental
Units
2 story
1200 sq/ft
3 bedroom
Habitat Homes

2 story habitat units
site walls provide private gardens
painted cementitious fiberboard on SIPS
front porch
@ street

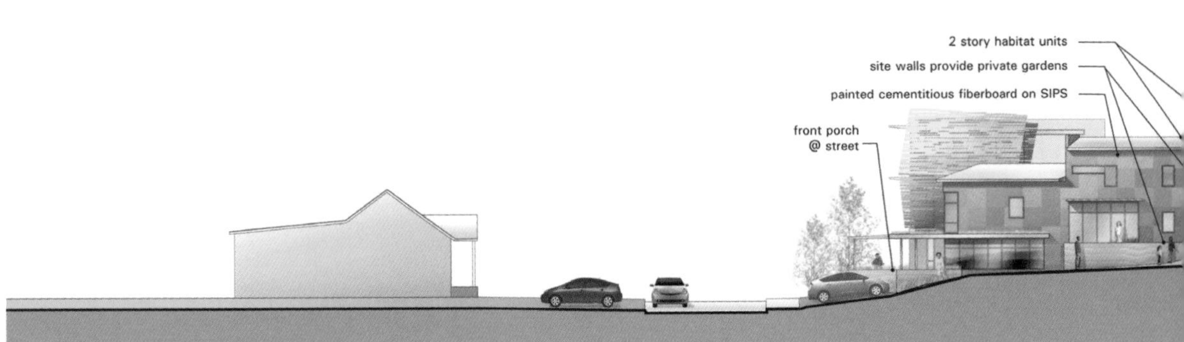

Watershed Architects ***Slip Stitch***

The Urban Habitats competition proposal Slip Stitch by Watershed Architects of Richmond, Virginia, is not explicitly set up to allow for change or to facilitate flux at the neighborhood scale. The site plan is organized around structured parking, which requires a large up-front investment and is financially feasible only if the entire project gets built out at once. At the dwelling scale, however, the surprising similarity among the proposal's unit types may be what best qualifies it to accommodate residents' changing needs.

This one, basic layout is clever and precisely worked out, in terms of dimensions, flexible living spaces, and necessary features, such as storage space. In the 1,200-square-foot affordable condominium units, all three bedrooms are accessible from more than one point, allowing them to be connected or separated as desired and clearly separating bedroom from living room areas. Kitchen, dining and living areas in turn are open to each other but arranged so that partitions could easily be built between them to create several smaller spaces. The slightly larger, 1,400-square-foot market-rate condominiums are laid out in the same way, but all rooms are slightly more generous in size. In the two-story, three-bedroom Habitat units, the layout manages to create equally sized and therefore flexible room dimensions while minimizing corridor space.

OPPOSITE
Floor plans of the "threads" of housing extending from Carlton Avenue to Midland Street. Each thread comprises commercial space as well as market-rate and Habitat dwellings.

BELOW
Site section looking east. The threads of housing straddle the underground parking and mediate between Carlton Avenue (right) and Midland Street.

NEXT PAGE, TOP TO BOTTOM
Diagram of the site plan components. Site plan showing the roofs.

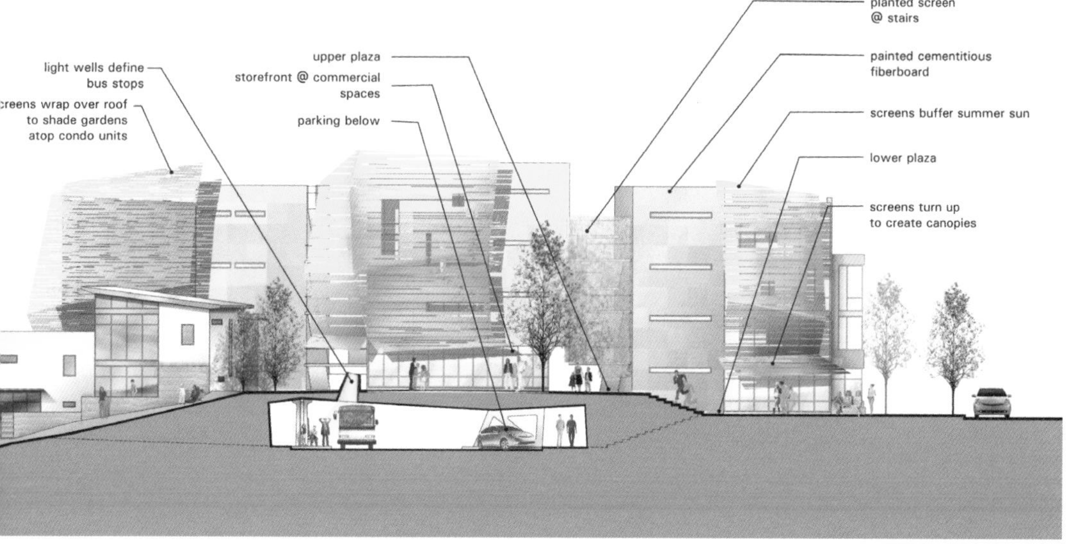

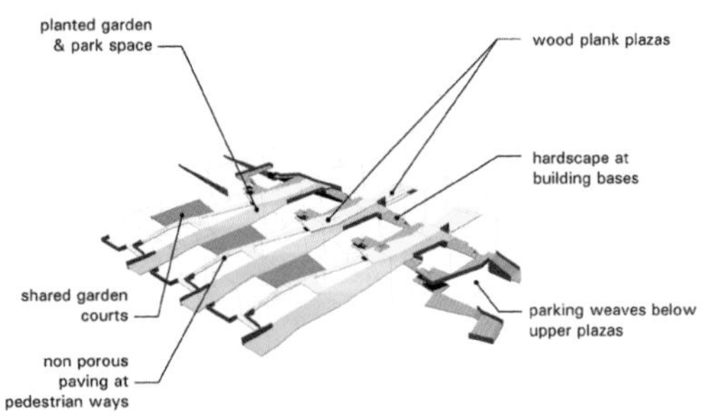

LANDSCAPE

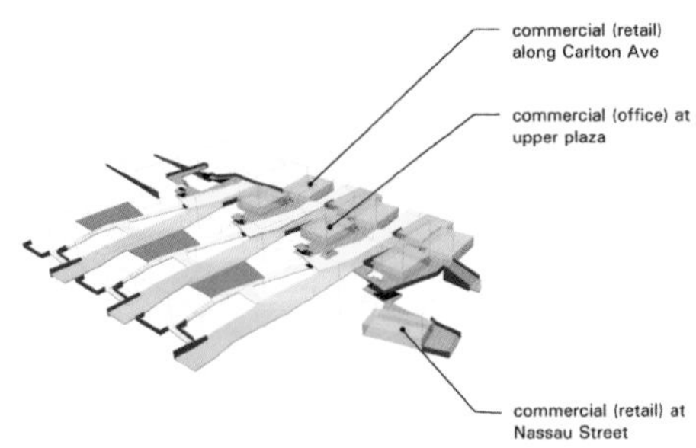

COMMERCIAL

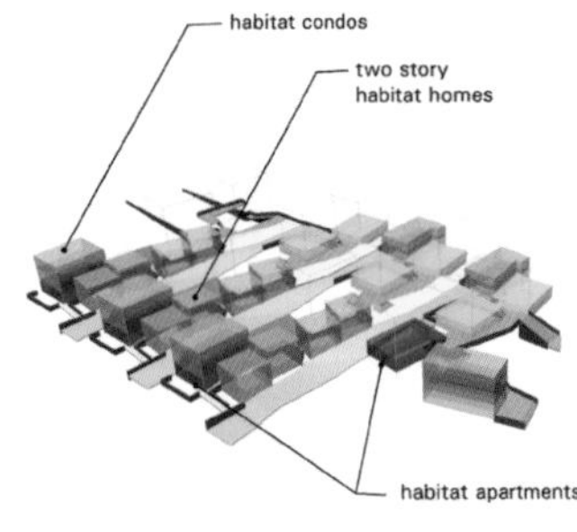

HABITAT

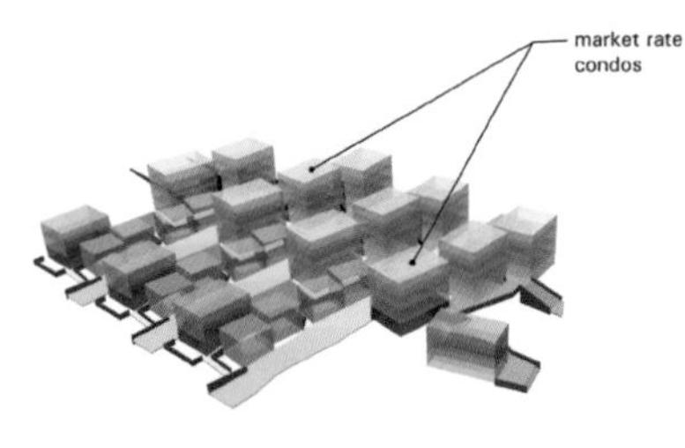

MARKET RATE

Extension
Damon Pearson

Damon Pearson was partner-in-charge for the Urban Habitats competition entry while at Watershed Architects. He has since become an owner of Tektonics Design Group, an architectural design and fabrication firm also located in Richmond, Virginia.

What role does / did the Urban Habitats competition play within your practice?

Typically, we did (and still do) competitions for marketing and research purposes. We chose competitions that were at least somewhat related to the work we did, but different enough to make it interesting for everyone. The Urban Habitats competition fit this mold because we were doing almost entirely custom single-family housing, yet we wanted our firm's ethos of environmental ethics to be applicable to a broader spectrum of people and project types.

Have you been able to further develop the concepts you put forward in your entry?

Yes and no. We chose this project because of the opportunity to develop some economical building assemblies that met our standard for environmental conservation (as was partially dictated by the Earth Craft House guidelines set forth in the agenda). We quickly realized, however, that due to the complexity of the program and the site, we would have to direct our efforts mostly toward that end. We were quite happy with the end result, yet ultimately, the project was very schematic with only the promise of being built well—a frustration for us since quality, affordable construction had been our initial goal.

Oddly, this issue was similar to some of my frustration as a partner at Watershed. Despite our best efforts to make "green" available to a broader spectrum of people, we never did. This was partly (in my opinion) due to media sensationalization of the "green" movement leading to clients who were willing and even anxious to pay a premium for it. In Richmond, it became a bit of a boutique industry for architecture, material suppliers, specialists, etc. I point to things like bamboo plywood, which is quite popular, costs around $250 a sheet, and yet has a very questionable role in sustaining our local environment. Instead of these products coming down in price, they often went up with the ever-increasing demand.

Now, my focus at Tektonics is to do projects where we have a very high level of involvement in the building and fabrication process, specializing in everything from architectural hardware to entire buildings. The shining star has been a shop-fabricated housing system that we have developed as a result of entering the 99K House Competition. This has turned into a very real system that can be built and configured in a multitude of different ways for varying income levels and program requirements, including the 1,300-square-foot version that we designed to cost $99,000.

Have you been able to realize any projects that are related to the Urban Habitats project, be it in scale, approach, client, philosophy?

The shop-fabricated housing system is related in philosophy and, as we have adapted our housing system to the scale of developments, in scale and approach as well. It is not a one-size-fits-all solution to architecture, but it does have promise in quite a few scenarios.

BELOW LEFT
Floor plan of a shop-fabricated house developed by Tektonics.

BELOW, TOP TO BOTTOM
Perspectives showing the house's components and how they are assembled.

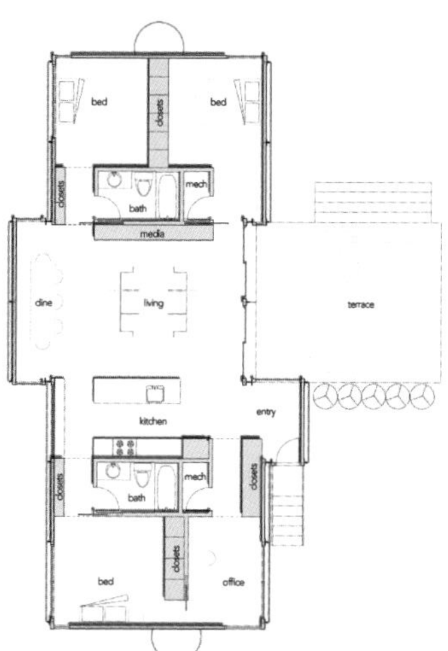

1 – pier foundation

2 – first pod installed

3 – windows installed

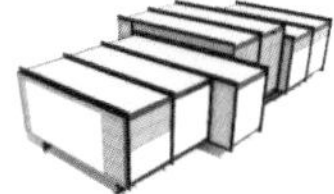
4 – remaining pods, trim, and windows installed

5 – roof installed

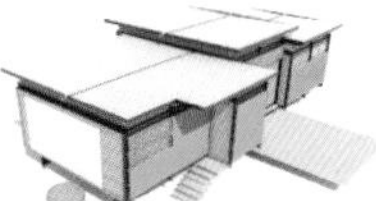
6 – final finishes installed

Chapter 4—

Sustainable
The Two Greens

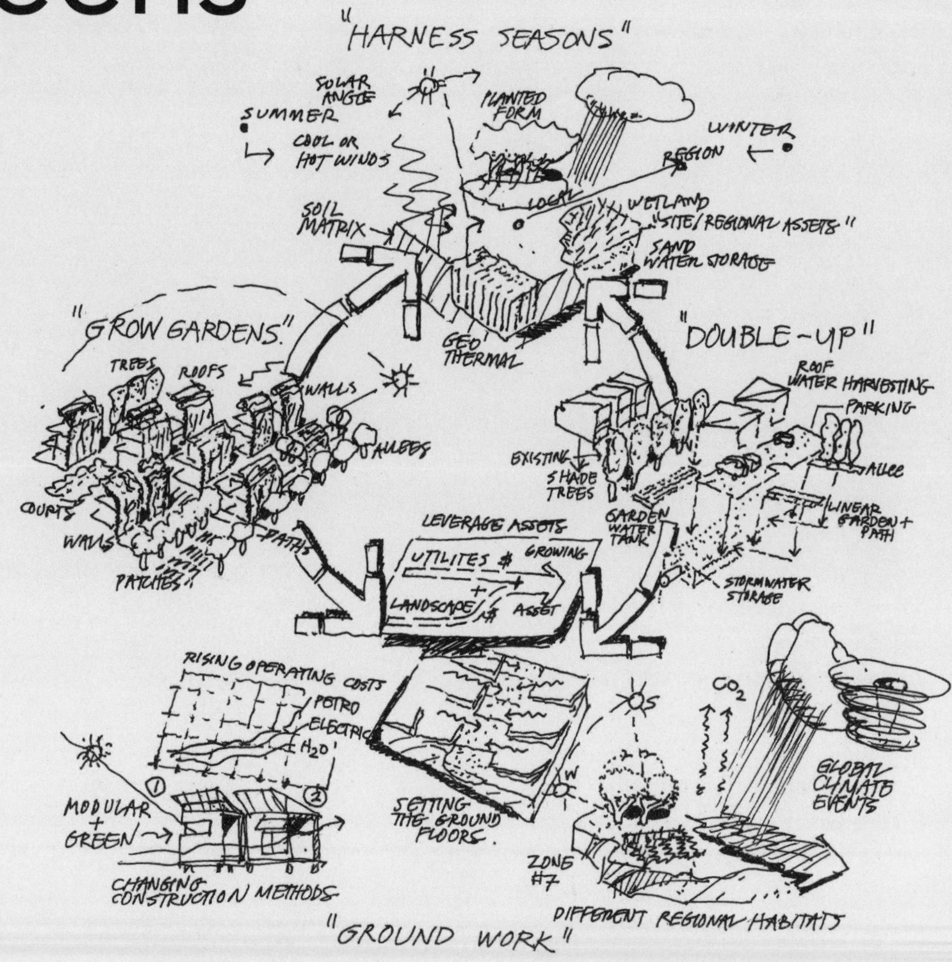

1—Casey Trees Endowment Fund, The Case for Trees, www.caseytrees.org, accessed May 2008.

In some ways you can construct a much more realistic understanding of what it means to be in an environment—to be an inhabitant in a complex, rich world— if you can strip away the image of what you have and instead see if there are other ways to get into the systems that we really experience.

Mark Anderson and Peter Anderson, Anderson Anderson Architects,
Growing Urban Habitats Symposium, September 2005

Urban habitats are grounded in sustainable building. A frequent challenge to the task of building more sustainably, however, is "Who will pay?" Who will pay for the additional costs—presumed or real—that are associated with planting bigger trees, better-performing equipment, higher-quality materials, unconventional layouts? Is cutting quality to save on upfront capital costs the best method for making housing affordable?

Let us think a moment about a simple tree. While it requires some level of attention and maintenance to get established, if properly planted it largely takes care of itself. But why talk about trees?

Neighborhood trees save energy and money. Homes with three well-placed shade trees enjoy summer air conditioning costs up to 40% lower than homes without them.

Street trees create better neighborhoods. Research has demonstrated that residents living in greener communities report lower levels of fear, anxiety, and crime.

Neighborhood trees aid growth and health. Children [...] are better able to concentrate, complete tasks, and follow directions after playing in natural, outdoor "green spaces." Natural environments improve adult health, as well: patients return home more quickly from hospitals where trees are visible.

Neighborhood trees increase property values. Residences with healthy trees sell for 10-20% more than those without them.[1]

These are only four of 19 benefits provided by a healthy urban tree canopy as listed by the Washington, D.C.-based Casey Trees Endowment Fund. The Fund works to inventory, restore, enhance, and protect the tree canopy of the Nation's Capital, which has lost 64% of its urban neighborhood tree canopy in the last 25 years.

In spite of these quantifiable benefits, adding a tree canopy to a typical affordable housing project is considered cosmetic, a superfluous cost in a developer's financial worksheet. Shade trees are not calculated into the heating and air conditioning budget, nor do they show up in allowances made for security. Rather, they are typically budgeted under landscape, which is considered an amenity, making them especially susceptible to elimination when the inevitable cost cutting begins.

Sustainable building requires the same logic as planting urban trees: upfront investment in design time and development costs for long-term pay back. Doing so results in two "green" benefits, one ecological, the other economic. These two greens are inextricably linked. Environmental smartness is invariably financial smartness.

This chapter outlines design opportunities for achieving the two greens.

It should be that simple

Better air, better ventilation, lower energy bills: they seem so banal when you enjoy them. It's only when these advantages are suddenly made apparent by their absence—bad air quality, drafty rooms and outrageous utility bills—that you begin to understand how crucial "sustainable features" are. Sustainability, however, is not about features. It results from integrating goals into the project idea from the start, as a part of the budget, a topic of city agency discussions and, of course, as a driver of the project's overall appearance. The following two examples illustrate how this is achievable at very different scales. The first, a multi-family building in Santa Monica, California, employs alternative energy technology to make striking architecture. The second project, the product of a design-build initiative at the University of Virginia, demonstrates that employing state-of-the-art construction methods is equally relevant in the rehabilitation of a small single-family home.

Colorado Court is one of the first zero-energy buildings to be realized in the United States. View of building from Colorado Avenue.

Colorado Court is perhaps the signature example of sustainably built affordable housing to be realized in the United States in the past decade. Completed in 2001, it was one of the first buildings to achieve complete energy independence, meaning that it feeds as much electricity into the grid as it draws from it. The striking sparkling-blue photovoltaic panels shading the 44-unit, single-room occupancy building by architects **Pugh + Scarpa** for the Community Corporation of Santa Monica, demonstrate how energy-efficient construction can be an integral part of the overall design idea.

At the Urban Habitats Symposium in September 2005, architect Larry Scarpa fleshed out key lessons on the integrated process which led to the Colorado Court. First and foremost, he posited that sustainability can never be separate from the building concept. "I think it's part of a building that's no different than any other part," Scarpa remarked. "It should be that simple."

So how did Pugh + Scarpa conceive of Colorado Court? Scarpa's interest in an energy-efficient building has dual ethical and architectural aspects:

First, I thought it was the right thing to do, and I think all buildings should be that way. Second, I was really taken by the beauty of the panels themselves, and we decided to use them in a prominent fashion to give the building richness. The reality is that if I were to propose a glass skin on an affordable-housing project, I would be thrown out of the state. "It's excessive, you shouldn't be

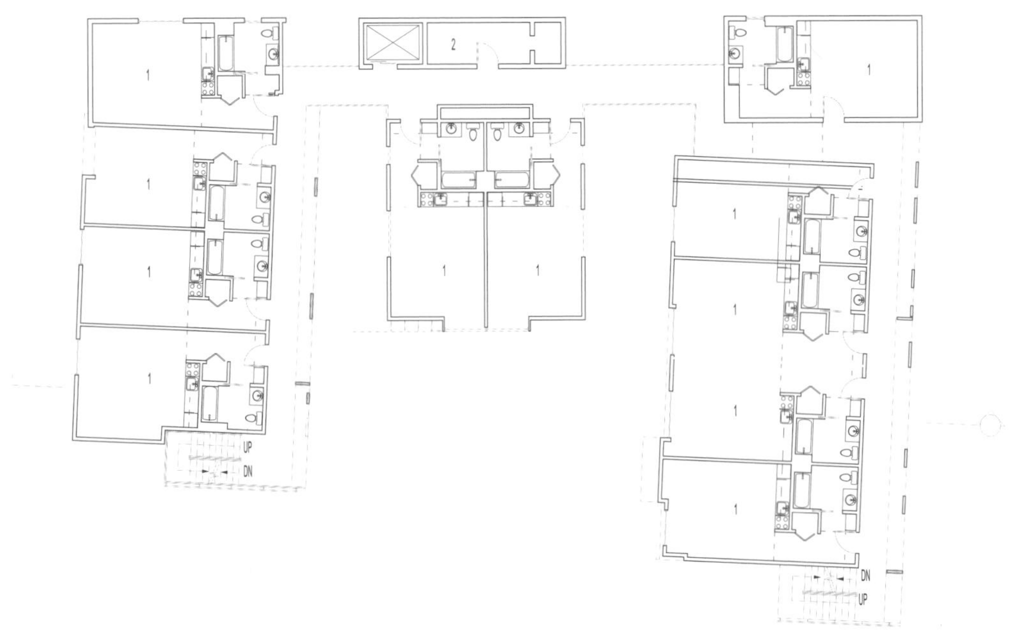
1
2
1
1
1
1
1
1
1
1
1
1
1
1
UP
DN
DN
UP

spending that money, affordable housing shouldn't be that fancy," is the response I would get. Because the glass skin was made of the PV panels, however, that was another story.

The architects' stroke of genius was to take the sustainable technology at their disposal and turn it into something more by applying it in an unconventional way. The four-story stucco apartment building is sustainable because it was laid out according to common sense: units benefit from cross-ventilation, and gallery access faces the interior of the site and creates shaded walkways. But the building's uniqueness was created by applying the blue panels to the facades, not hiding them, as is typically done, on the roof.

Scarpa did not hesitate to acknowledge that design always involves trade-offs. In the balancing act between comfort and efficiency, costs and aesthetics, form and operation, the architect and client must continually make choices. As Scarpa summarized, these can turn expectations on their head:

OPPOSITE, ABOVE
Typical floor plan.

1 Living unit (375 square feet)
2 Trash / recycling unit

OPPOSITE, BELOW
View of the building from 5th Street.

BELOW
Ground floor plan.

1 Lobby / lounge
2 Common courtyard
3 Kitchen
4 Office
5 Entry
6 Storage room
7 Mail room
8 Laundry
9 Mechanical
10 Parking
11 Electrical room
12 Trash / recycling collection

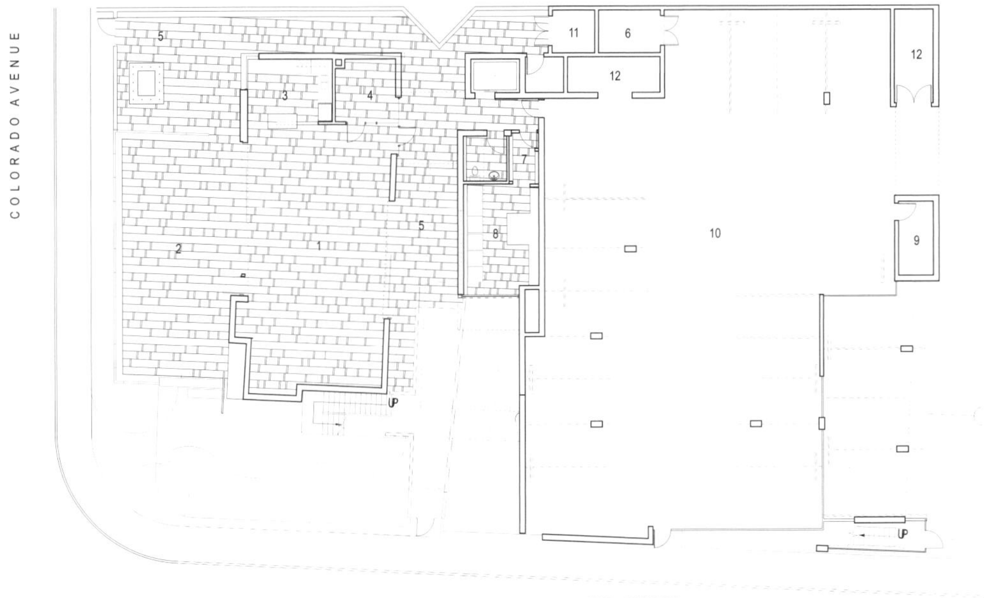

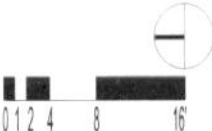

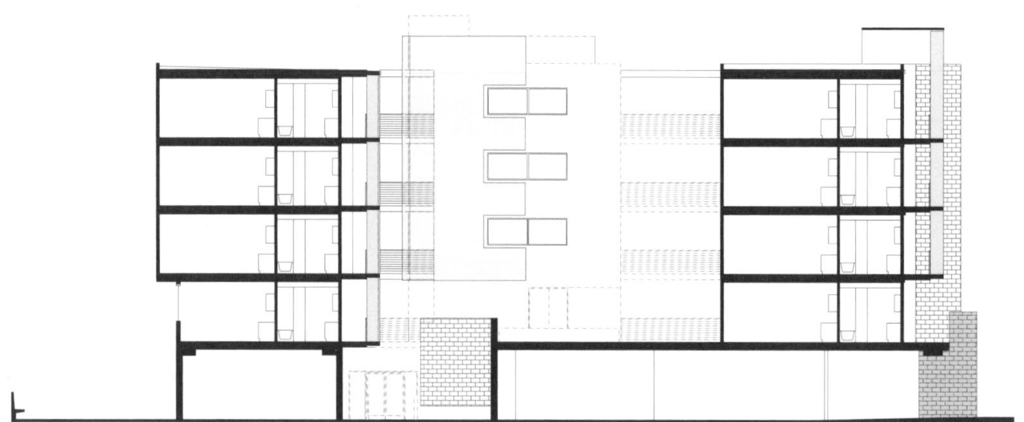

0 1 2 4 8 16

I get asked a lot: "Isn't it less efficient to put solar panels facing west? Isn't it less efficient to put them vertically?" Well, yes. But I argue that making buildings that people like is what really matters, not energy efficiency. I think you have to make good architecture out of the buildings; it can't simply be a building that is environmentally good. So we will make sacrifices in efficiency if it makes places better for people.

In the end, monitoring the building during its first two years of operation showed that the vertically installed panels had a major benefit: they were less likely to accumulate dirt than panels installed at an angle on a roof, thereby reducing necessary maintenance. Finally, Scarpa suggested that when charting new territory, numbers, because they are objective and hard to argue with, will turn out to be your best friend in pushing your agenda.

When our engineers call me up threatening to quit, I know they're doing their job, because what they are doing is working on the design criteria. We got our engineers to reduce their electrical load, for instance, so that it didn't have safety factor upon safety factor. I think that if there's something you can do, it is to actually look at the data of your engineers and, without thinking too hard, you'll be able to make it about 50% more efficient simply by working the numbers.

The lessons of Colorado Court are clear: Learn to think boldly, integrate all aspects of the project, leverage the numbers and the two greens come within reach. These are lessons that can also be learned from ecoMOD, an applied research project at the University of Virginia's School of Architecture, although at a very different scale. While Colorado Court was realized using conventional on-site construction techniques, ecoMOD aims at improving the quality of manufactured homes.

OPPOSITE, ABOVE
Building section.

OPPOSITE, BELOW
Close-up view of photovoltaic panels with access galleries beyond.

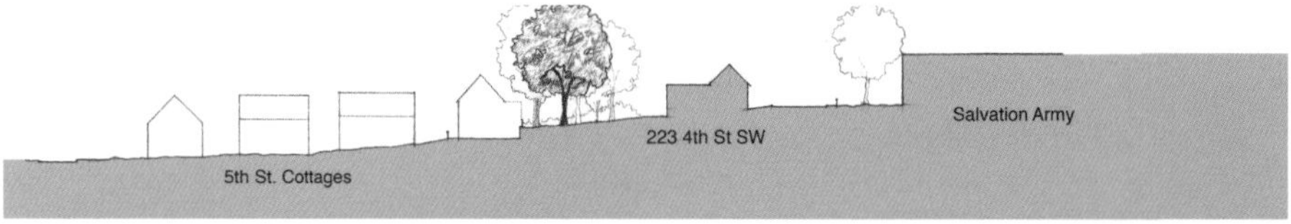

Salvation Army
223 4th St SW
5th St. Cottages

5th St.
4th St. SW
Dice St.
North
223 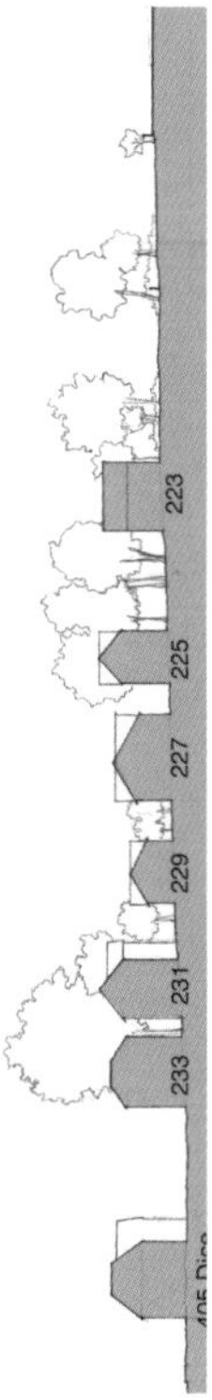
225
227
229
231
233

Since 2004, John Quale, Assistant Professor of Architecture at the **University of Virginia**, and P. Paxton Marshall, Professor of Engineering there, have been directing **ecoMOD**. Its primary goal is to create processes for building modular homes that cost less to operate and maintain than conventional homes, respect their environment, and appreciate over time. These goals may sound self-evident, but they stand in stark contrast to the qualities of today's most affordable prefabricated home—the trailer. As Quale emphasizes, present-day construction of trailers and their variants tends to prioritize short-term cost above all else, but the dramatic, long-term costs of an "Always Low Prices" ethos are becoming as clear in manufacturing circles as they are in low-income housing. Although easy to install and seemingly adaptable to any environment, these aggressively "site-less" structures waste resources, suffer from inherent indoor air quality problems and do not take into account local sun, wind or water patterns.

Completed in the spring of 2008, the SEAM House, ecoMOD's third realized project, explores the full spectrum of the two greens way of thinking at the scale of an individual structure. The project is located in Fifeville, a working-family African-American neighborhood of Charlottesville. It unites a small, mid-19th century house thought to be a former slave quarters with a modular addition as well as a new modular accessory unit behind it for elderly residents, laid out according to Universal Design criteria.

As the house was being restored, debris was not thrown away, but instead studied for potential reclamation, refurbishment and reuse. New design features include an evacuated tube solar hot water system coupled with on-demand water heating, a modular green roof system and highly insulating ThermaSteel wall panel construction. The concept of modularity extends into the landscape with the "seed packet," a tool for managing site conditions that describes how to cool the house, store water and reduce storm water run-off. All of these strategies were employed in the modular addition of the SEAM House.

Most importantly, and in contrast to many modular systems, the seed packet illustrates how ecoMOD elements can be customized for different locations. Window openings and fenestration are aligned with existing trees and new gardens, so that their shade cools the hot summer air. The operable windows on the south side are placed low on the exterior wall, while on the north side, operable windows are located higher up to help draw the heat out.

OPPOSITE, ABOVE
The SEAM House involved the renovation and expansion of an existing home thought to be a former slave quarters. The photograph shows its condition prior to the ecoMOD intervention.

OPPOSITE, BELOW
Context plan and sections showing the heterogeneous setting of the small home.

BELOW
EcoMod's working criteria are summarized in a pentagonal diagram. It is used for aiding key decisions during project development as well as guiding the post-occupancy evaluation. The example compares the benefits of three exterior wall systems.

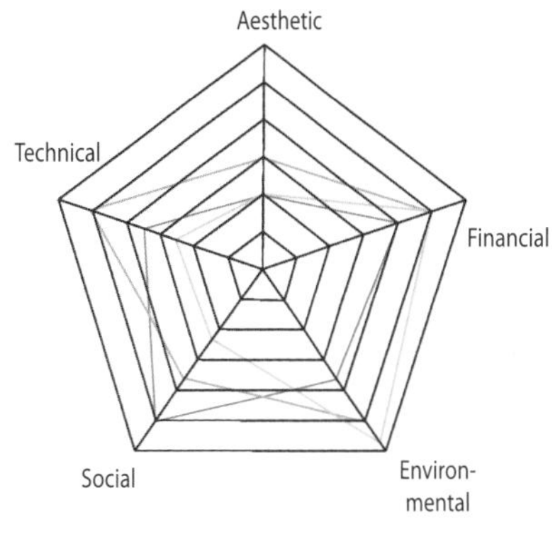

Design for Deconstruction by Layer

Green Roof System:
Planting trays can be dug out and reused in other green roof systems.

Plywood Sheathing:
Screwed into Thermasteel panels. Easily disassembled.

Thermasteel Roof:
Steel and foam panels assembled with screws. Simple connections leads to easy disassembly.

Wood Flooring:
Reclaimed from existing house on site to be renovated. Closes the loop on construction waste.

Floor Framing:
Lumber assembled with screws and can be easily disassembled and reused.

Site Framing:
Lumber assembled with screws and can be easily disassembled and reused.

Concrete Block Piers:
Raises the building off the sloped site. Touches lightly to the ground and therefore lessens environmental impact.

Module Layers

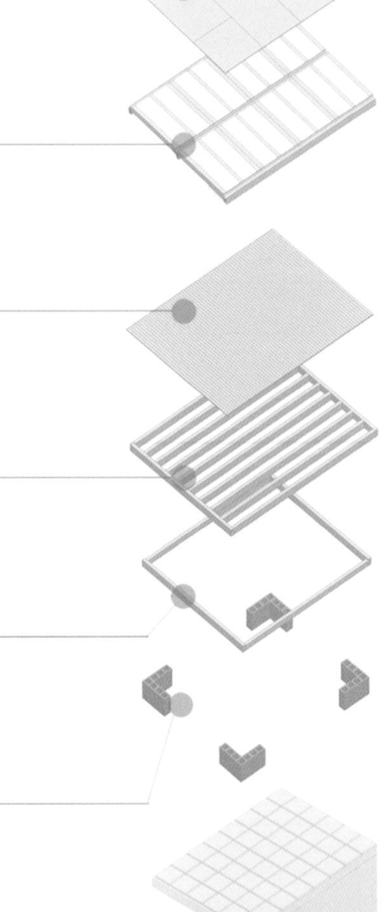

Thermasteel Roof Design for Deconstruction:

Disassembly of panel into foam and steel.

Disassembly of panels from beams.

Thermasteel Wall Design for Deconstruction:

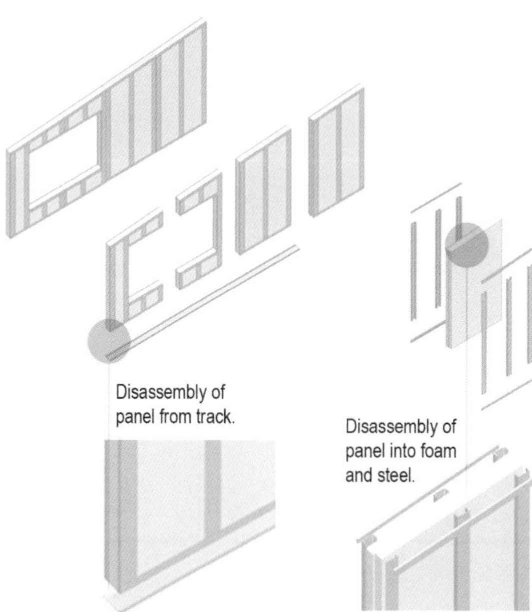

LEFT
A key concept of the ecoMOD process is Design for Deconstruction. A project is assembled so that can easily be disassembled and its parts reused elsewhere. The exploded axonometric shows the elements and materials that were used to build the SEAM House's accessory unit.

BELOW
Photographs of students and professionals collaborating in the off-site construction of the modular elements.

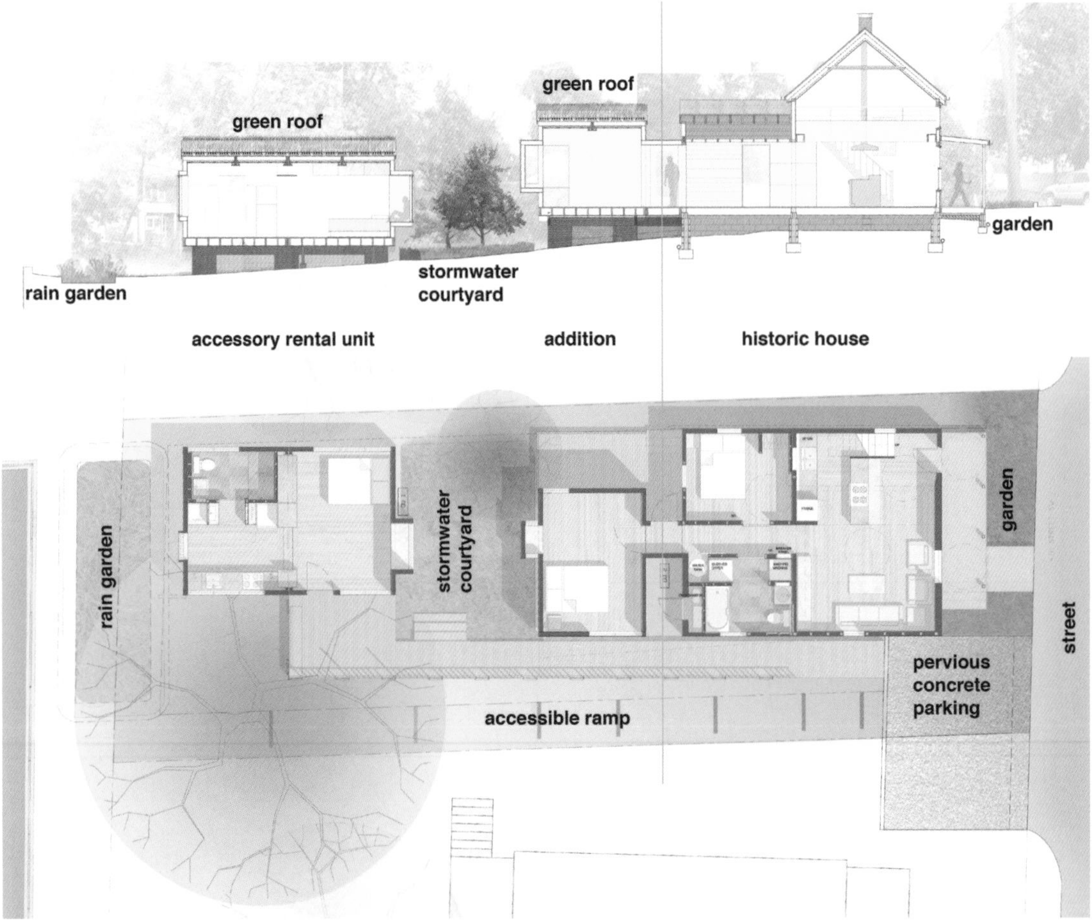

green roof
green roof
rain garden
stormwater courtyard
garden
accessory rental unit
addition
historic house
rain garden
stormwater courtyard
garden
street
pervious concrete parking
accessible ramp

The two greens approach does not end with the construction, however. The SEAM House was sold to an elderly couple by project partner Piedmont Housing Alliance, a non-profit housing provider, and occupied in the summer of 2008. Data from the ecoMOD building performance monitoring system will be evaluated for everything from energy and water usage to the effectiveness of passive heating and cooling systems. The evaluation phase will also assess the operating cost of the units, the ability of the green roof to reduce storm water runoff and the homeowner's satisfaction with the layout of the small housing units. The residents will be active partners helping gauge how money is spent managing the home on a day-to-day basis. The results will be published on the ecoMOD website and used in future projects by the project partners.

OPPOSITE
Plan and section of the SEAM House.

OPPOSITE BELOW AND BELOW
Photographs of the on site installation of the modular elements, as well as exterior and interior views of the completed project.

Count Again
:Ground Work

Landscape, or why it's your project's financial foundation

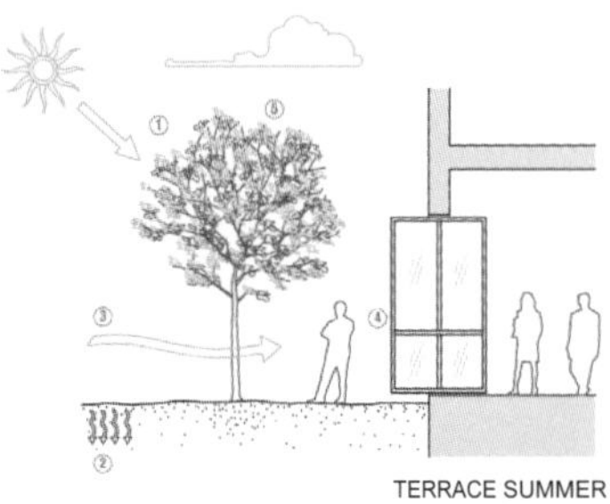
TERRACE SUMMER

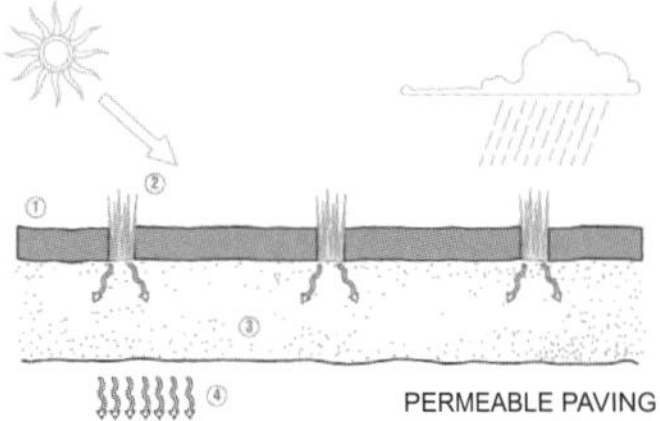
PERMEABLE PAVING

Accommodating new infill development and estimating site development costs for non-standard sites is more complicated than building on a clean slate. While this takes time, it is also a frequently overlooked opportunity to set up a productive long-term investment. How to turn site work into your project's financial foundation?

:Budget landscape.

As indicated in the introduction to this chapter, relocate cost. Slip landscape elements into the building budget and you'll find it much easier to get them paid for. Have the trees included in the safety budget. The bushes can fit into HVAC. The water feature blends nicely into sanitation. In this way, your landscape will become an indispensable part of your overall project.

:Capitalize landscape.

Think of your landscape as part of your hard and soft working capital. Don't dismiss what you have. New landscapes grow best from the existing. What ground forms are found on site, and how can you build on them? Can you uncover buried waterways and reconnect them to an open stream? How might water be retained to irrigate new landscapes?

Don't dump good soil from the site. Utilize cut and fill from site development as building material for new landscapes.

Don't fret over soil remediation. Soil analysis will determine whether your site needs remediation (removing residual toxins) or amendment (adding nutrients). Design the soil treatment process as a first-phase landscape, providing a positive way to land bank.

Don't fret over the market. It may be slow, your project may have to be phased, but the open portions of the site can be programmed with interim uses. You might use the extra land as a tree nursery, and as the market becomes active again, the matured and acclimated trees can then be relocated on the site. A word of caution, however: it may be hard to let go of popular first phase activities.

:Turn grading into place-making.

The grading plan for the project is more than a civil engineering exercise in which land is cut into standard flat parcels upon which buildings are placed. Grading sets the dimensions of buildings and open spaces. See grading as a place-making process to convert your site into a mosaic of social and environmental microclimates that accommodate the flow of people, water, sun and air, and align the new project within the existing urban landscape.

DIRT Studio
Greenola

In 2006, Global Green USA held an open design competition called Greenola for the sustainable redevelopment of a 1.2-acre site, adjacent to the Mississippi levees in New Orleans' lower Ninth Ward. In her landscape plan for Greenola, Julie Bargmann's DIRT Studio (Design Investigations Reclaiming Terrain) of Charlottesville, Virginia, worked closely with the architects, workshop / apd of New York, to establish landscape as an integral part of the overall project. *(See also the second placed design proposal by Eskew + Dumez + Ripple, p. 156.)*

DIRT Studio's grading and landscape architecture transforms the site from its abandoned industrial use into a new base for five single-family homes, an 18-unit apartment building, and a community center. To gradually reinsert the site into the surrounding Holy Cross neighborhood, the project was organized into three layers, or phases. Each layer links the necessary but seldom celebrated preliminary site work to the inauguration of a memorable element of the project. A landscape can be the first building on site.

The project's first layer, "Ground Work," connects the remediation of the toxic soil from past river industries to the construction of a community center and educational laboratory. It includes a remediation garden, to be tended by residents, with plants that absorb the chemicals in the soil. In several years, this soil will be clean and can again be gardened for vegetables and flowers. This community garden is planned as a demonstration site for residents and neighbors alike.

The second layer, "Site Re-Building," involves shifting soil to create masses that will locate the project's different activities and housing types. In this way, the new landscape sets the foundations for the actual buildings. These planted forms establish microclimates within the site and the edge environments on its four very different sides. The west side of the parcel will be planted with large shade trees to filter the strong western sun from the front porches of the new homes lining the street. On the north side, flowering trees celebrate the more public side of the project, creating a visual amenity for the community center and market place.

The third layer, "Neighborhood Re-Generation," extends the plan into the surrounding community to encourage planting street trees and enhancing backyards with plants native to the adjacent Mississippi River. In a humid

OPPOSITE
The diagrams show examples of landscape elements that are easy to budget. A well laid-out terrace helps with cooling, the use of permeable paving manages storm water.

BELOW
Aerial photograph of the Holy Cross site, adjacent to the Mississippi levees.

BOTTOM
Model view of Greenola. The architecture, designed by workshop / apd of New York, includes five single-family homes, an apartment building, and a community center.

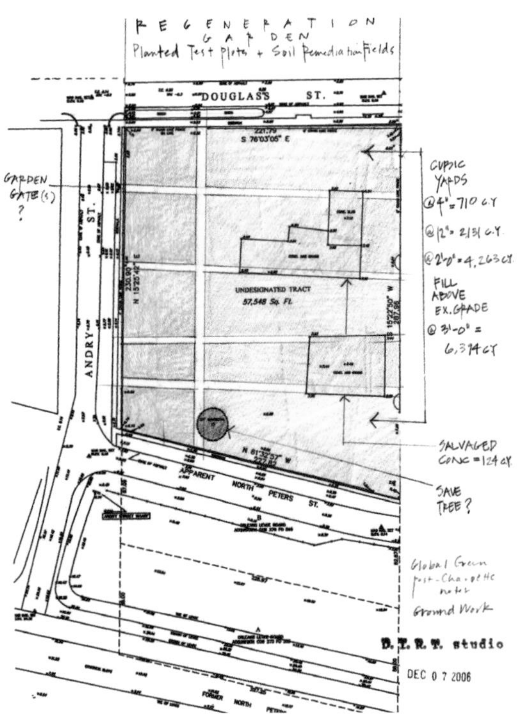
REGENERATION GARDEN
Planted Test plots + Soil Remediation Fields
DOUGLASS ST.
GARDEN GATE(s) ?
CUBIC YARDS
@4" = 710 C.Y.
@12" = 2131 C.Y.
@2'-0" = 4,263 C.Y.
FILL ABOVE EX. GRADE
@ 3'-0" = 6,394 C.Y.
UNDESIGNATED TRACT
57,548 Sq. Ft.
ANDRY ST.
SALVAGED CONC = 124 C.Y.
SAVE TREE?
APPARENT NORTH PETERS ST.
Global Green post-Charette notes
Ground Work
D.I.R.T. studio
DEC 0 7 2006

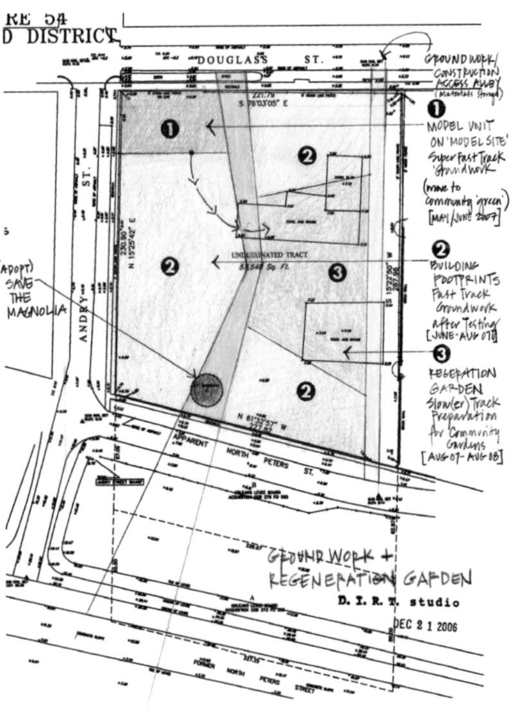
D DISTRICT
DOUGLASS ST.
GROUNDWORK/ CONSTRUCTION ACCESS ALLEY (Materials Storage)
1 MODEL UNIT ON 'MODEL SITE' Super Fast Track 'Groundwork' (move to community 'green') [MAY/JUNE 2007]
2 BUILDING FOOTPRINTS Fast Track Groundwork after Testing [JUNE-AUG 07]
3 REGENERATION GARDEN Slow(er) Track Preparation for Community Gardens [AUG 07-AUG 08]
(ADOPT) SAVE THE MAGNOLIA
UNDESIGNATED TRACT
ANDRY ST.
APPARENT NORTH PETERS ST.
GROUNDWORK + REGENERATION GARDEN
D.I.R.T. studio
DEC 2 1 2006

environment like New Orleans, large canopy trees with a rich ground cover of grasses are critical to managing the rainfall that comes in cloud bursts or hurricanes.

Once the project is complete, the three layers, included in the budget because they are indispensable to the overall development, will create the varied landscape so emblematic of New Orleans.

OPPOSITE, LEFT AND RIGHT
DIRT's site plan sketches illustrate the three layers of the landscape work at Greenola. The first phase, Ground Work, organizes the remediation of the soil. By setting up a Regeneration Garden, this process becomes a tangible experience for neighbors and future residents.

BELOW, LEFT
In a second phase, Site Re-Building, the remediated soil is moved to create the permanent landscape forms. These set the foundation for the future buildings.

BELOW, RIGHT
In a final phase, Neighborhood Re-Generation, trees and other landscape elements that have been located on site are extended into the neighborhood.

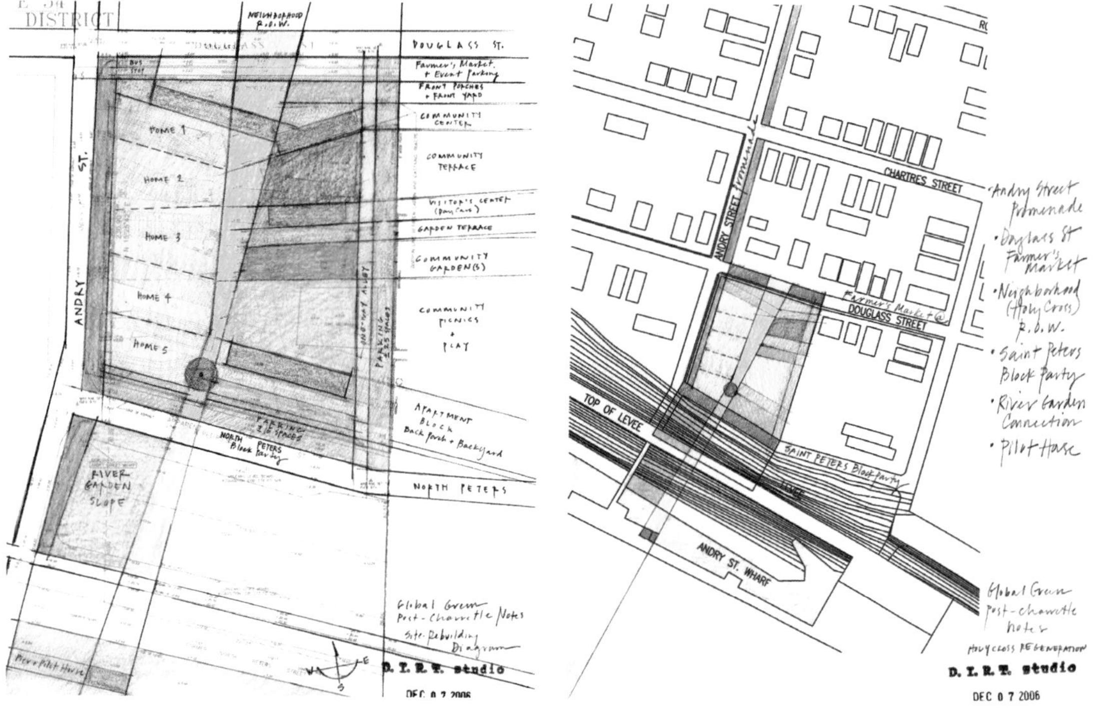

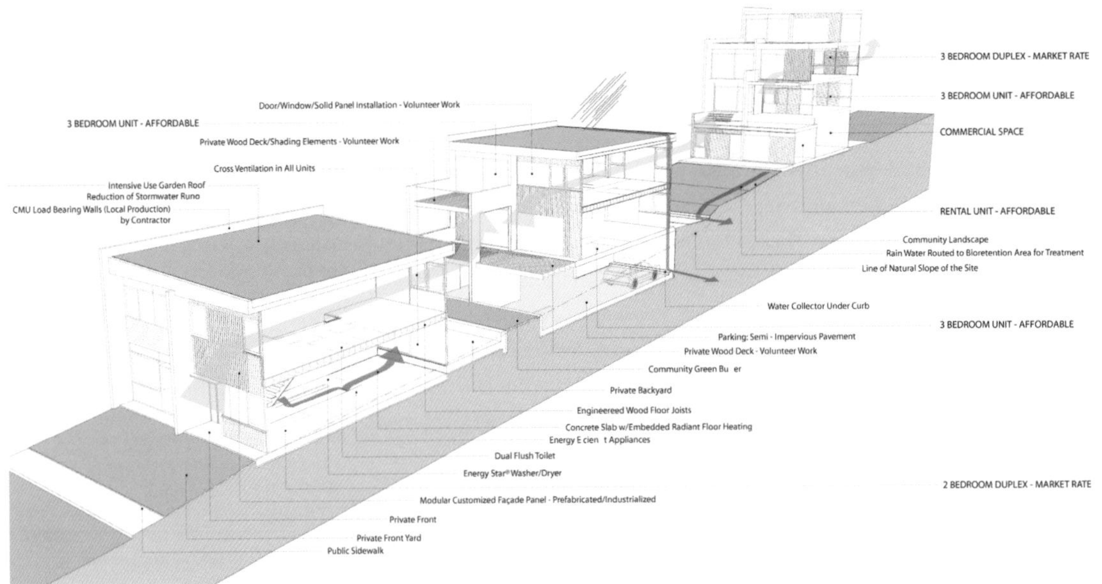

Section through a typical segment. Each segment uses the site's grade to accomodate residential and commercial uses and maximize passive cooling and heating. The underground parking connects the segments.

CARLTON AVENUE

MIDLAND STREET

RIVES STREET

NASSAU STREET

Site plan showing ground floor uses.

CAN Architecture
Sequential Landscapes

The Urban Habitats competition proposal by CAN Architecture of Brooklyn, New York, takes another approach to ground work and finding a budget for landscape. The buildings themselves are the site's grading elements, blurring the distinction between landscape and architecture. The site is divided into 33-foot-wide "segments," each of which incorporates multiple housing types as well as commercial space staggered from the highest to the lowest part of the site. In so doing, the buildings can never be considered without the site. Underground parking connects the various structures. Although the competition brief explicitly excluded structured parking, here it creates usable open space at ground level, and ties the landscape site work to the structural foundations of the architecture.

Views of the interior landscape.

Honorable Mention

Team Members
Mauro Bianucci, Anna Dietzsch, Carlos Salinas Weber, Robert A. Golda, Adam John Grosshans

Statement
The site presents a challenging "in-between" condition within the city structure, a transition between a typical suburban setting and the more natural and unique landscape of Monticello. Transverse parallel axes organize the project's composition. Within this system a series of adaptable segments redefine the site. Each segment synthesizes the main intentions of the project, as well as the programmatic requirements, acting as the catalyst for the central idea. Repetition, diversity and transition are the three main directions of our approach.

The strategy ranges from the collective to the individual to achieve a vibrant counterpoint between public and private; natural and built. The contiguous sequence of segments and the variety developed in section are spontaneous in its relationship to the rich natural diversity of the site.

The construction system is consistent with the concept. The main structural system is the same for all of the units, providing uniformity to the whole. The possibility of selecting different facade panels, as well as finishes, provides variation to the composition and the participation of volunteers in the construction process. The accessible roof gardens complete the main idea.
Our ultimate goal is to create a sustainable place for community life, where the whole always reaches beyond the sum of the parts.

Jury Comments
Many times we think of housing in terms of number of units laid more or less indiscriminately on the site. This project proposes, by contrast, an interweaving of units, landscape, parking, topography and recreation. This proposal incorporates ideas about the ground plane currently under investigation in architecture, which might actually be affordable in the real world.

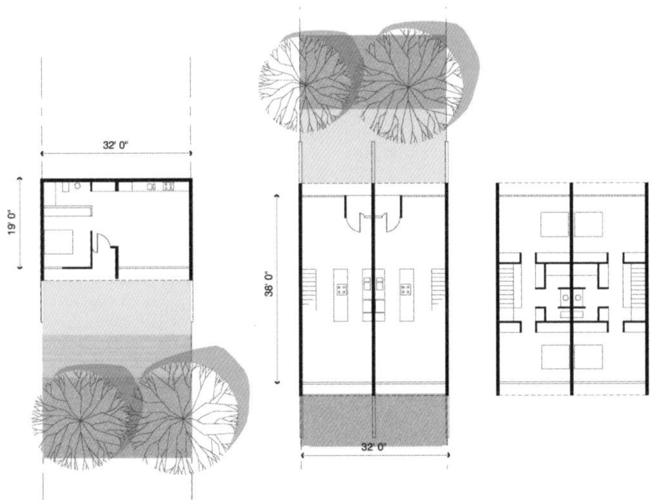

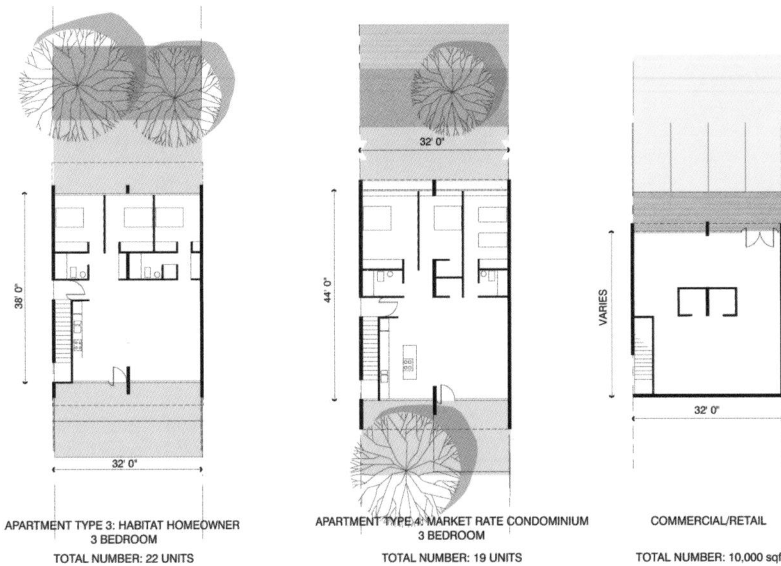

Floor plans of the different unit types.

Extension
CAN Architecture

CAN architecture was formed by architects Mauro Bianucci, Anna Dietzsch and Carlos Salinas Weber with the Urban Habitats Competition as a testing field for their shared ideas. Since this collaboration, they have continued to work separately on related themes.

What role does / did the Urban Habitats competition play within your practice?

We believe in architecture as a common ground for social life and we want to insist in its strength as a collective action. If we belong to the polis, we are political. We believe in architecture as a response to specific and real social conditions and we advocate that the role of the architect be an active one. As architects, our goal is to create unique intersections of materials and ideas, resulting in places that shape our everyday lives and feed our memories.

This 'manifesto' was included in our submittal and, even though we are not currently working together as an office, it remains relevant today.

Have you been able to further develop the concepts put forward in your entry?

Since the competition, Anna Dietzsch and Charlie Salinas have been involved in several projects that continue to explore said themes. For instance, Anna Dietzsch (with Marshall Brown and Alex Felson) worked on the UNITY Plan for Atlantic Yards (2004-08). Created in opposition to a 22-acre development in the heart of Brooklyn, the UNITY Plan is the response of a community effort, endorsed by elected officials and 25 community organizations. Questioning the principles of abusive eminent domain and the development of extensive public land by one developer, the proposal opens new streets through the site to subdivide it into eight different parcels, reuniting different neighborhoods and enabling multiple developments. The program is diversified with public, cultural and civic components. Low-income housing is increased in the residential and commercial mix.

Have you been able to realize any projects that are related to the Urban Habitats project, be it in scale, approach, client, philosophy?

Mauro Bianucci has taken principles in the manifesto and brought them to the sphere of fashion and product design, demonstrating that they are not proprietary to the field of architecture. Carga, his handmade collection of bags, is being batch-produced in a socially responsible, family-run workshop in his native Argentina. Using environmentally friendly materials (natural wool felt, vegetable-dyed leather), the collection has played a role in helping local craftsmen protect and keep alive their artisanal production methods while earning a living wage.

Designing for social responsibility is not limited to buildings. Mauro Bianucci founded Carga Bags to design and produce bags. The bags are hand-made in Argentina. Craftsmen are paid a living wage.

Mix It Up
:Double-Up

Systems, or how one can be two can be three

Mechanical systems frequently consume the largest share of a project budget. At the same time, they are painstakingly hidden and hardly contribute to the project's pleasures. Challenge this course of action by making your systems work in more than one way. It's a matter of saving space, saving money and making your project look good. How?

:Lay them bare.

Infrastructure may not seem attractive to you. Try to think of your building systems another way. Consider them, for a moment, as your key features. Your photovoltaic panels may become your main aesthetic device. Or, take what is necessary and celebrate it as the key organizational principle: add a water filtration system and a rainwater catchment basin to your roof drain and suddenly you have a garden. Plumbing, venting, heating, cooling: link your equipment and endow it with more than one meaning.

:Start multi-tasking.

Doubling-Up also refers to using space in more than one way. Why should a parking lot be a sea of asphalt only serving cars? Why can't the playground take part? Try to describe what happens in a space 24/7, and how activities can overlap or take place one after another. Think about what doesn't yet happen there, but could. Often, multi-tasking has less to do with building, than with how you organize what's going on.

:Continue asking.

Rethink every piece of the pie one more time. What does your roof do for you? Could it do more than keeping the rain out? Could it become a planted area by altering its slope? What does that window do for you? Would it ventilate more effectively if you introduced another operable lite? Would it light your desk if it were a little wider, a little higher?

Office dA
Intergenerational Learning Center

OPPOSITE
View of the two interlocking ramps.

LEFT
View from the community center across the planted roofs of the single-story homes.

BELOW
Model view.

Doubling-up can mean combining uses so that they mutually sustain each other. An excellent example is the Intergenerational Learning Center proposed by the City of Chicago to combine Head Start classrooms, housing for seniors with custody of grandchildren, and a Satellite Senior Center offering legal, medical and social services. Various City departments had realized that their constituents were falling through holes in existing social support systems. Specifically, over 41,000 citizens 60 years or older were responsible for grandchildren under the age of 18. Over 51% of these households earned $25,000 per year or less. Meanwhile, guardians of minors were automatically disqualified from senior public housing. How to serve these citizens?

In 2003, the City organized a design competition to tackle this task. As competition director Denise Arnold emphasizes, “It was only through the joint effort of different city departments that it was possible to secure a site, political support, and the funding for a competition and construction.” In their winning proposal, Office dA of Boston demonstrates how doubling-up systems can drive a design functionally and aesthetically. In the community center, the architects literally intertwine the programs of the senior and child care centers: interlocking ramps allow young and old to see each other as they move within their own parts of the buildings. Meanwhile, key facilities like the auditorium are shared by both, guaranteeing maximum use of these spaces.

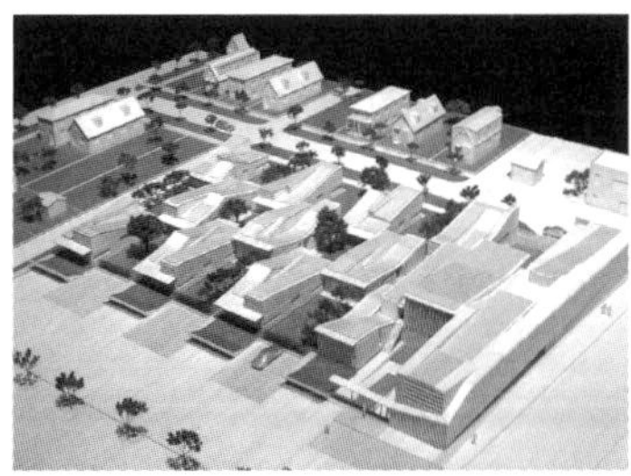

The nine one-story residences adjoining the Learning Center are staggered around gardens, each dedicated to a unit and yet also bordered by walkways and neighboring units. Internally, the three- and four-bedroom units are laid out to separate parent from children’s sleeping rooms, and to allow for

D
E
50
51
3B UNIT
3B UNIT
3B UNIT
4B UNIT
4B UNIT
4B UNIT
3B UNIT
4B UNIT
4B UNIT
18 17 16
12 11 10
6 5
21 20 19
15 14 13
9 8 7
D
22 23 24 25 26 27 28 29 30 31 32 33 34 35 36 37 38 39

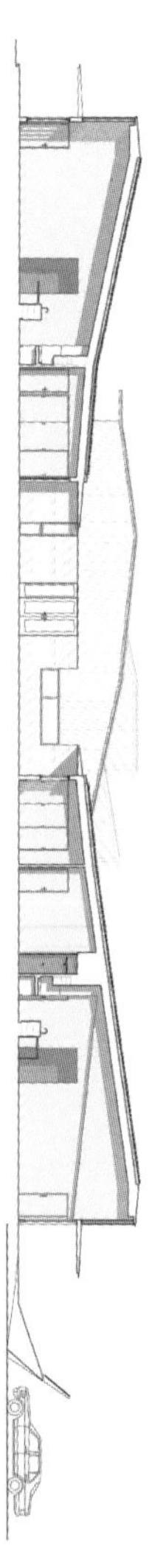

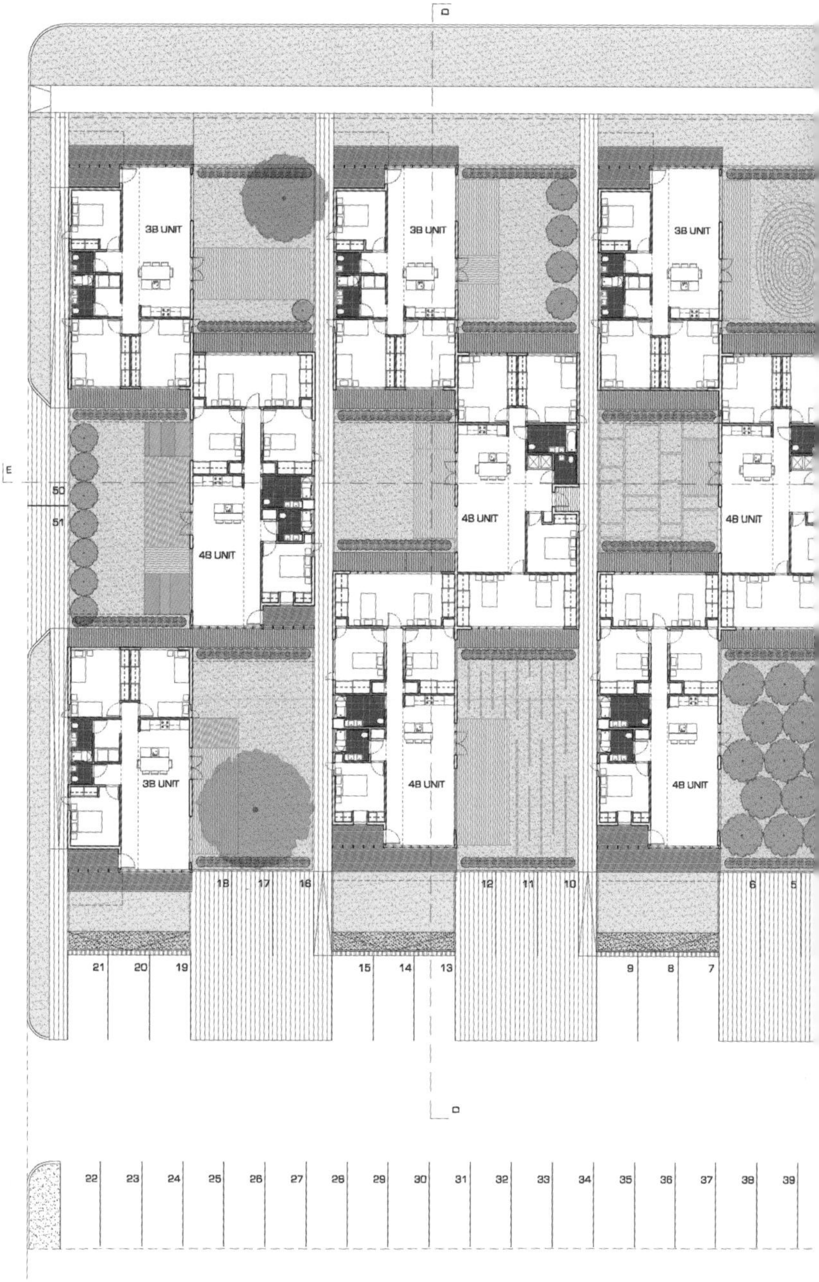

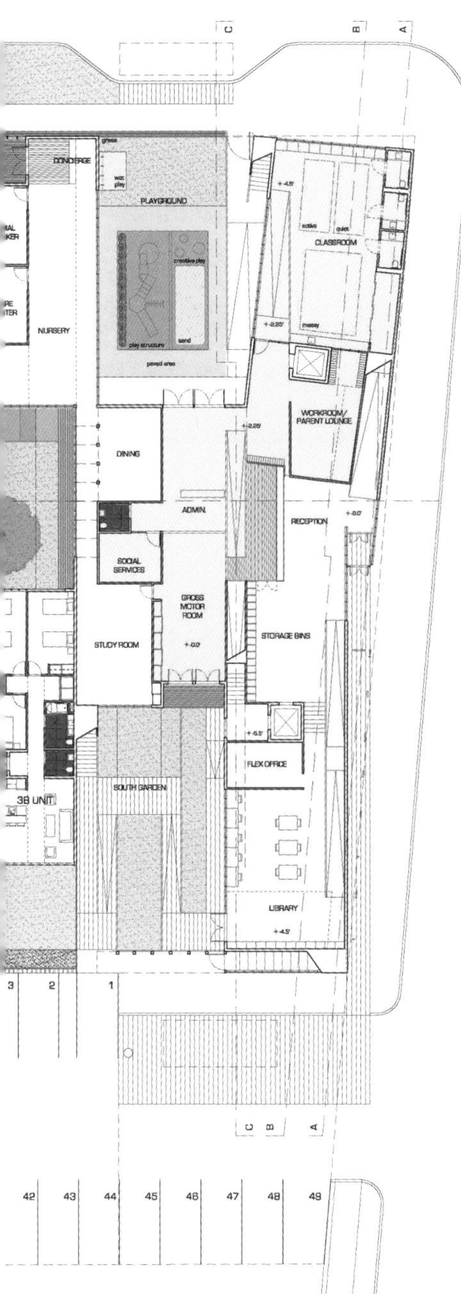

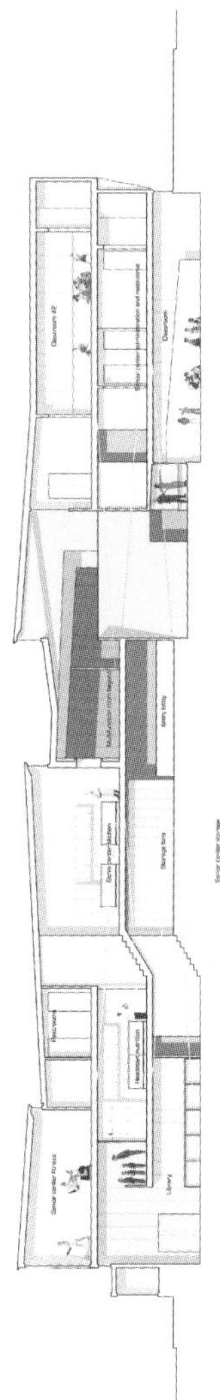

THIS SPREAD

First floor plan with section through houses at left and section through community center at right. The ramps are shown with dashed lines.

Split mechanical systems

Phase II subdivision of units with shared laundry

Side entry 4 bdrm. unit phase I and phase II

an easy later subdivision into two smaller units. To that end, the houses are equipped from the get-go with two separate HVAC systems. The houses' offset angled roofs provide several environmental benefits: the planting above insulates and minimizes storm water run-off, while the varying room heights allow for cross ventilation within. More than $11 million had been raised for construction when the future beneficiaries' needs were put into question and critical Head Start funding was withdrawn. The site has since been sold.

OPPOSITE
Diagrams showing the location of the two HVAC units that enable the subdivision of a large unit into two smaller ones. Floor plans of a three-bedroom and a four-bedroom unit.

BELOW
Second and third floor plan of community center.

Site plan.

From left to right: Condominium townhouses, upper level plan; lower level plan; plan of condominium flats; view of courtyard.

CK-Architecture
Sunrise

The Urban Habitats competition scheme by CK-Architecture of Los Angeles is based on a site laid out according to principles of solar and wind orientation, and buildings that integrate state-of-the-art technology. Both site and building design double-up systems. For instance, the landscaping of the parking areas doubles as an acoustical buffer, and in the buildings, circulation areas such as the gallery access at the upper levels of the stacked townhouses, are arranged to create thermal barriers. At the systems level, solar energy is captured through photovoltaic panels, but rather than placing these on the roofs, the panels are mounted at an angle in front of the building facades so that they double as sunshades for the apartments behind.

Honorable Mention

Team Members
Christoph Kapeller, AIA, Jayna Cooper

Statement
Site Development: Porous site design allows pedestrian and bicycle networks to intertwine Sunrise Park with surroundings, serving as linkage system and model for future developments. Commercial development along Carlton creates buffer towards industrial area. Building heights follow natural topography, sun-angles, views of surrounding hills and prevailing wind direction. Mixture of parking courts and private carports provide child-friendly environment with maximum land-use efficiency while allowing controlled parking adjacent to homes.

Floor Plans: Healthy mix of low-income and market-rate units as townhouses and fully accessible flats stimulates diverse cultural environment. Habitat homeowner units as individual buildings are easily constructed. Natural topography employs rental units as retaining elements and foundation for habitat units. Café, retail and day care generate diverse commercial activity.

Bioclimatic Features: Heat reduction / rainwater retention through permeable parking surfaces. Rainwater recovery system provides "gray water" for irrigation and non-drinking purposes. Active / passive solar energy. Photovoltaic panels as sunshades. Thermal/ acoustical buffer formed by circulation, service spaces and parking courts. Maximum natural ventilation due to building orientation and through air-flow.

Jury Comments
The jury respects the rigor of this proposal. The details in the perspective views show a sympathetic residential environment. The parking "rooms" incorporating permeable materials, the community spaces and the tree canopy along the perimeter were very appealing.

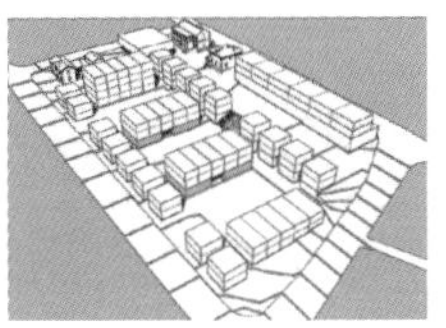

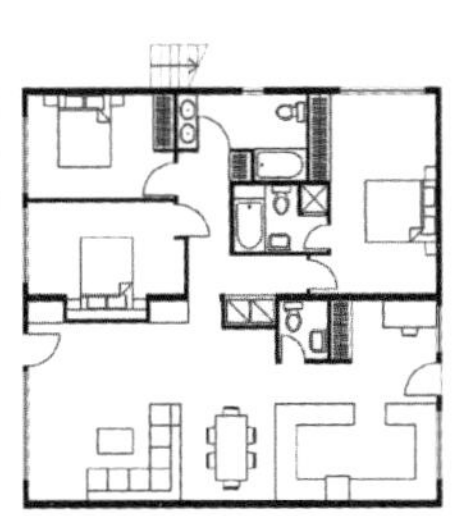

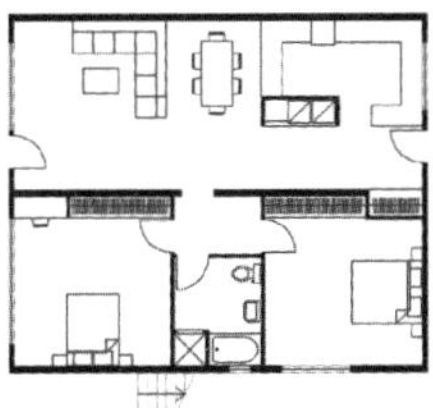

Extension
CK-Architecture

CK-Architecture is a design practice based in Los Angeles. Over the past 20 years, principal Christoph Kapeller has developed expertise in places as diverse as Norway, Egypt and the United States. Recently, CK-Architecture has focused on design within campus contexts, including the newly completed Robert H. Timme Graduate Research Center at the USC School of Architecture. In addition to his practice, Kapeller teaches architecture at USC.

What role does / did the Urban Habitats competition play within your practice?

I have thought a lot about this competition, and we have had some follow-up on it in our office. In 2006, we participated and became finalists in the Small Lots-Smart Design competition in Los Angeles. *(For more details, see p. 85.)* This competition was directly related to a new city ordinance that allows developers to sub-divide lots into very small parcels for independent development. To be able to design townhouses on these lots reduces cost, making home ownership accessible to many people who previously could not afford it.
We proposed an easily replicable, modular system for subdivision and densification. Units range from 480 to 1,500 square feet. Rooftop living and open decks combined with natural day lighting and cross ventilation for all rooms are ideal elements for the mild Southern California climate.

Have you been able to further develop the concepts put forward in your entry?

In 2007, we participated in the Europan competition in Gleisdorf, Austria: Gesellschaft und Ökologie, Generationen Wohnen (Society and Ecology, Intergenerational Living). In this competition, we directly applied lessons learned from the Urban Habitats competition. We created flexible indoor/outdoor rooms for each unit that could be used as meeting places between different social groups and age groups within the 70-unit development.

Currently, we are working with a non-profit developer on a small, two-unit residential and commercial mixed-use project here in Los Angeles to provide transitional housing for the homeless.

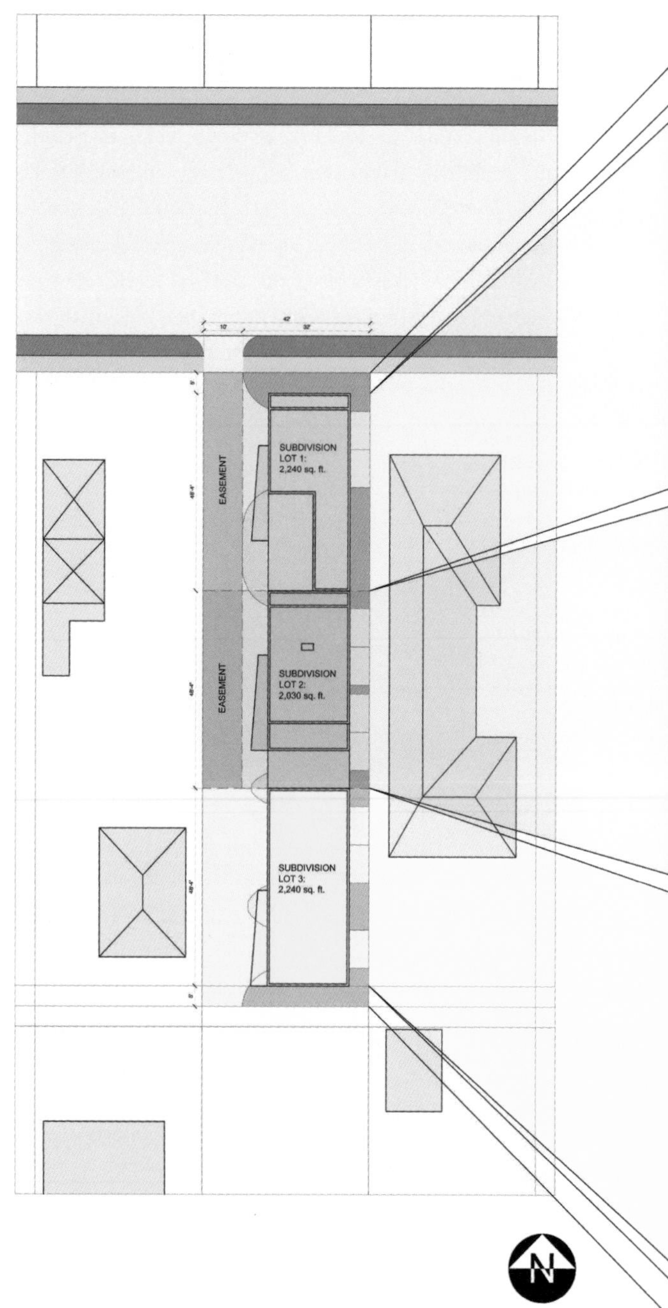

CK-Architecture's competition proposal for five units and on-site parking on a prototypical 42-by-155-foot lot in Los Angeles.

Subdivision Lot 1
3-bedroom unit (1,517 square feet)
2 parking spaces

Subdivision Lot 2
3-bedroom unit (1,296 square feet)
1-bedroom unit (586 square feet)
4 parking spaces

Subdivision Lot 3
3-bedroom unit (1,220 square feet)
Efficiency unit (478 square feet)
3 parking spaces

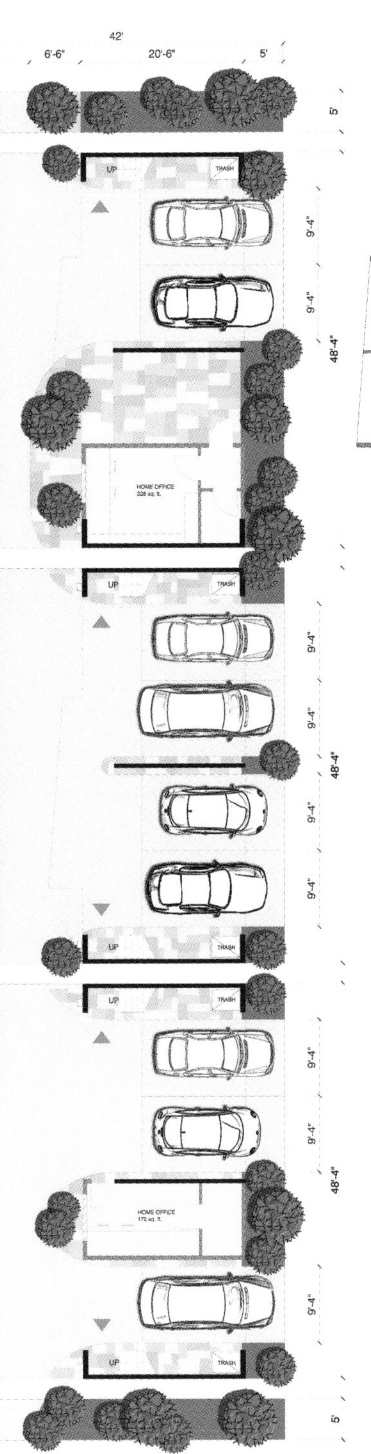

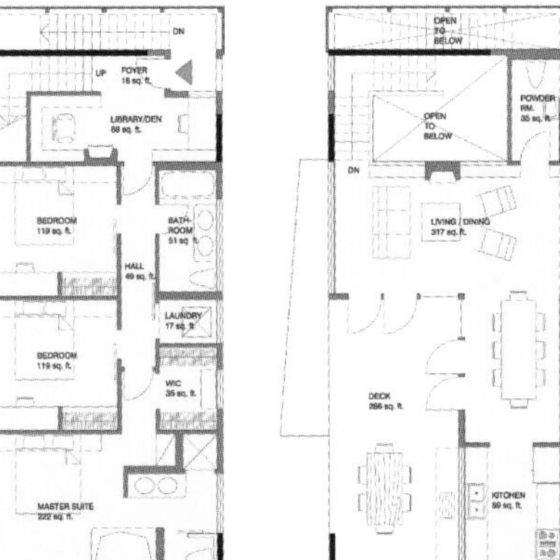

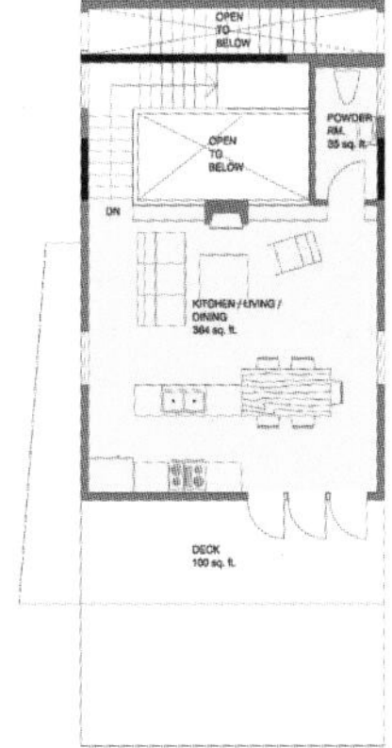

GROUND FLOOR PLAN 2ND FLOOR PLAN 3RD FLOOR PLAN 4TH FLOOR PLAN

Expand Options
:Grow Gardens

Plants, or cultivating the balcony

"Where did the yard go?" is a common refrain when Americans look at multi-family housing. Compact living seems to restrict the dream of an individual garden. Not so. Growing gardens can happen on decks, walls, roofs. How?

:Start with a container.

Make sure it drains. Add soil. Insert plant. Water as required. Watch sunlight, heat, humidity. This is the kernel of your garden. Tomatoes, flowers, fig tree follow.

:Move down to the ground.

Somewhere next to your apartment, underneath your home, there is the ground. Between the ground and your unit there is a wall. Pick up a piece of that pavement next to that wall. Set down the roots. Roses will climb. Ivy will climb. Your wall will be green.

:Get up on the roof.

Not every roof was built to be occupied. Negotiation may be required. Access and safety may have to be provided. But it will be worth it. Where else will you find such peace? On the how, consult guidebooks. One we particularly liked: Guide To Setting Up Your Own Edible Roof Garden, by Alternatives and Rooftop Gardens Projects in Montreal, published in 2008.

Phipps Rose Dattner Grimshaw
Via Verde

The 221-unit, mixed-income housing development, Via Verde, located in a formerly ravaged area of the South Bronx, may seem unrelated to the small-house neighborhoods discussed in this book. It is precisely the intensity of its urban location between vacant lots, new and old housing and institutional buildings, however, which demonstrates how critical the cultivation of gardens can be, even in a 221-unit high-rise building.

The project is the winning response to the New Housing New York Legacy competition, held in 2006 by the City of New York. PRDG, the architect-developer team, comprises the non-profit housing developer The Phipps Houses and Jonathan Rose Companies, a for-profit developer with a track record of sustainable, low-income projects. Dattner Architects of New York and Nicholas Grimshaw & Partners of London are responsible for the design. Together, the team formulated a courageous approach to green urban living. The project integrates 150 rental and 71 co-op units that are linked through a network of individual and shared gardens.

In fact, the project is inspired by the integration of garden and city. The connected rooftops of low-rise town homes, a mid-rise duplex building and the 20-story tower will be used to harvest rainwater, grow fruits and vegetables, exercise and relax. The gardens take a variety of forms, including balconies, backyard gardens, semi-private courtyards, and public learning and gardening space. Scheduled for completion in 2010, the project's success will hinge on whether or not residents avail themselves of this vast array of opportunities to garden.

OPPOSITE
Growing gardens in the South Bronx.
View north from Via Verde's roof-top gardens.

BELOW
Site plan showing roofscape.

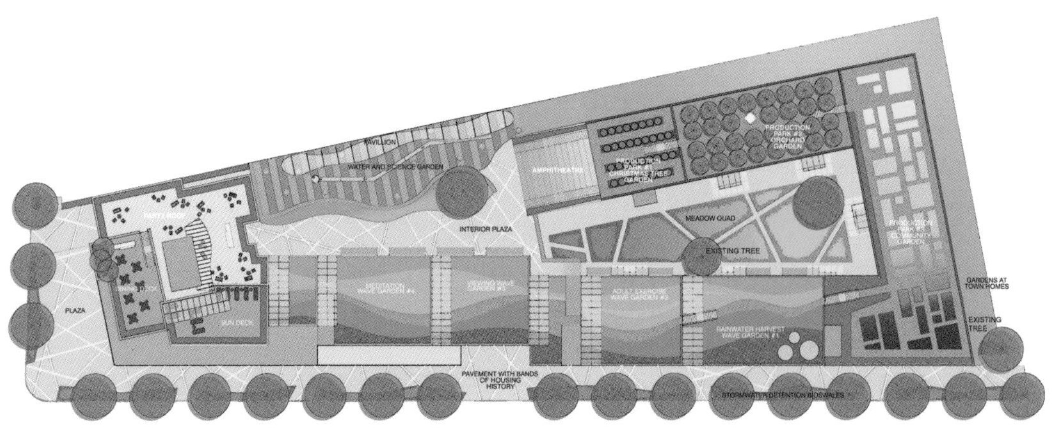

PAVILION
WATER AND SCIENCE GARDEN
AMPHITHEATRE
PRODUCTION PARK #1 CHRISTMAS TREE GARDEN
PRODUCTION PARK #2 ORCHARD GARDEN
INTERIOR PLAZA
MEADOW QUAD
EXISTING TREE
PRODUCTION PARK #3 COMMUNITY GARDEN
GARDENS AT TOWN HOMES
PLAZA
SUN DECK
MEDITATION WAVE GARDEN #4
VIEWING WAVE GARDEN #3
ADULT EXERCISE WAVE GARDEN #2
RAINWATER HARVEST WAVE GARDEN #1
EXISTING TREE
PAVEMENT WITH BANDS OF HOUSING HISTORY
STORMWATER DETENTION BIOSWALES

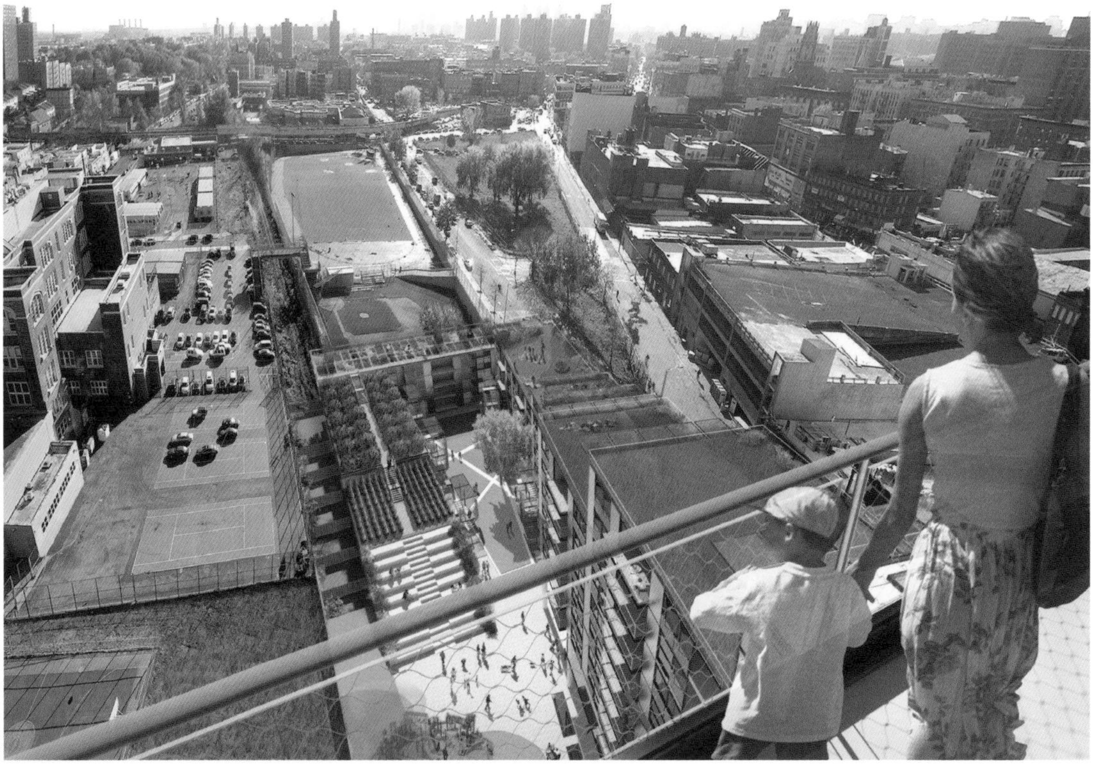

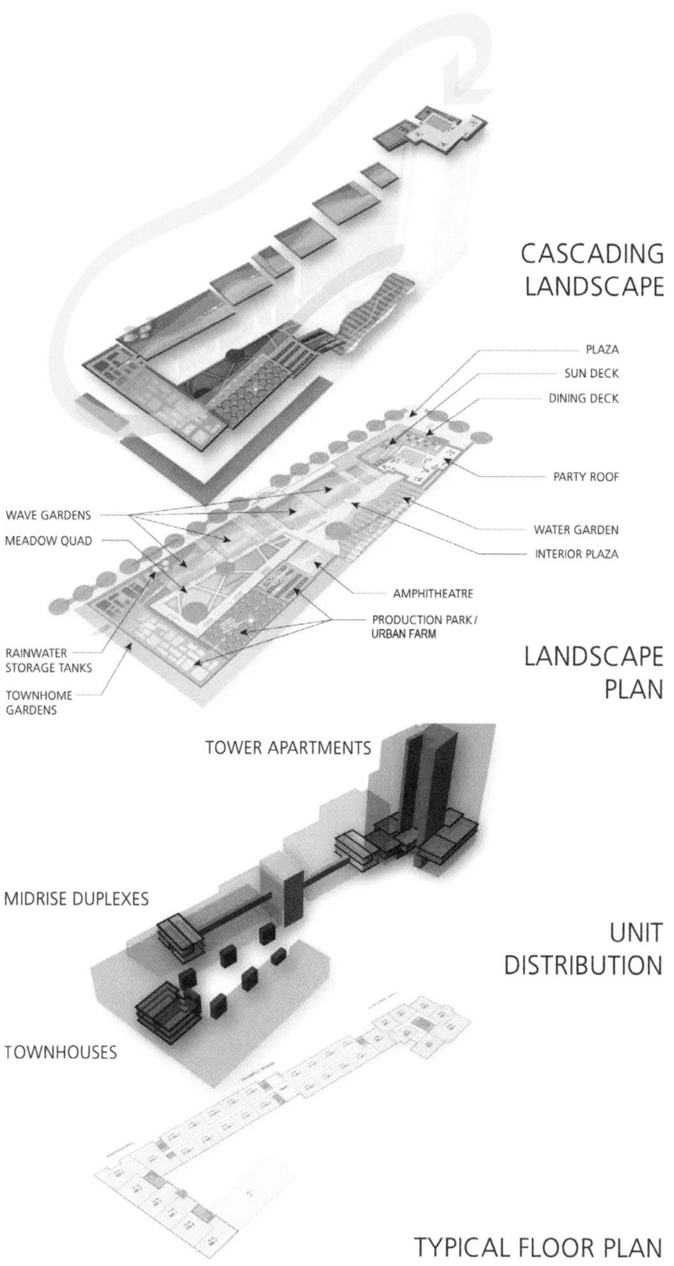

OPPOSITE, ABOVE
Plan of terraced roofs showing different gardening areas.

OPPOSITE, BELOW
View south from the tower toward Manhattan.

LEFT
Exploded axonometric explaining the key relationships between landscape, building massing, and unit distribution.

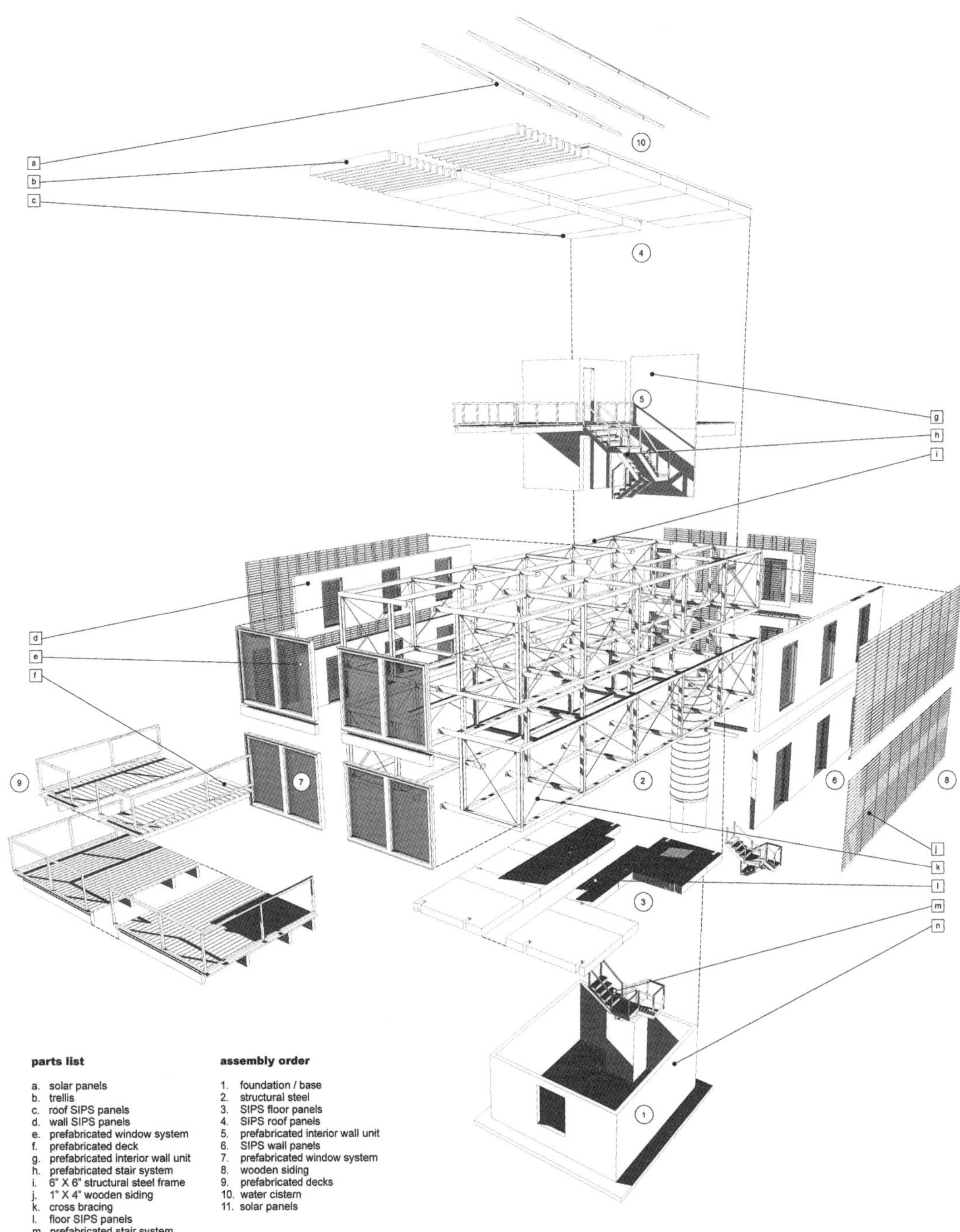

Exploded view of a prefabricated building unit showing components and assembly.

Anderson Anderson Architecture
Organic Urban Living Field

The Urban Habitats competition entry by Anderson Anderson Architecture shows how every part of a development can contribute to a landscape of productive gardens. This cultivation of gardens starts with the overall treatment of the site. Again, creating planted forms as the basis for the buildings is a first and fundamental move. Upon this groundwork, the architects superimpose an "agrarian orchard grid planted with fruit-bearing shade trees." Based on the Jeffersonian ideal of integrating an agricultural landscape with urban, civic life, this continuous orchard then supports a network of shared gardens and outdoor spaces.

Third Place Finalist

Team Members
Mark Anderson, AIA, Peter Anderson, AIA (principals in charge), Hitasha Bhatia, Aaron Brumo, Christopher Campbell, Lawton Eng, Chia Chieh Lee, Dennis Oshira, Brent Sumida

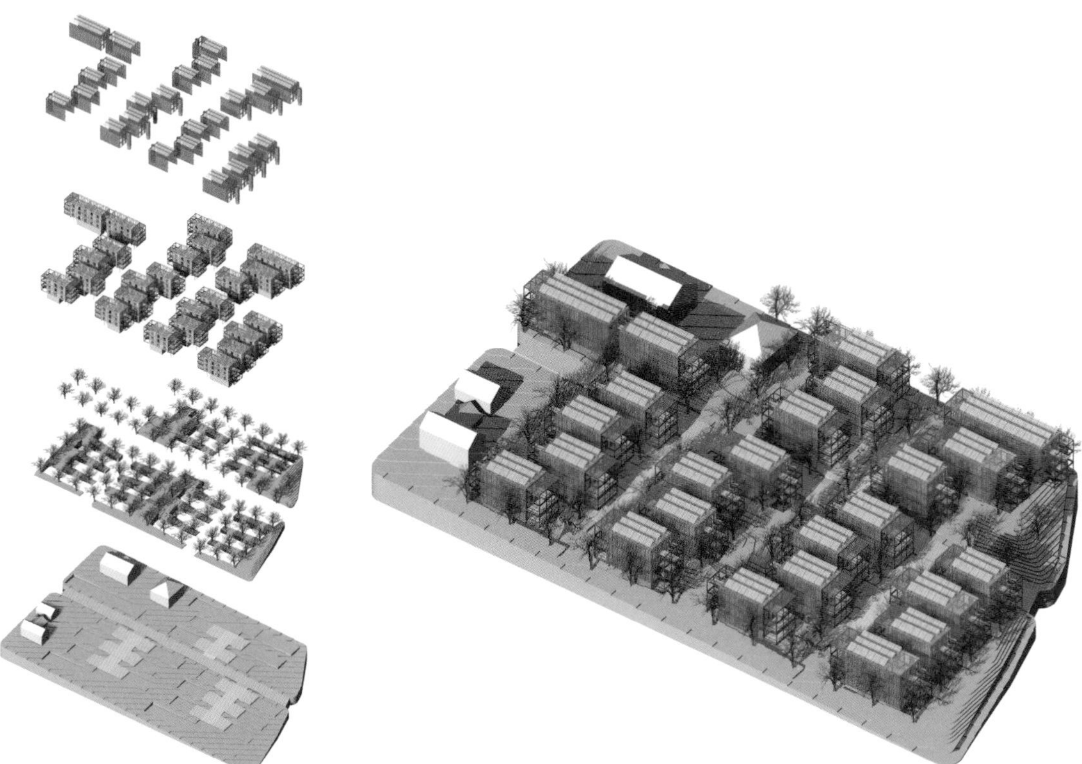

Exploded view of the site strategy. Shading screens, solar panels, and rain barrels; Prefabricated building units; Orchard and landscape berms; Existing site with new streets and excavation. At right, aerial view of completed site.

Carlton Avenue

1102 CARLETON AVENUE

1106 CARLETON AVENUE

Rives Street

512 RIVES STREET

512 RIVES STREET

Midland Street

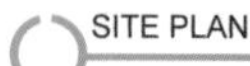

1. Flexible street front retail/ restaurant space
2. Common residential stairs and balconies
3. Street-level accessible residences
4. Mechanical space and utilities
5. One bedroom or studio residence
6. Two bedroom, one bath residence
7. Three bedroom, one bath residence
8. Three bedroom, two bath residence
9. Three-plus bedroom, two bath, two-story townhouse residence
10. Residential balconies
11. Community playground
12. Parking; Electric car station; City Car Share station
13. Bicycle parking
14. Recycling and trash center
15. Community center and day care
16. Community vegetable gardens
17. Community compost center
18. Rain barrel water catchment and filtration tanks

Site plan showing first floor plan.

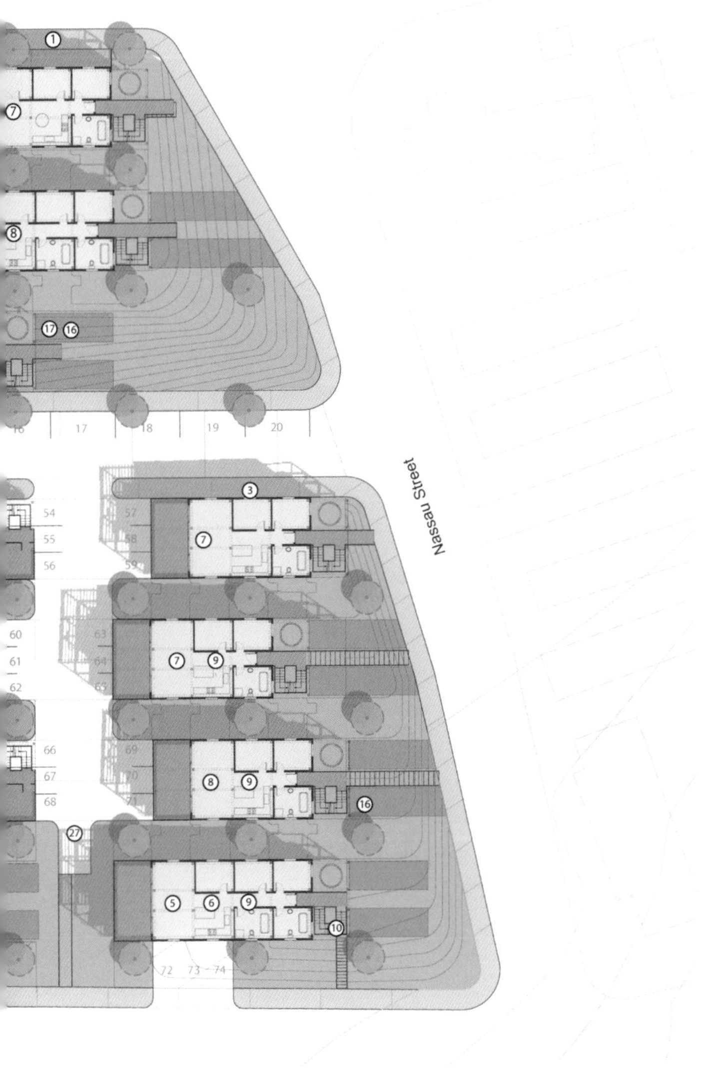

19 Black water sewer pre-treatment tanks
20 Household gray water filtration and irrigation recycling tanks
21 Street run-off storm sewer pre-treatment tanks
22 Balanced cut and fill rolling landscape berms
23 Community outdoor gathering space
24 Rooftop photovoltaic solar collection panels
25 Natural ventilation corridors
26 Fruit-bearing shade tree orchard
27 Community basketball hoops/hard surface play area

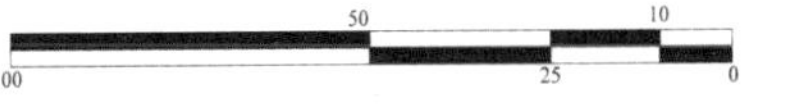

Statement

This high-density urban housing landscape will be fabricated almost entirely off-site using a hybrid, steel-frame / structural insulated panel system. The individual building units will be efficiently manufactured in two, road-legal halves per typical three-bedroom flat and then stacked by crane as complete three-story, three-family units on top of semi-buried, prefabricated, composite concrete basement vaults. Earth excavated for building foundations is redistributed as rolling landscape berms creating a unified outdoor common space flowing around the individual house blocks. Earth cut and fill is balanced in order to minimize cost, energy expenditure and existing community disruption, while simultaneously enhancing the rich symbolism of a community rooted in the local Jeffersonian earth.

Dwelling units share a common geometric order defined by a superimposed agrarian orchard grid planted with fruit-bearing shade trees. Within the regular orchard grid, the slightly sliding house positions create a readably syncopated rhythm, allowing the common open space to shrink and swell across the rolling berms, creating variously sized outdoor gardening, picnic and play areas.

The entire manufacturing and prefabrication process can be completed off-site within a 5-month, just-in-time delivery framework, overlapping with a total 3-month on-site construction period.

Jury Comments

While all of the designs reference landscape as an organizing principle, this design is organized rationally with a central route that gains access to site, including large open spaces that are clearly defined. Secondary spaces link parking, dwelling areas and major office spaces. The plan very clearly defines the potential for layering sustainable architecture and landscape systems through use of energy efficient units, louvers, trees, berms and water collection systems.

But Anderson Anderson takes the gardening further. The 23 buildings placed within the orchard each form a large trellis to support plant growth. For each building, the structural purpose of the three-story trellis is to support the prefabricated dwelling units. However, by articulating open spaces between the dwellings, both as sunrooms, which provide entry to the units, and as private balconies at the short ends of the buildings, the trellis becomes a multi-story garden.

With this framework, the architects aren't just inviting plants to occupy every corner of the site and every building level, they are inviting participation. The success of the scheme depends on residents actively cultivating their gardens. The gardens form the "primary image of the site;" if they are not tended, it will show. The project's gardens beautifully highlight how operation and maintenance are just as important to a housing development as its design and construction.

OPPOSITE
View of trellis and prefabricated dwelling units from the community gathering space.

BELOW
Building section describing water and energy management across the site.

4 Mechanical space
10 Residence
13 Car parking
14 Bicycle parking
19 Rain water tanks, used for irrigation
20 Black water tanks, treated pre-sewer
21 Household gray water tanks filtered before use for irrigation
23 Berms balancing cut and fill
24 Photovoltaic panels
25 Community gathering space

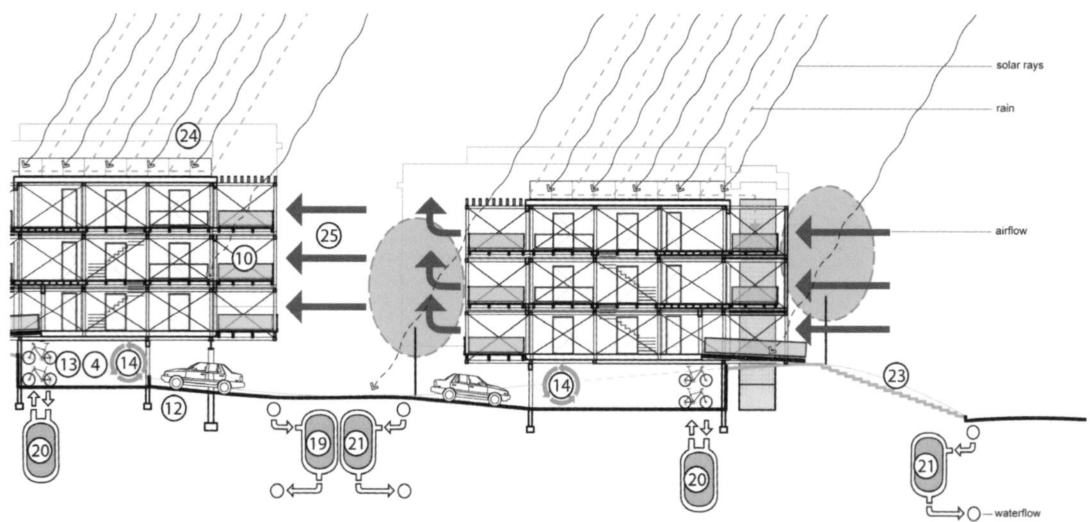

HOUSE TYPE 3.2 - 3 BEDROOM, 2 BATH
enclosed living space 1,179 s.f.
exterior balcony space 276 s.f.

HOUSE TYPE 3.1 - 3 BEDROOM, 1 BATH
enclosed living space 892 s.f.
exterior balcony space 123 s.f.

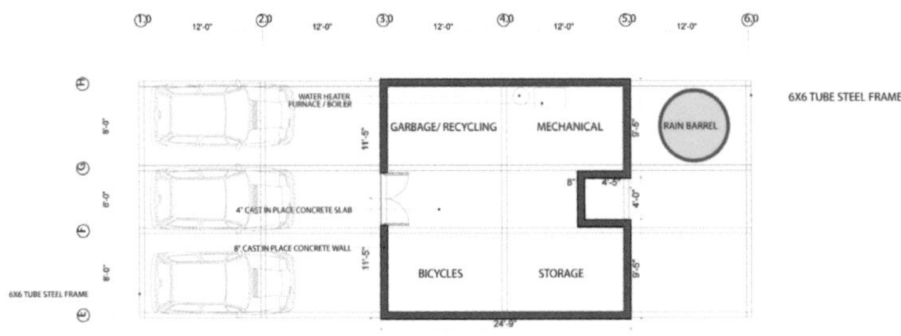

SHARED HOUSE BASEMENT
enclosed living space 548 s.f.

OPPOSITE AND THIS PAGE, CENTER
Floor plans of selected unit types.

LEFT
View from a balcony across the site.

BOTTOM
View from a dwelling interior out across its balcony.

Extension
Anderson Anderson Architecture

Mark Anderson and Peter Anderson started their firm as a design-build construction company in 1984. The practice, based in San Francisco and Seattle, has since grown into a firm with diverse experience collaborating with general contractors, manufacturers, artists, fabricators and technical specialists. Their current work is particularly focused on urban housing and public waterfronts.

What role does / did the Urban Habitats competition play within your practice?

Coming out of our single-family, steel-frame prototypes, the Urban Habitats competition was a very important step in the development of many of the steel frame multi-family projects that we have worked on since. These include our design for high-density housing, one of two winning entries in the "Designing the Future of New Orleans" competition, organized after Hurricane Katrina by Architectural Record and Tulane University. The project was featured in the US Pavilion at the 2006 Venice Biennale and other venues, enabling us to exhibit prototypes of our SpongeComb inflatable levee system, an integral part of the project's ecological and water management systems.

Have you been able to further develop the concepts put forward in your entry?

In part as a result of the Urban Habitats competition, we have been invited to propose a number of similar projects, both in international invited competitions, and for developer projects in the United States. We have also been invited to work with Habitat for Humanity on a number of related projects that have not yet come to fruition, but which also seek to provide affordable, high-density housing in areas that are prone to the flooding and other natural threats, common to lower income areas in many cities. We recently completed two housing proposals in China based on similar prefabricated, modular steel systems, and a tower proposal for the History Channel's "City of the Future" invited competition for a high-rise neighborhood of San Francisco. All of these projects focus on affordable, sustainable construction systems adapted to unique urban sites with extreme environmental conditions.

Have you been able to realize any projects that are related to the Urban Habitats project, be it in scale, approach, client, philosophy?

Soon after the New Orleans competition, it seemed that there was some good momentum towards construction of the project, and toward bold new thinking about how to redevelop the waterfront. Priorities have shifted since, and there is more effort going into rebuilding than starting new projects or creating greater density on the city's traditional high ground. In the meantime, we have worked extensively with developers in Tulsa, Salt Lake City, Los Angeles, Shanghai and Wuhan. The proposed systems are highly sustainable and very cost-effective if employed at a significant scale, but there are hurdles to overcome, both in terms of the investment risk and design review processes. Currently, new projects in both China and Korea are likely to move forward, while the projects in the United States have been slowed by the housing downturn and increasingly risk-averse lending.

A further opportunity that grew out of the Urban Habitats project and the Venice Biennale exhibition is a collaboration with the Autodesk Corporation, the makers of the Revit, Building Integrated Modeling (BIM) software, and other parametric modeling and environmental analysis tools. While we have not built any of these projects at full size, we have still been able to move forward into advanced engineering and modeling analysis, allowing the modular systems to become increasingly comprehensive and predictable in terms of their implementation in a wide variety of sites and climates. This sort of modularization and site adaptability modeling of our design work increases its affordability and hence the likelihood of construction for future projects.

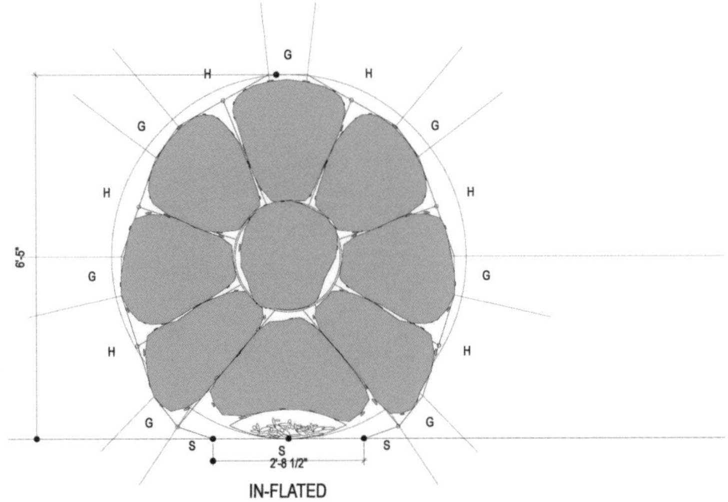

Cross sections through the SpongeComb showing different inflation levels.

Looking from above on to prototypes of the SpongeComb inflatable levee system deployed at the U.S. Pavilion at the Venice Biennale 2006.
Anderson Anderson developed the SpongeComb for multi-family housing in New Orleans. If the river rises, SpongeComb fills with water, preventing a flood.

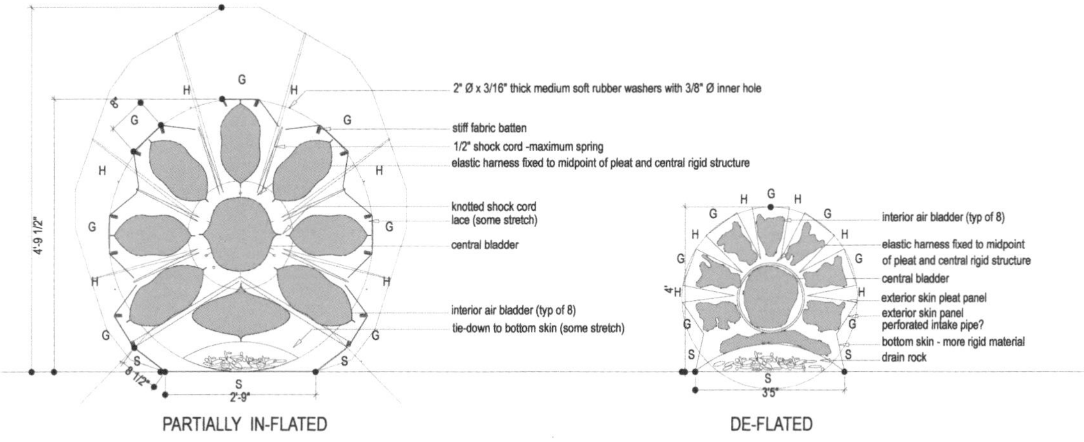

Build for Change
: Harness Seasons

Energy, or how to create a productive building

Buildings account for 40% of the nation's overall energy use. Reducing this consumption is a major task of redevelopment projects. How can you harness seasons to create a productive building?

: Employ wind, light, rain, heat.

It's self-evident and yet it's rarely implemented. Make use of all the free energy at your disposal, and be aware of what each season has to offer. Being able to cool your bedroom with a simple breeze, being able to cook your dinner without turning on the light, being able to heat your bathroom with water warmed in pipes underground.

: Reuse, recycle.

This too has been said before and it is worth repeating. Perhaps the most sustainable development approach is to reuse existing building stock. Rather than trying to start from scratch, work with what is there. It's likely to be close to infrastructure, it's likely to be centrally located and it's likely to have a history and patina that you'd never be able to create anew.

Zoka Zola
Zero Energy House

The Zero Energy House, designed in 2005 by architect Zoka Zola of Chicago, is an example of how to build for change and harness seasons at the scale of a single-family residence. Its goal was to design a zero-carbon emission building for Chicago's climate, characterized by very cold winters and hot, humid summers. The smart, elegant, split-level house does so by making full use of passive as well as active strategies.

The passive heating, cooling and ventilation were achieved primarily by intelligent layout decisions. Organizing the main house into two main zones negotiated by a central stair allowed the architects to work with varying floor-to-floor heights which can modulate light, air flow and acoustics. Generous living areas are located to the west, while compact bedrooms and bathrooms are stacked in the east. The kitchen is a single-story extension connecting to the multi-functional building. Clearly separating it from the living spaces limits odors and maximizes natural light. By organizing the building around a courtyard and locating openings deliberately, interior spaces receive sunlight in the winter but remain shaded in the summer. Shading is optimized by the location of trees and recessed windows at southern exposures. The building's active systems include a geothermal system for heating and cooling, solar thermal panels for producing hot water, as well as photovoltaic panels and a wind turbine to generate electricity.

OPPOSITE
View from the courtyard of the Zero Energy House toward its living areas.

BELOW
Overall view showing how building envelope and vegetation intertwine to maximize benefits of sun, wind, and shading.

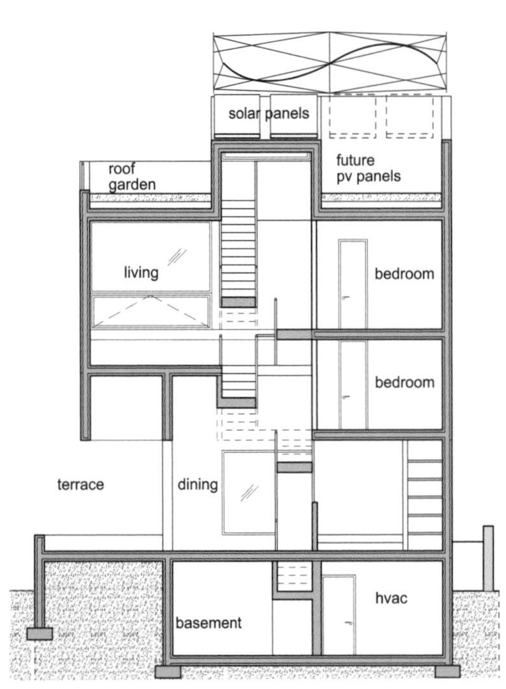
air turbine
solar panels
future
pv panels
roof
garden
living
bedroom
bedroom
terrace
dining
basement
hvac

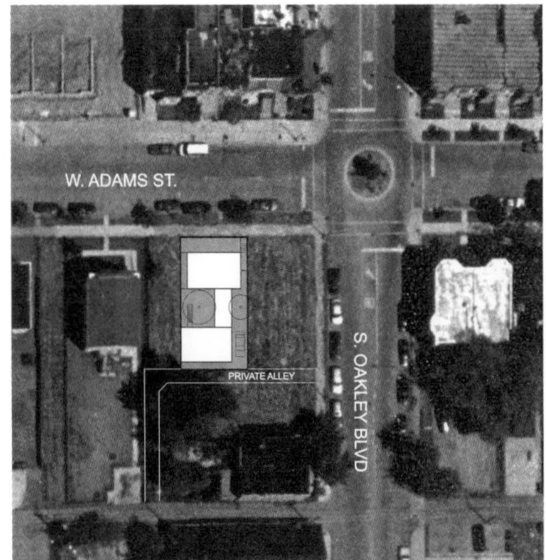
W. ADAMS ST.
S. OAKLEY BLVD
PRIVATE ALLEY

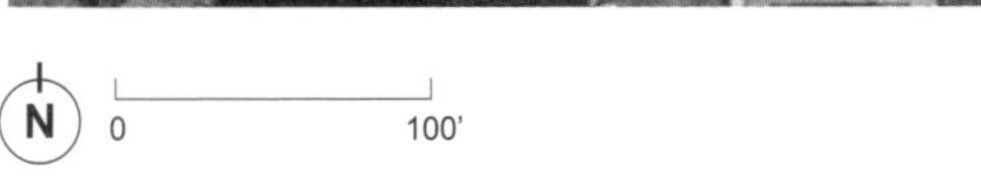
N
0
100'

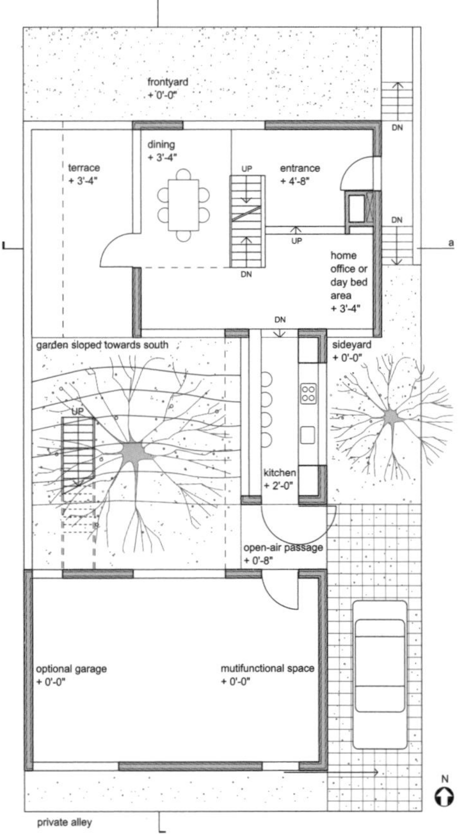
adams street
frontyard
+ 0'-0"
terrace
+ 3'-4"
dining
+ 3'-4"
entrance
+ 4'-8"
home
office or
day bed
area
+ 3'-4"
garden sloped towards south
sideyard
+ 0'-0"
kitchen
+ 2'-0"
open-air passage
+ 0'-8"
optional garage
+ 0'-0"
mutifunctional space
+ 0'-0"
private alley

OPPOSITE, ABOVE
Building section through main living areas.

OPPOSITE, BELOW
Site plan.

BELOW, LEFT TO RIGHT
First, second and third floor plans.

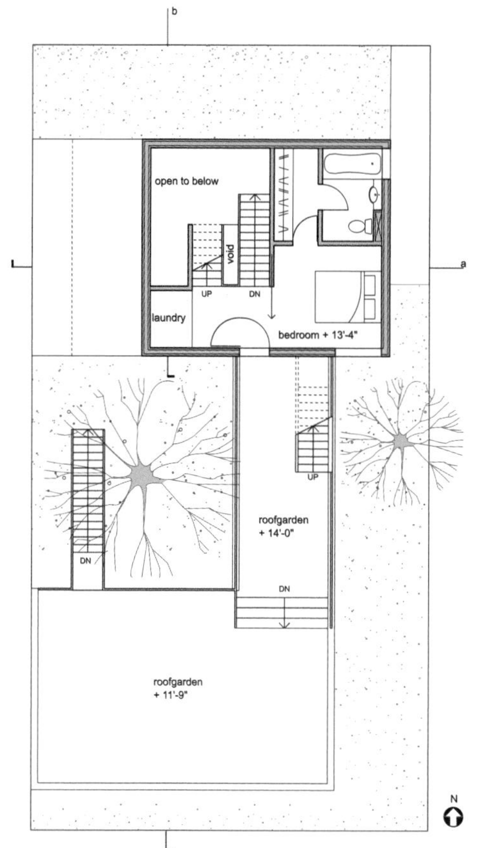

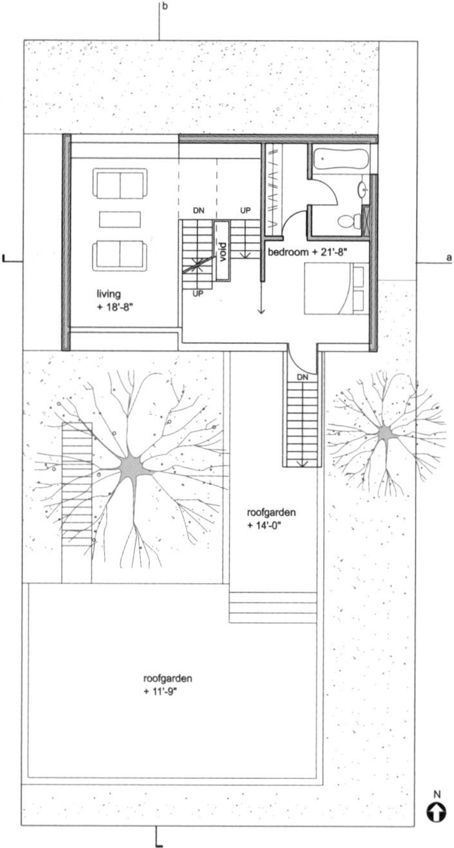

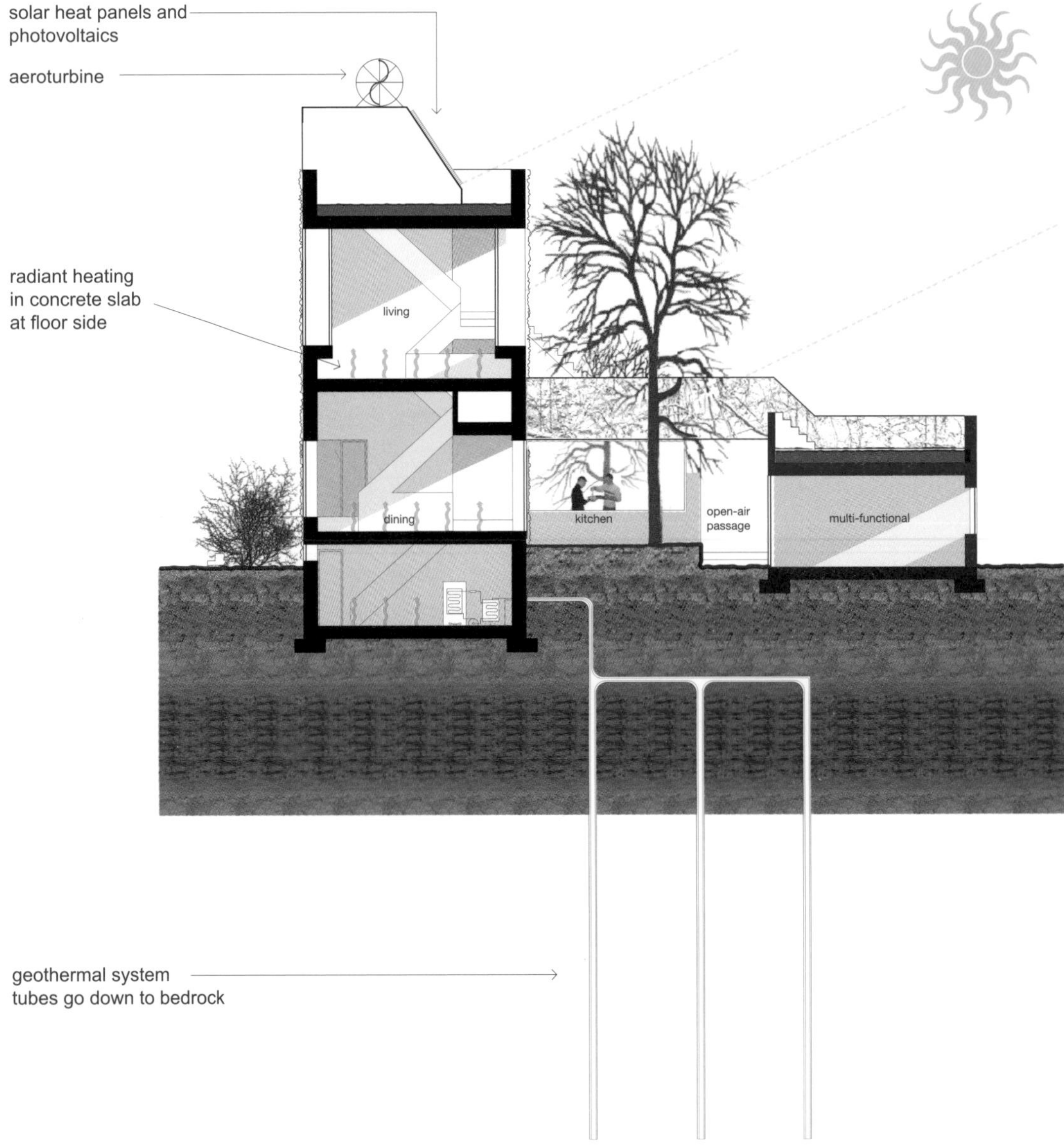
solar heat panels and photovoltaics
aeroturbine
radiant heating in concrete slab at floor side
living
dining
kitchen
open-air passage
multi-functional
geothermal system tubes go down to bedrock

Besides harnessing the seasons in this way, the project also addresses the questions of urban renewal and long-term change. The choice to site the project on two adjacent vacant lots in an area of Chicago characterized by severe disinvestment but fully serviced by infrastructure, helps rebuild an existing neighborhood and conserves land, energy and transportation resources. Furthermore, the architect addresses what she calls "intergenerational responsibility" by providing the space and structure for both a ground-level "grandparent" addition and another story on the building. The design also anticipates the future conversion of the 19-by-30-foot accessory building.

Despite the specificity of its location, this project was designed as a prototype. Its principles have been applied to speculative multifamily development in Chicago. A further iteration has also been worked out for a site in Malaysia.

OPPOSITE
Section showing building performance in winter.

BELOW
Section showing building performance in summer.

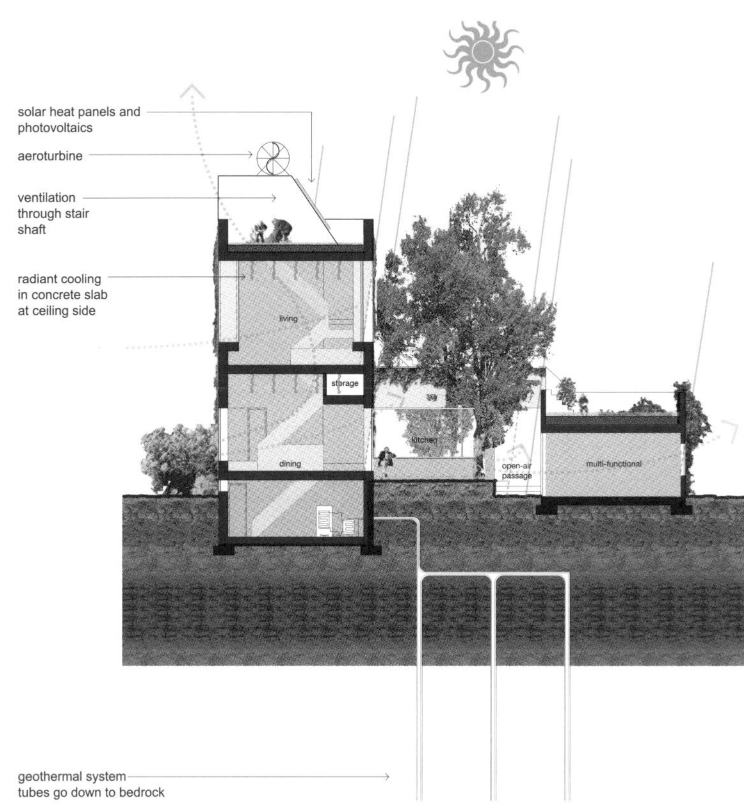

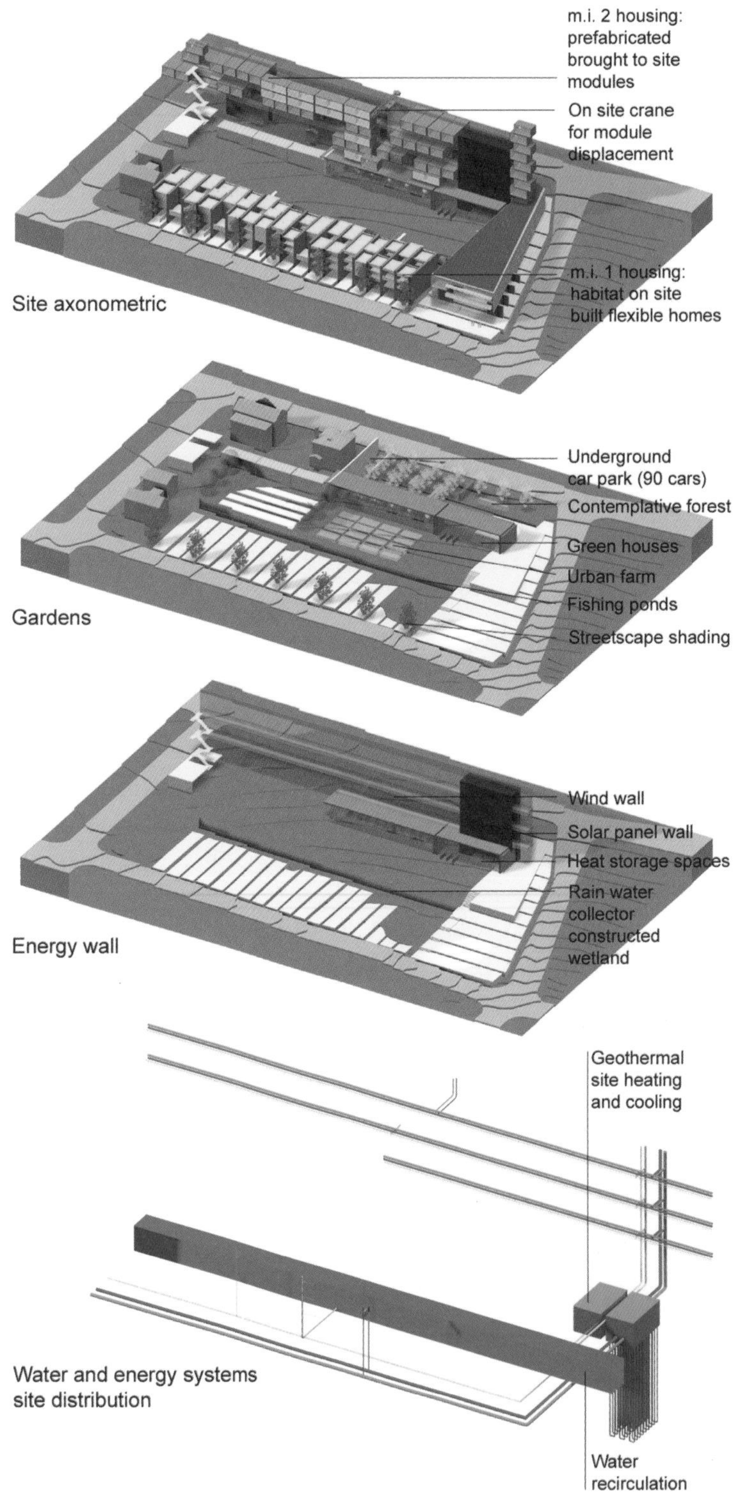
m.i. 2 housing: prefabricated brought to site modules
On site crane for module displacement
m.i. 1 housing: habitat on site built flexible homes
Site axonometric
Underground car park (90 cars)
Contemplative forest
Green houses
Urban farm
Fishing ponds
Streetscape shading
Gardens
Wind wall
Solar panel wall
Heat storage spaces
Rain water collector constructed wetland
Energy wall
Geothermal site heating and cooling
Water recirculation
Water and energy systems site distribution

Carlo Carbone + JLP et Associés
Urban Farm

The Urban Habitats competition entry Urban Farm by Carlo Carbone + JLP et Associes Architectes of Montreal, Canada, addresses building for change and harnessing the seasons on two levels.

On one level, as its name implies, the proposal is based on turning Sunrise Trailer Court into an energy-producing site. "This urban farm imposes the cultivation and the harvesting of the site's potential energy sources: geothermal (for heating and cooling), solar energy (for electricity and for year round food production) and constructed wetlands (to reduce load on city systems)." The proposal foresees, quite literally, an urban farm, harnessing not only energy, but producing crops and foodstuffs.

On a second level, the project acknowledges cycles of growth and decline, and the vagaries of changing residents and their changing tastes. The proposal is geared to allow redevelopment without replacing any existing infrastructure, buildings or structures, since this is one of the most energy-consuming and expensive consequences of obsolete buildings.

With this in mind, Urban Farm proposes two types of dwelling units to anticipate change. The first, built on-site by Habitat volunteers along Midland Street, would be permanent. Although permanent, the dwellings could be easily customized on the interior, since floors are inserted as required between structural party walls that contain all the necessary infrastructure. The second type is targeted at market-rate residents and would be manufactured off-site before being "placed and removed as required" along Carlton Avenue. A project goal is to express the inevitable, constant change, and these removable dwellings would "provide an ever-changing colorful display of personalities and lifestyles. As lifestyles evolve so too will the Sunrise Urban Farm."

This kind of constant rebuilding seldom works as smoothly as intended. The logistics of moving heavy components is cumbersome and relies too much on one system of parts. Nevertheless, the scheme highlights that the biggest enemy of sustainable development may be the obsolescence of buildings. As the architects wisely conclude,"Sustainability in the housing market is a function of how developments can evolve over time without having to completely overhaul a site."

OPPOSITE
Exploded view of site showing key components to harness seasons, including a geothermal system, solar panel wall, and rain water collector. The site's central open space is used for agriculture.

BELOW
While Habitat units (m.i. 1) are flexible, but constructed to remain permanently on site, market-rate units (m.i. 2) are assembled off-site and come and go with their residents.

FOLLOWING PAGE, TOP TO BOTTOM
Sectional perspective of a Habitat house; sectional diagrams showing the type's inherent flexibility due to structural party walls that contain all services; floor plans.

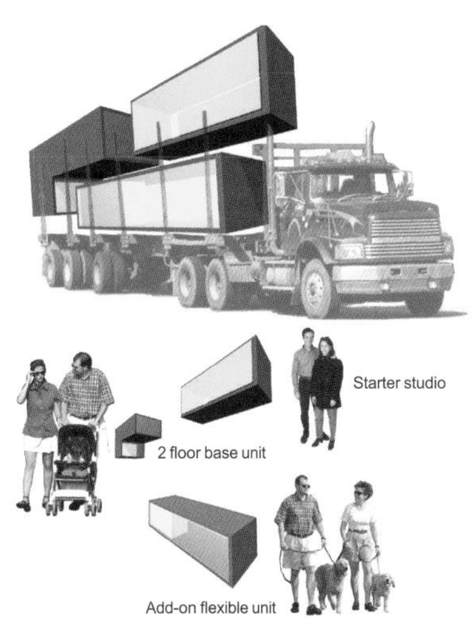

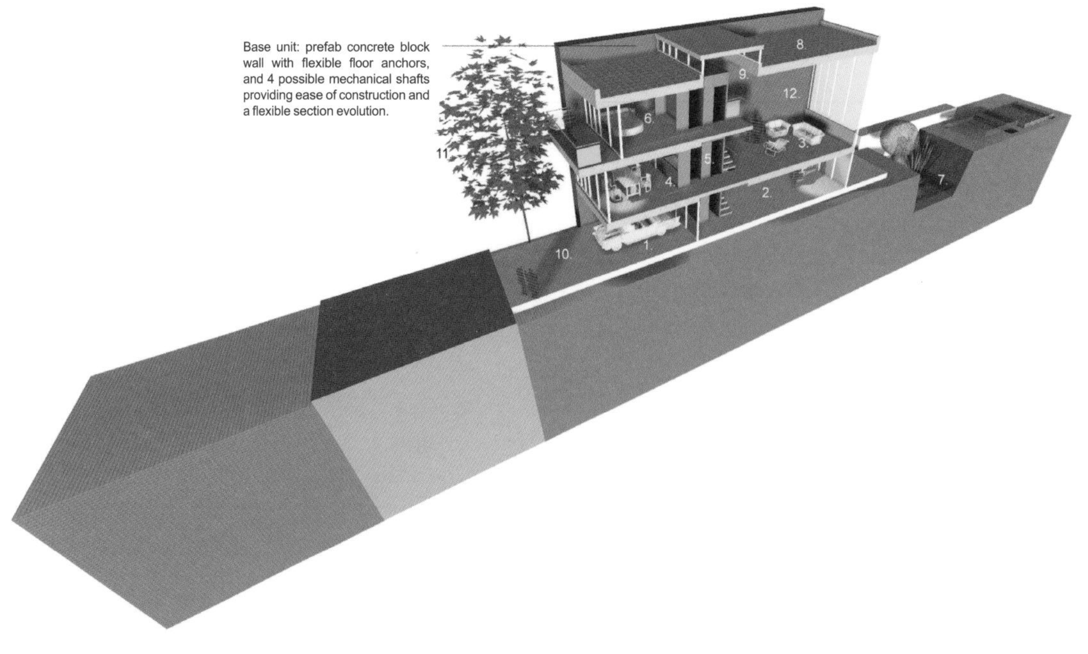

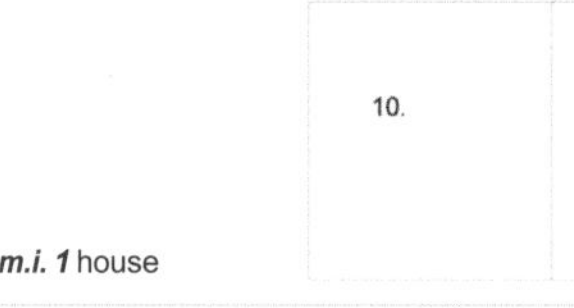

m.i. 1 **house**

1. flexible space (rental, office, commercial)
2. office / evolving space
3. living room
4. kitchen / dining
5. bath
6. bedroom
7. water garden
8. green roof
9. natural air shaft
10. carpool parking
11. streetscape shading
12. concrete and echanical wall

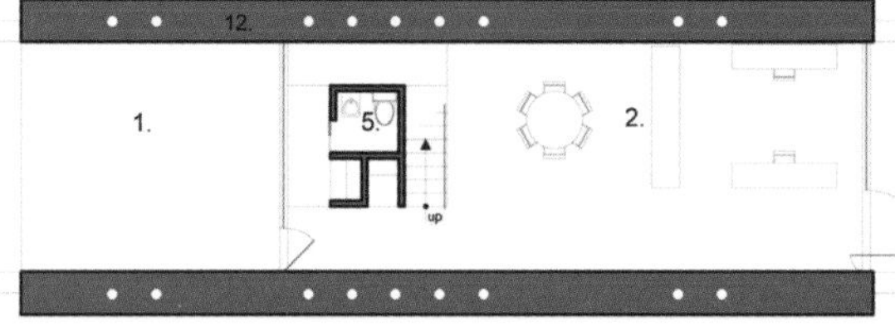

Ground floor plan

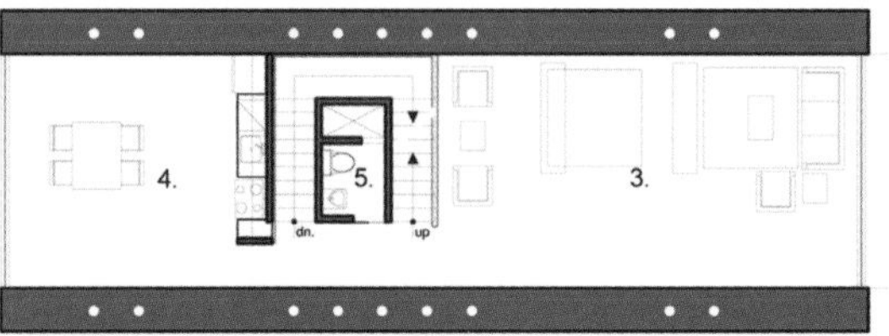

First floor plan

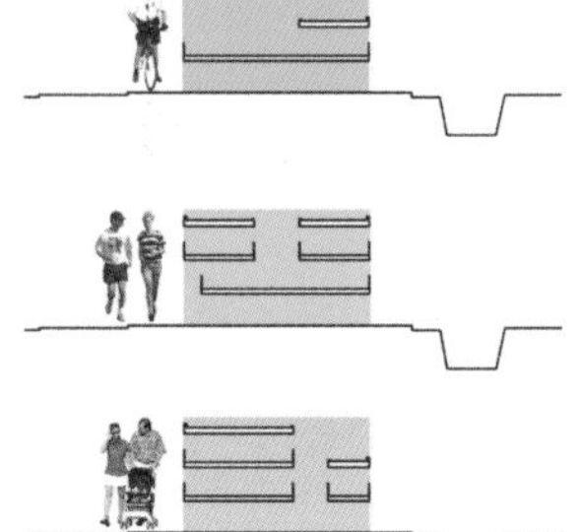

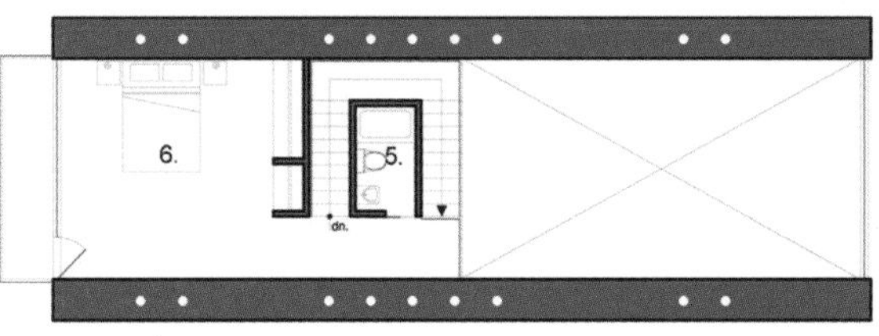

Second floor plan

Extension

Carlo Carbone

Carlo Carbone is an architect in Montreal, Canada. He founded his own practice, Atelier C2, in 2001, and has been working with Jodoin Lamarre Pratte et associés architectes since 2002. He teaches at the University of Montreal and is a member of the editorial committee of ARQ, the Quebec Architecture Journal.

What role does / did the Urban Habitats competition play within your practice?

The competition gave me an opportunity to explore an integrated community that proposed a combination of all family types and all age groups with a multitude of activity and community space. The competition also gave me a framework within which I was able to define a type of home that could be easily built and modified by its owner.

Have you been able to further develop the concepts you put forward in your entry?

I have started a chapter of Habitat for Humanity with a couple of local architects and we are presently helping a non-profit organization with a community planning project. We generated several proposals for the project in a design charette with the University of Montreal.

Have you been able to realize any projects that are related to the Urban Habitats project, be it in scale, approach, client, philosophy?

No, but I am in the process of trying to develop a prototype with a local contractor. The prototype would be loosely based on my proposal—a design excellence winner—for the Portland "Living Smart: Big Ideas for Small Lots" design competition, held in 2004. *(For more details on the competition, see p. 97.)*

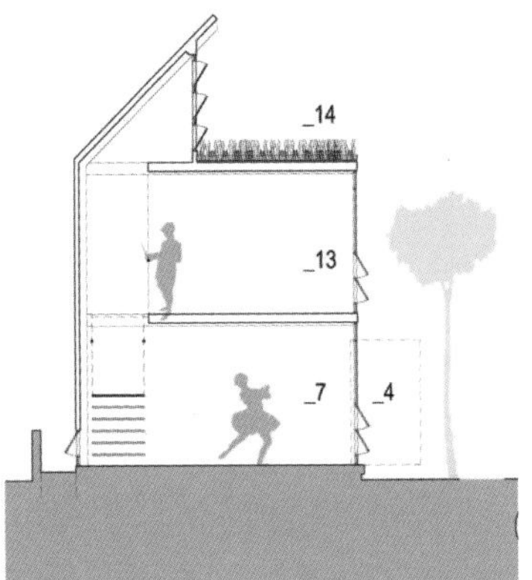

LEFT
Based on an award-winning proposal for Portland's Small Lots competition, Carlo Carbone is currently refining a prototype for an energy-efficient, low-cost house. Section.

BELOW
First and second floor plans.

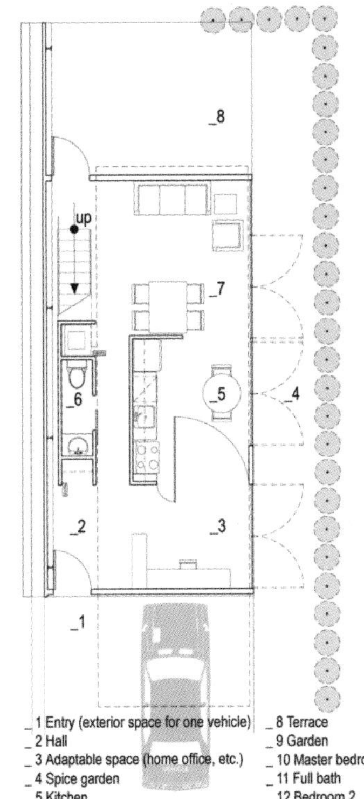

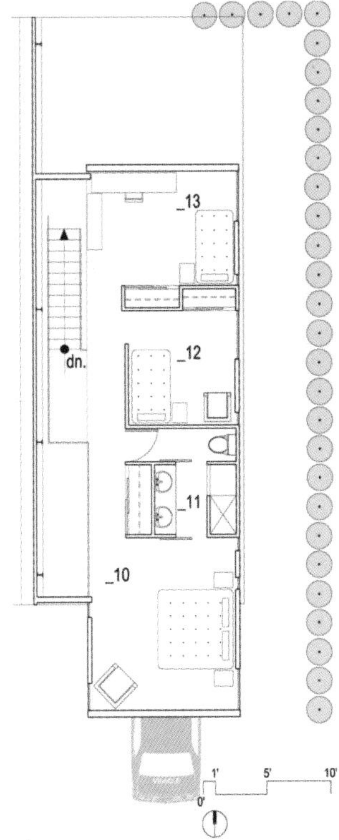

_ 1 Entry (exterior space for one vehicle)
_ 2 Hall
_ 3 Adaptable space (home office, etc.)
_ 4 Spice garden
_ 5 Kitchen
_ 6 1/2 bath
_ 7 Living / dining room
_ 8 Terrace
_ 9 Garden
_ 10 Master bedroom
_ 11 Full bath
_ 12 Bedroom 2
_ 13 Bedroom 3
_ 14 Roof garden

NISSAN

Epilogue
Shifting Gears

Will the future be like Aspen, Colorado, overwhelmingly affluent [but] where moderate and lower income workers simply cannot afford to live and are forced to commute long distances to their jobs? Or will it be more like Austin, Texas, which has established a healthy balance between the affluent and the workers who make that community a social and economic success? This stark choice is still in the hands of the community, but the 'tipping point' draws closer every year.

Habitat for Humanity of Greater Charlottesville, www.cvillehabitat.org, July 2008

The Urban Habitats competition did not end with a public symposium and exhibition. As the competition results were presented to the public, the Board of Habitat for Humanity of Greater Charlottesville (HHGC) conducted interviews with the three finalist teams, whom they had not yet met, to get a sense of how to move forward. HHGC was intrigued by the multidisciplinary planning approach of Metropolitan Planning Collaborative (MPC), a group comprised of two planners, an architect and a landscape architect. They were equally intrigued by the architecture proposed by Genter Schindler. In April 2006, HHGC decided to engage both the first and second place finalists to further develop the project as a team. HHGC commissioned MPC to take the lead in a first master planning phase, culminating in a Planned Urban Development (PUD) submission. Genter Schindler, who had brought the project to Utile, the Boston firm where they were both employed, would then take the lead in a second, construction phase.

The post-competition process leading up to the revised master plan provides an excellent case study of the promise and challenges of implementing the urban habitats goals outlined in this book. Above all, the design team needed to re-focus on laying the multiple foundations necessary for achieving integrated density, dimensional diversity and the two greens.

Moving into Reality

Shifting from writing the program for compact affordable housing at Sunrise and organizing a design competition, to the actual implementation of such a pilot project, involved some soul searching for HHGC. The organization and key figures behind the Sunrise project at the time—Lynne Conboy as President of the Board and Overton McGehee as Executive Director—realized that they needed to restructure internal operations in order to take on a project of this size, and created the new position of Chief Operating Officer. At the same time, HHGC decided to move forward on its own, discontinuing its working relationship with the Charlottesville Community Design Center (CCDC) and its then-director Katie Swenson, who had initiated and expertly managed the Urban Habitats competition process. To facilitate decision-making, HHGC considered appointing an Executive Committee for Sunrise from within its 22-member Board, but ultimately they opted for an Advisory Committee of community members with expertise in real estate, construction, and non-profit finance.

In terms of the program for Sunrise, HHGC felt the need to revisit the mix of housing and other uses outlined in the competition. To do so, HHGC invited a local real estate firm to conduct an assessment of Charlottesville's housing market. HHGC was interested in identifying which type of developments—row houses, condominiums, lofts—were selling at what prices. The study was indeed descriptive of current trends, but it could not supply any insight into housing types that were not already on the market. When the design team proposed a "micro condo," a market-rate studio unit, to be pitched at both first-time home buyers and people interested in just a pied-à-terre in Charlottesville, realtors were delighted. To actually aggregate the niches of a solid program requires input from all sides, but also a leap of faith as to new forms of housing. In fact, the development team needed to keep reminding itself that the Sunrise project is in and of itself a new type of development, responding to a new niche, which requires much explanation to potential residents.

Moving toward a master plan for Sunrise after the successful completion of the competition involved revisiting the development program and re-engaging stakeholders. Workshops were held at various locations in Charlottesville and the final presentation was hosted by the Charlottesville Community Design Center. A physical model proved invaluable to communicate the project goals.

Determining the mix of housing types, the number of housing units, and which non-residential uses should be accommodated is not an easy task. How many units are desirable from a social point of view? How many are necessary to make the project financially feasible? While HHGC was debating quality versus quantity, the design team tried to support the deliberations by visualizing options. In terms of site layout, this meant using a wider array of unit types than had been used in the competition proposals, and generating options with different unit counts for HHGC to consider. Visualizing the associated trade-offs, however, proved to be a lingering challenge. On the one hand, developers and realtors indicated that a market-rate, single-family house would need to be larger than what was being proposed in order to be sold at a price high enough to cross-subsidize the Habitat homes. The tighter the site became, they argued, the less likely it was that the single-family houses would be spacious enough to attract buyers. In other words: Less units, more revenue. At the same time, there was a debate as to whether free standing single-family homes should be provided at Sunrise at all. Charlottesville taxes single-family homes at a higher rate than attached homes. Because of recent increases in property values, property taxes for some Habitat homes now far exceed the mortgage payments on the house, creating serious financial hardships for the owners. In other words: Let's not build single-family homes.

Ultimately, HHGC arrived at a delicate balance of residents and housing types. Eight elderly households would be provided with an accessible, rental unit; these households include many of the current Sunrise Trailer Court residents. Habitat houses would accommodate 18 families, while 15 households with incomes of up to 120% of the area median income (AMI) would be able to buy a Creative Housing home (see explanation of Creative Housing below), and another 15 units would be sold outright at market rate. This led to a total of 54 units, a marked decline from the 72 units that the Urban Habitats competition brief had requested. The great majority of units would not to exceed three stories so that they can be built using volunteer labor. Some condominium units, however, would be reserved for professional construction and can therefore rise higher than three stories. The argument less is more had won.

The debate within HHGC, however, continues as we write this book. Some board members argue that it would be more feasible economically and in terms of later management, to divide the site into a number of fee-simple parcels, either developed by HHGC or sold off to developers. They argue that it is preferable to avoid organizing a shared ownership model, such as a condominium, between households of different income. If HHGC were to fall back on this traditional form of development, individual parcel by individual parcel, they would undermine the fundamental premise of Urban Habitats: creating a new housing development model.

While these deliberations were going on, HHGC and the design team proceeded with further community and political outreach. MPC initiated a master planning process structured around three public workshops which were held between late July 2006 and February 2007. The idea was to re-evaluate the implications of the financial and design requirements discussed above, with the community, elected officials, and Charlottesville planners, to ensure that the project had been vetted by all parties before it was to be submitted for official planning review.

The public workshops generated some relevant feedback for the revised master plan. For instance, a central point of discussion during the meetings was how open, in terms of access and in terms of views, the site should be to its surroundings. While "openness" may sound appealing at first, no one wants to have strangers walking through their yard. From experience, current residents were concerned about drivers taking a short cut through the trailer court instead of using public roads. How to reconcile the wish for openness or "porosity" with the demand for security and privacy? Another question was whether the residents could remain on site during construction, which would require phasing the work, or whether they would be offered intermediate housing until the entire project was ready for occupancy. The revised plan tried to address these issues.

Looking back, other forms of outreach could have been developed, especially since the current residents of Sunrise and the immediate neighborhood had already played a central role in setting up the program for the Urban Habitats competition *(see Chapter 1 for a more detailed description of this process)*. Rather than addressing this group only, why not try to involve the future members of the Sunrise community? Why not solicit the thoughts and preferences of those who are not yet able to afford to live in Belmont, but constitute the target group of the Sunrise project: nurses, firemen, and teachers who work nearby? This kind of pro-active, upfront outreach would have required a larger organizational effort, but it would have provided excellent marketing for the project and HHGC.

The Revised Plan

Landscape plays a central role in the revised Sunrise plan. Two main landscape elements structure the site, respond to residents' concerns and wishes, and create new options. The first is the canopied "Easy Street" running from Carlton Avenue to Midland Street. It is an iteration of the multi-functional "woonerf" used for car and pedestrian access, parking, and community activities alike, proposed by MPC in the Urban Habitats competition. Easy Street also creates a central visual axis across the site. Besides accommodating multiple uses, it is designed to double as a storm water drainage and retention system. Bioswales, a porous parking surface, numerous large trees, and gradual grading are designed to maximize the use of the on site water resources for irrigation.

In contrast to the more public Easy Street, the second main landscape element is the "Big Back Yard". Its large, gently sloping lawn provides a gathering and playing space for Sunrise residents only. The adjacent "Grove",

In revisiting the program to be realized at Sunrise, discussions revolved around how many of which type of dwellings would need to be built in order to make the project financially feasible and socially desirable. Size of dwellings was also an issue. Living small was very much in the air, as the cover of CVille Abode (November 2006) shows.

organized around a large existing tree and community gardens, is conceived as a sheltered, exterior space, tucked between buildings' patios and porches, a place where the elderly and children living at Sunrise may interact out of sight of the larger neighborhood.

Private open space is included in a variety of ways, appropriate to each type of housing. Some homes have private yards opening directly off their living spaces, others have porches overlooking the shared areas, and still others have decks oriented towards the best views and breezes. Careful grading proved to be the most important way to organize the relationship of private and shared open space. Strategic planting at three levels —trees, shrubs, and ground cover—was another important tool to define different qualities of open space. As an example, the nine free-standing houses along Nassau Street are organized in three groups of three. Each group of three houses sits on a plateau connected to Easy Street by a common foot path. The yard and/or porches of each house are oriented in a different direction, so as to ensure privacy. A planted incline separates each plateau visually and in terms of access from the one below it. The need for fences or walls has been eliminated.

The architecture complements the open, yet organized gesture of the landscape. Four groups of housing respond to particular qualities of site and location. The resulting narrow, high houses, as well as the multitude of interlocking, stacked unit types, are reminiscent of types proposed by Genter Schindler in the Urban Habitats competition. Side-by-side duplexes combining two single-family homes engage lively Midland Street. On the terraced slope between Easy Street and Nassau Street, in contrast, the single- and two-family homes are freestanding and take advantage of multiple frontages and views. For the sites fronting one of the major streets and the Grove, a third type of housing was developed: these cluster buildings combine smaller and larger units to bring different household types together within one building. Finally, a four-story condominium building at the busy corner of Carlton Avenue and Nassau Street is a landmark anchoring the site in its neighborhood. It combines ground floor commercial or community uses with a variety of multi-story apartment options above.

A key concept in the design of the housing was to create a limited number of types which could be recombined in numerous ways. Thus the single-family homes that are paired as duplexes along Midland can be reworked as parts of clusters, or can be deployed as free-standing units. Another key concept was that all residential units should be walk-ups, giving each household a

Site section through the Midland Houses, Easy Street and the Nassau Houses looking north.

Landscape plays a central role in the revised Sunrise plan. Site section through the condominium building and the Nassau Houses looking west.

true front door on a public street. This holds true for the condominium building as well, where access for all units is from one common deck avoiding the need for shared interior circulation. Still, the designs allow for, indeed demand, further work. The team felt that rather than issuing a buildable product, the purpose of a master plan was to define the key relationships between public and private uses and interior and exterior spaces. These qualities were described by providing a set of schematic design drawings, including landscape plans with planting and rough grading, as well as dimensioned floor plans and sections for each housing type. In addition, HHGC received an appendix of cut sheets for sustainable building practices presented in an expandable binder so that changes and new information could easily be incorporated.

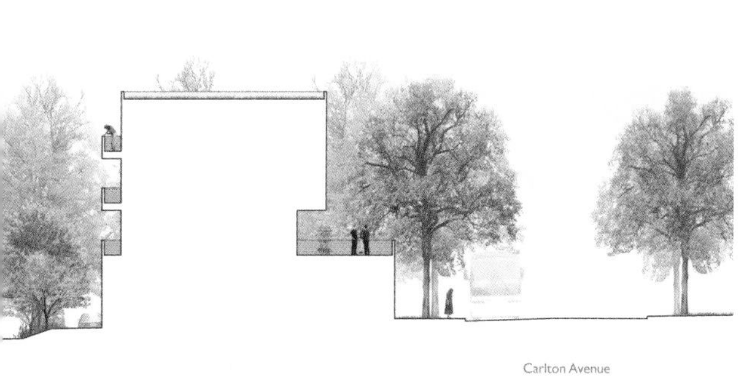

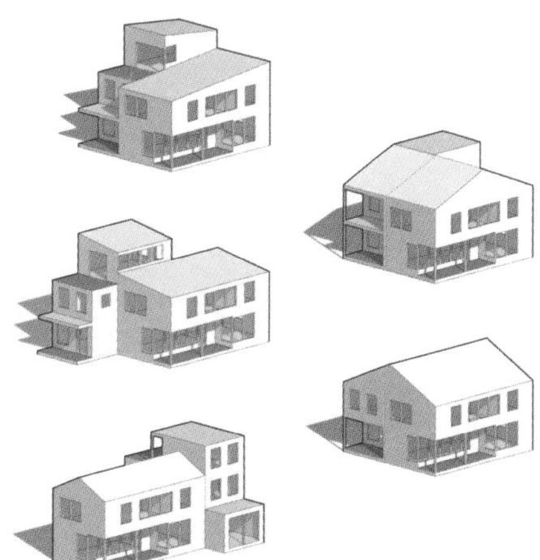

A fundamental idea was to generate maximum variety on the basis of a limited number of housing types. The axonometric drawings show possibilities for joining two single-family homes.

New Developments

As the redevelopment of Sunrise moves towards implementation, many challenges remain. Market trends have dramatically shifted since the project was initiated, making the underlying premise of cross-subsidizing affordable units with market-rate units difficult. At the same time, the mortgage crisis and the thousands of households who have lost their homes as a result, have made it clear to all that there is enormous need for housing protected from untenable, profit-maximizing lending practices.

HHGC has shown resolve in its mission to create innovative affordable housing options. Sunrise seems to have triggered HHGC's entrepreneurial edge.

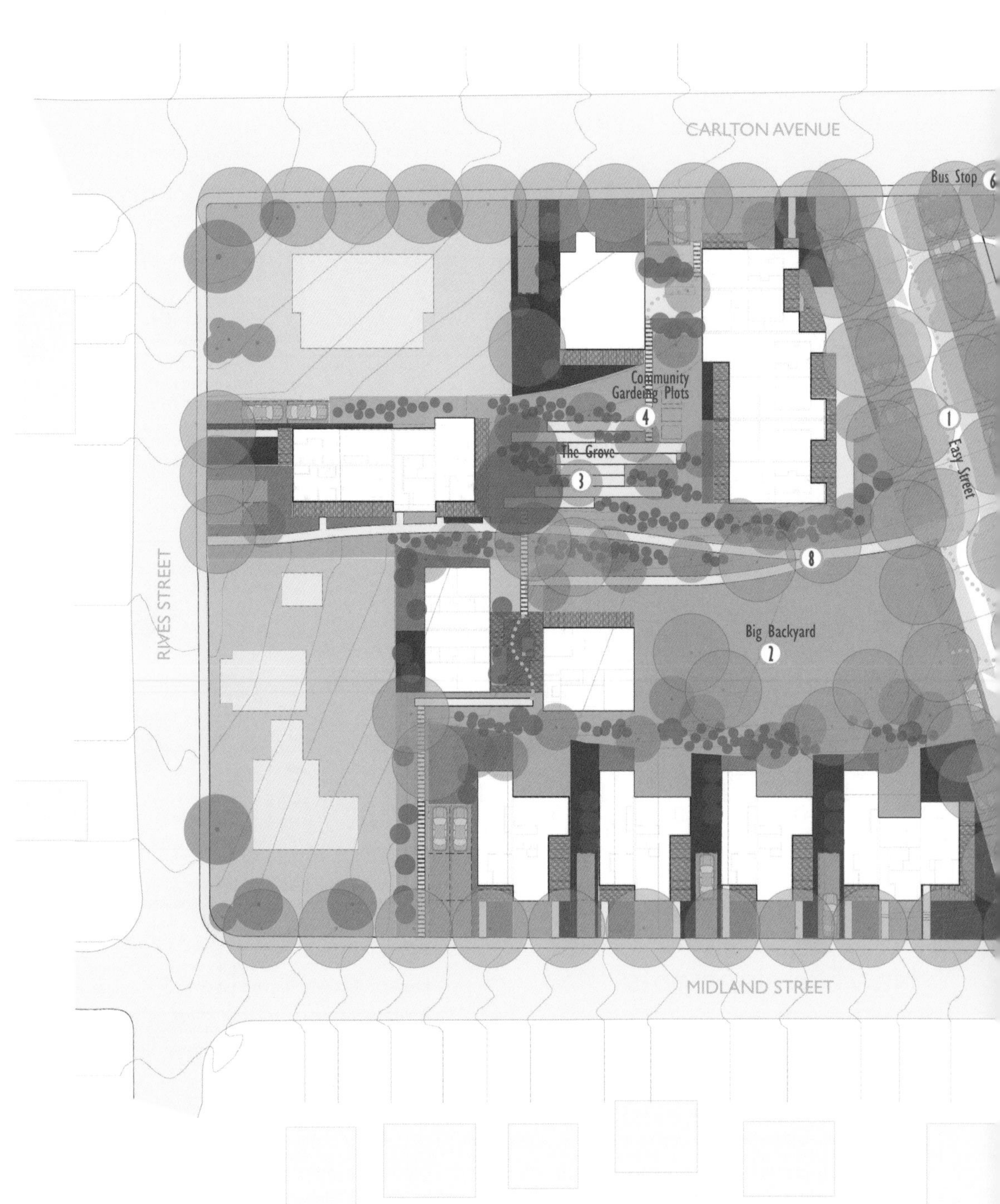
CARLTON AVENUE
Bus Stop 6
Community Gardening Plots
4
The Grove
3
1
Easy Street
8
RIVES STREET
Big Backyard
2
MIDLAND STREET

LEFT
The revised site plan for Sunrise as presented in February 2007. The plan shows the major landscape elements. These include:

1 Easy Street. Taking its identity from the active street that runs through the site now, Easy Street fills many needs. Offering parking and seating, it encourages casual socializing and play. Porches line the edge, and all the Nassau and Carlton units feed onto the street so there's lots of coming and going. A double allee of ginkgo trees provides ample shade during the summer and buoyant fall color. Wide planting areas collect storm water run off and prevent the street from feeling like a parking lot.

2 Big Backyard. Large and open, this lawn is great for running around and for quiet sitting. Mostly sunny, trees provide shady pockets along its edges.

3 The Grove. Under the Big Tree a generous terrace encourages small gatherings for BBQs, games, and conversation. It's enclosed by a grove of flowering understory trees and low shrubs.

4 Community Gardening Plots. Just to the east of the Grove sit community garden plots, while small shared gardens act as thresholds for the occupants of the Internal and Carlton clusters.

5 Commercial Space. At the busy corner of Carlton and Nassau, ground floor space that can be subdivided for commercial and / or community uses allows for on-site work spaces and provides an active interface with the surrounding neighborhood.

6 Bus Stop. A new transit stop is located at the corner of Carlton and Nassau to serve the growing Sunrise community and reduce the residents' dependence on cars.

8 Pedestrian Paths. The overall Sunrise site is accessible to passers-through by a network of pedestrian paths. While open in this way, the position of the buildings and their decks and porches, ensure that the site is always safe.

Private Open Space: Every unit at Sunrise enjoys a private yard, porch or deck. Set off from the shared open spaces by small embankments, these yards are great for relaxing and independent pursuits.

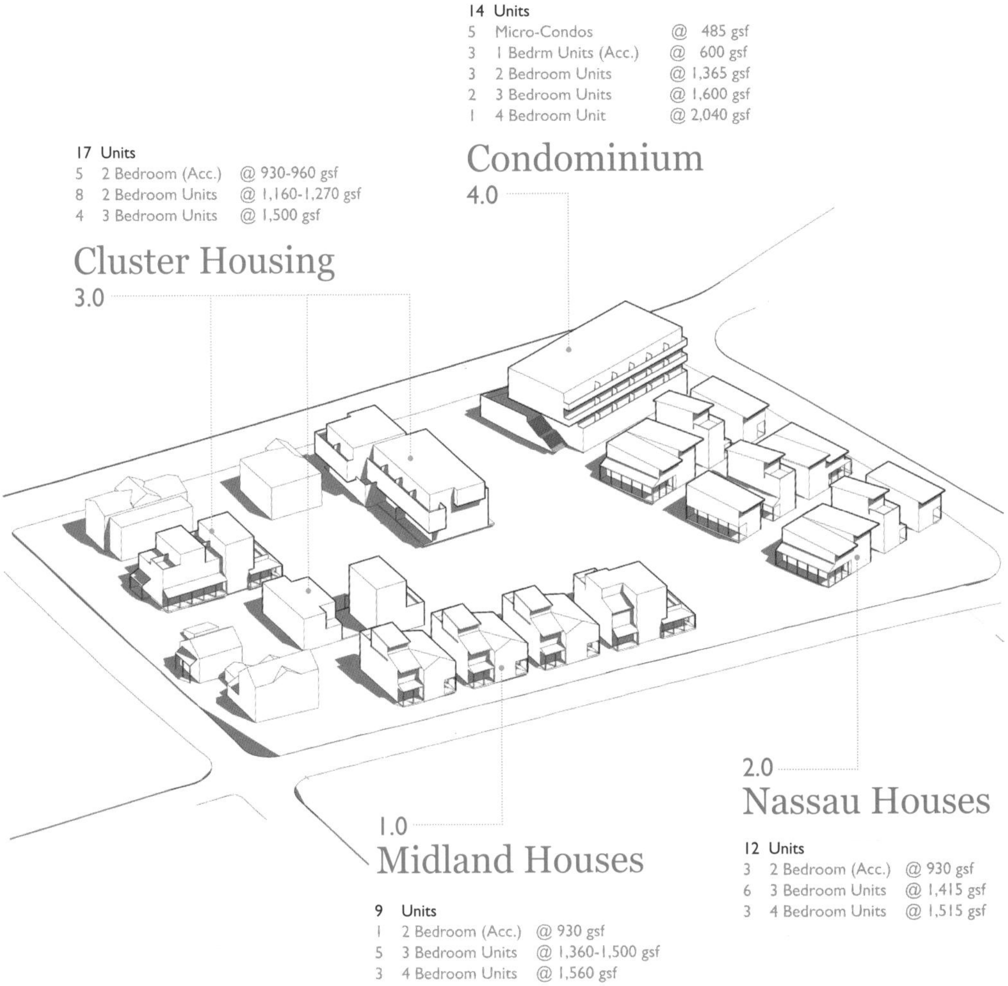

Condominium
4.0

14 Units

5	Micro-Condos	@ 485 gsf
3	1 Bedrm Units (Acc.)	@ 600 gsf
3	2 Bedroom Units	@ 1,365 gsf
2	3 Bedroom Units	@ 1,600 gsf
1	4 Bedroom Unit	@ 2,040 gsf

Cluster Housing
3.0

17 Units

5	2 Bedroom (Acc.)	@ 930-960 gsf
8	2 Bedroom Units	@ 1,160-1,270 gsf
4	3 Bedroom Units	@ 1,500 gsf

Nassau Houses
2.0

12 Units

3	2 Bedroom (Acc.)	@ 930 gsf
6	3 Bedroom Units	@ 1,415 gsf
3	4 Bedroom Units	@ 1,515 gsf

Midland Houses
1.0

9 Units

1	2 Bedroom (Acc.)	@ 930 gsf
5	3 Bedroom Units	@ 1,360-1,500 gsf
3	4 Bedroom Units	@ 1,560 gsf

Site axonometric showing numbers, types and locations of dwellings with the revised Sunrise plan.

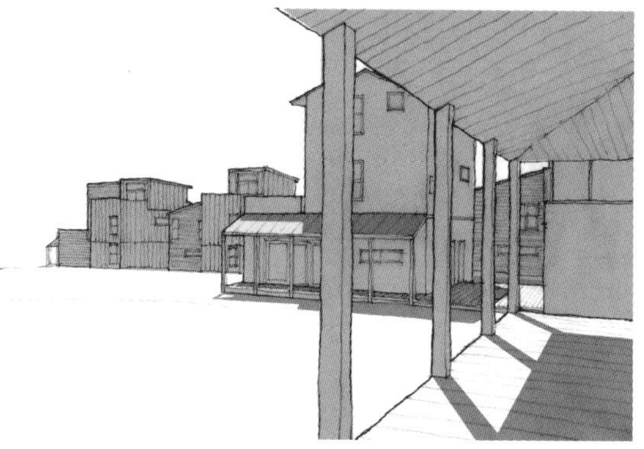

OPPOSITE BELOW, ABOVE
Sketches were used to illustrate the relationships between interior and exterior space. From left to right: The side yard of a Midland House. The side yard of a Nassau House. The porch of a Cluster fronting the Grove and Big Back Yard. The balcony of a micro-condo.

The organization launched a new sister organization, Creative Housing, as a for-profit development arm in 2006. The goal of Creative Housing is to serve households with an annual income of around $80,000, or 120% AMI, to complement the traditional Habitat target group, families with annual incomes between 30 and 60% AMI, or $20,000 to $40,000. Just like the Habitat homes, Creative Housing homes are constructed in part by volunteer labor, and in fact make use of the surplus of volunteer labor HHGC receives. However, they are sold at a higher return, and the income generated is used to fund more Habitat homes. By summer 2008, two Creative Housing homes were under construction in the Fifeville neighborhood of Charlottesville.

An even more impressive undertaking was launched in early 2007, when HHGC purchased a one-hundred-acre trailer park called Southwood located just south of the city of Charlottesville. The extended site accommodates approximately 2,500 residents who live in more than 375 mobile homes. HHGC plans to redevelop the site in conjunction with other housing providers, tripling the number of housing units. Accordingly, the project will have a significant impact on the availability of affordable housing in the Charlottesville area. The successful implementation of the Sunrise plan, with "only" 54 units of housing, therefore, is being watched all the more closely.

Given all these developments since the Urban Habitats competition was launched in 2005, Ryan Jacoby, HHGC's project manager for Sunrise, does not hesitate to underline the lasting value it has brought to HHGC: "It heavily promoted community feedback and collaboration, which is crucial. We can develop a model that we can drop in, but if the community resists it, we have not done our job. The Design Center's community engage-ment process promoted the integration of the project into broader community." Further, he says, the design work generated by the competition helped HHGC to refine its goals and priorities.

Many of the principles that drove the original designs of MPC and Genter Schindler still constitute the strength of the revised plan. In addition, the enthusiasm generated by the Urban Habitats competition energized not only local stakeholders, but the design team as well. Despite the geographic distance of MPC and Genter Schindler and Utile, Ryan says, "to their credit, they are still

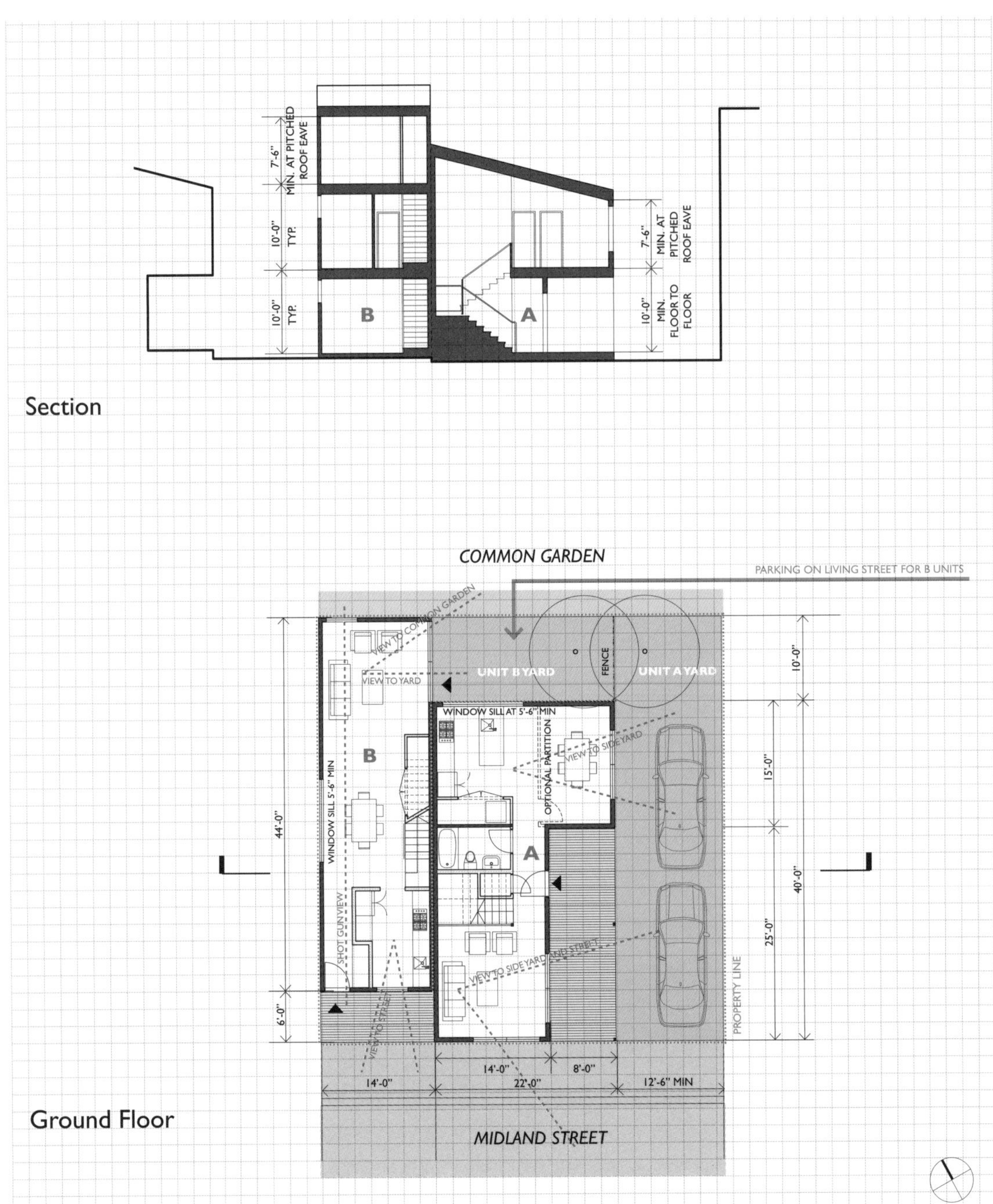

Plans and sections of a Midland House as described in the housing guidelines that were submitted as part of the master plan.

dedicated to the project three plus years later—their passion for the ultimate outcome has not waned at all."

Finally, the Charlottesville Community Design Center (CCDC) has prospered as a result of the Urban Habitats process. The public success of the ideas competition attracted institutional support for the CCDC as well as more demand for their services. In 2006, for example, the City of Charlottesville and local business leaders engaged the Design Center, in conjunction with the Central Virginia Chapter of the American Institute of Architects (AIA), to develop a competition to explore new models of green, mixed-use urban development for a difficult, two-acre parcel in the heart of Downtown. "Market Value" attracted over fifty entries from around the world, with finalists and a public exhibition announced in October 2007.

In the process, the City learned how the CCDC could help them translate its planning regulations and policies into physical and conceptual models, which in turn could be used in public forums and improve the City's ability to work with developers and neighbors. Since the competition, the municipality has granted the CCDC an annual $25,000 subsidy towards its operations. In 2008, the Design Center and the City merged their efforts to design and build a permanent "green" public workshop space called City Space, half of which is now occupied by the CCDC. Together, the City and the Design Center program educational and design events and hold public meetings. This effort has, in turn, attracted additional funding from local foundations and community organizations seeking a place to envision design models for their future.

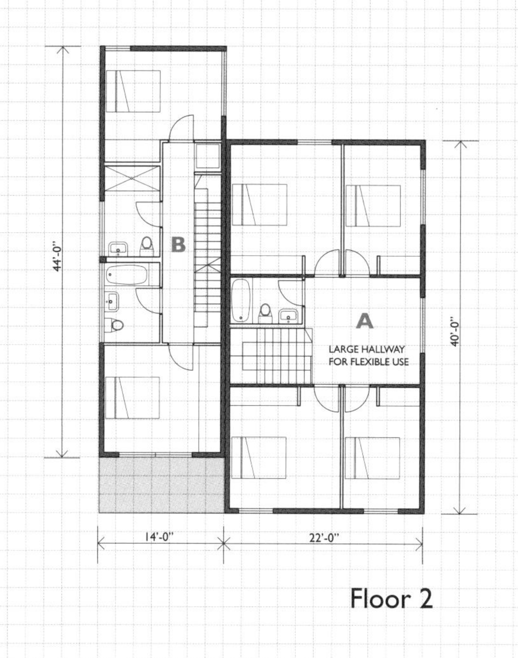

Floor 2

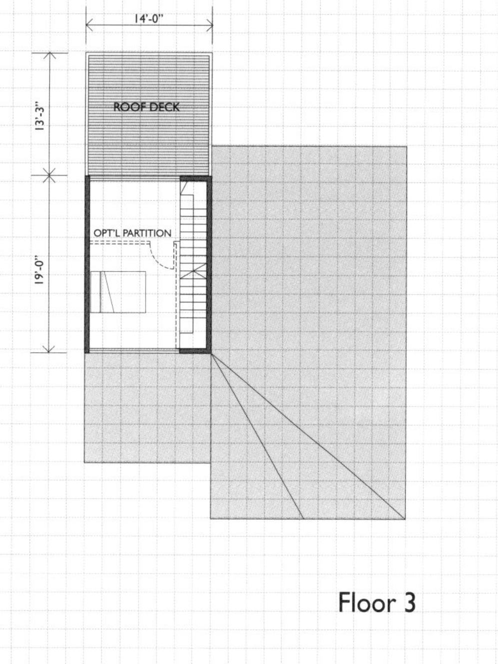

Floor 3

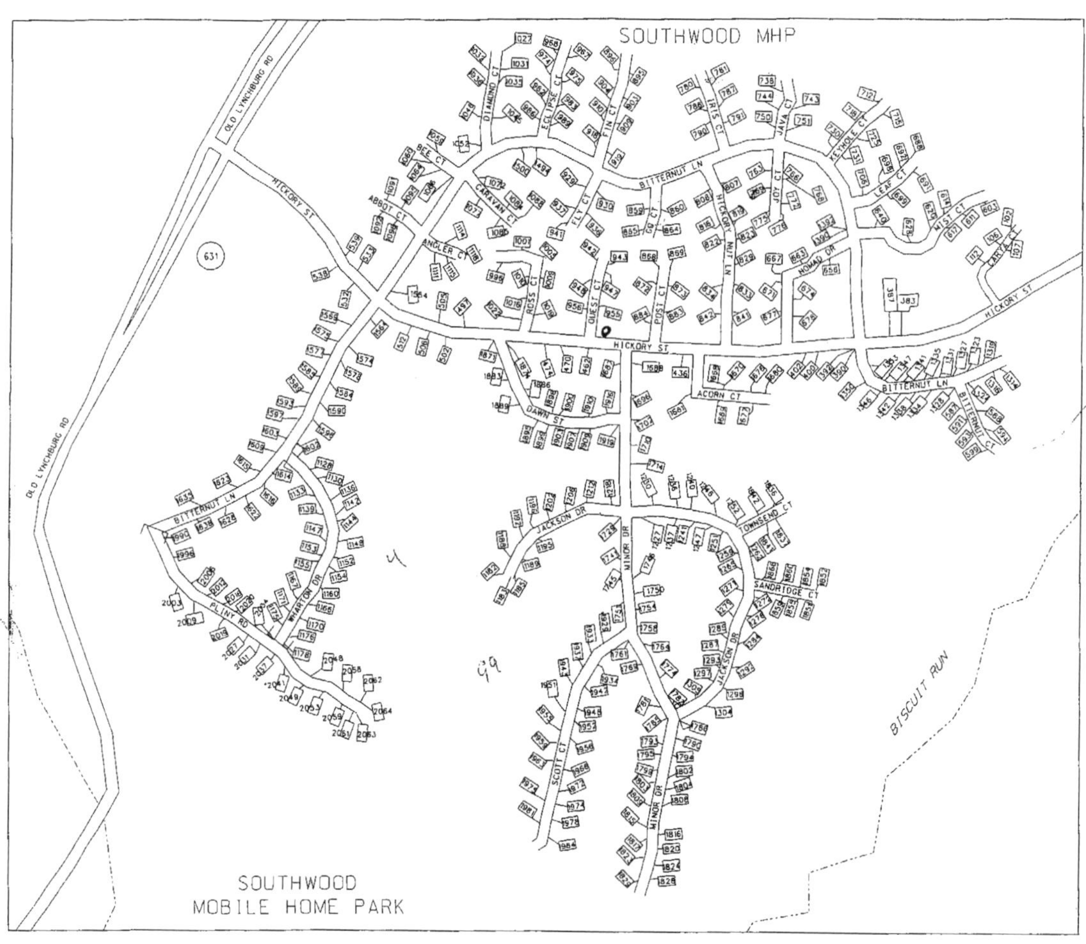

Southwood Charlottesville LLC

Plan of Southwood Trailer Park.

Will it be Aspen or Austin? Habitat owns the land, and is prepared to develop it for the benefit of future generations. However, this opportunity cannot be realized without a strong partnership between Habitat, other housing and service non-profits, for-profit builders, faith communities, major foundation and individual donors, the City and County, and thousands of volunteers—the entire Greater Charlottesville community. This may be the only opportunity for such a partnership in affordable housing. Failure to act would not only be a missed opportunity for Greater Charlottesville, but also for the nation.

Habitat for Humanity of Greater Charlottesville,
www.cvillehabitat.org, July 2008

Appendix
Participants in the Urban Habitats Competition

a + i design corp.
New York, New York
Stephen Nielsen, Hannah Purdy,
Kate Thatcher, Sommer Schauer,
Boone Lo, Danielle Rago
A-3 Madrid
Madrid, Spain
Sam Garcia, Benjamin Llana,
Patricio Rubi
aardvarkitects
Brooklyn, New York
Jesse Beacom, Minho Yang
Abruzzo Bodziak
Brooklyn, New York
Emily Abruzzo, Gerald Bodziak
Adapt
New York, New York
Sofia Zuberbuhler, Jorge Yafar,
Varun Kohli, Ed Wall, William Moraes
Allen + Killcoyne Architects
New York, New York
Stephen Killcoyne
amadeo
Washington, D.C.
Amadeo Bennetta
Anderson Anderson Architecture
San Francisco, California
Mark Anderson, Peter Anderson,
Brent Sumida, Lawton Eng,
Dennis Oshiro, Aaron Brumo,
Hitasha Bhatia, Chia Chieh Lee,
Christopher Campbell
Andrew Kraetzer
Philadelphia, Pennsylvania
Andrew Kraetzer, William Adair
Anna Conti Architecture
Firenze, Italy
Anna Conti
ARCH
Douliu, Taiwan
Nai-Feng Chen
ARCH 5217
Stillwater, Oklahoma
Sarah Holstedt
Archi S.L.K.H
Seoul, Korea
Hyon-Dok Son, Ewha Kim,
Hyoeng-Sik Hwang, Suyeun Lee
ArCS
Brookline, Massachusetts
Seanna Walsh, Patrick Casey
Army of One
New York, New York
Jason Gibbs

ARQ-UdeC
Concepción, Chile
Leonel Pérez Bustamante,
Mauricio Mendez Bustos
ASDF
Sendai, Miyagiken, Japan
Takahiro Tsuji, Roma Ishinabe,
Kouki Yokoyama, Noriko Yamamoto

B+P+P
Paris, France
Julien Paulre, Dan-Alexandre Becker,
Paul Pflughaupt
Bakke
Chicago, Illinois
Ryan Bakke
Bamssem
Seoul, Korea
Hyun Jong Park, Young Jong Joo,
Sang Eun Kim, Hyung Jung Kim,
Tae Kyun Kim, Dong Seo
Bateman Architecture
Rotterdam, The Netherlands
Ramon Knoester
Berry / Keller Architects
Beverly Hills, California
Andrea Keller, John Berry, Brian Karn
Blue Studio Hongik University
Seoul, Korea
Alice Choy, Tae Byoung Yim, Jin Hee Byun,
Joon Young Park, Young Kook Cho,
Yun Seung Seo, Mi So Yoo
BNIM Architects – Houston
Houston, Texas
Filippo Castore, Christi Anders,
Jara Kloucek
Boyarsky Murphy Architects
London, United Kingdom
Nicholas Boyarsky, Nicola Murphy,
Andrew Lyon, Joakim Skajaa
Honorable Mention
Brie & Galindo
Concord, California
Venessa Galindo, Melissa Brie
Bruce R. Wardell, Architect, PC
Charlottesville, Virginia
Bruce Wardell, Ryan Doone,
Lia Keesecker, Kurt Keesecker,
Mark Humbertson, Heather Stephenson

Calnitsky Associates Architects
Winnipeg, Manitoba, Canada
Ed Calnitsky, David Calnitsky,
Greg Woloszyn

Calnitsky Associates Architects
Winnipeg, Manitoba, Canada
Ed Calnitsky, Greg Woloszyn
CAN Architecture
Brooklyn, New York
Mauro Bianucci, Anna Dietzsch,
Carlos Salinas Weber, Robert A. Golda,
Adam John Grosshans
Carleton University
North York, Ontario, Canada
Cecilia Chui
Carlo Carbone + JLP ET ASSOCIES
Montreal, Quebec, Canada
Carlo Carbone
Chocolade
Douliu, Taiwan
Che-Wei Hsu
ChoShields Studio, Inc.
Brooklyn, New York
In Cho, Timothy Shields, Karena D'silva,
Michael Dox
CK-Architecture
Los Angeles, California
Christoph Kapeller, Jayna Cooper
Honorable Mention
Cnia Blue and Black
Needham, Massachusetts
Alexander Knox, Dale Travous,
Robert Knox
Concept 2
Douliu, Taiwan
Shih-An Weng
Conway + Schulte Architects
Minneapolis, Minnesota
Marcy Schulte, William Conway,
Mary Springer, Thomas Weitzel, Scott Ervin
Cooke+Millward
Brooklyn, New York
Erik Millward, Travis Cooke
Cottle Khan Architects with Travis Ridenbaugh and Jackson Kane
Altlanta, Georgia
Sabir Khan, Mark Cottle,
Travis Ridenbaugh, Jackson Kane
Crank
Minneapolis, Minnesota
Beth Nelson
CSAX
Charlottesville, Virginia
Cheyenne Sheafe

Darkan
Perth, Australia
Carly Barrett, Sarah May

David Rooth
Amherst, Massachusetts
David Rooth
DeByRe
Mexico, D.F., Mexico
Barry Espinosa Oropeza, Isela Sánchez Castro, Alejandro Arenas García
Design & Systèmes Constructifs
Montreal, Quebec, Canada
Aurélie Amable
Design & Systèmes Constructifs
Montreal, Quebec, Canada
Chaker Hamoudan, Michel Lepage
D-Fold
New York, New York
Shao W. Deng, Yu Wing Deng
DJSP
Englewood Cliffs, New Jersey
Jin Kwon Kim, Seung H. Lee, David Jaubert, Phanat Sonemangkhala
DKJC Studio
Jupiter, Florida
Daniel Kahan, John Conley
Dotproduct
Charlottesville, Virginia
Johanna Huang, James Sun, Luka Radakovich, Eric Craig
Dri Chevillard
Nancy, France
Angélique Dri, Christoph Chevillard
DRt
Hampton, Virginia
Reginald Truxon, Donald Roman

E4 Architects
Culver City, California
Ned Engs, Anita Engs, Audrey Mcewen, John Gaiser
EADG
Fargo, North Dakota
Bakr Aly Ahmed, Khaled Nassar, Ron Randell
Eugenio Hernandez
San Juan, Puerto Rico
Eugenio Hernandez

f/g/s
Melville, New York
Janine Sutton, Robin Fitzgerald-Green
Florencia de Lasa
London, Ontario, Canada
Florencia De Lasa
FMDTC
New York, New York
Scott Ferebee, Lewis Maverick Mcneel, Jonathan Duey, Brian Talbot, Jonathan Cielo
Forma Unica
Moscow, Idaho
Anne Clapperton, Dustin Rowland
Frederic Schwartz Architects
New York, New York
Frederic Schwartz
Funcion [T]
Cambridge, Massachusetts
Paul Tebben

GAINEAU
Nancy, France
Noémie Gaineau, Rebecca Pierre
Garbage
Douliu, Taiwan
Zhang-Ru Chen
GBArch
New York, New York
Elizabeth Bacon, Kent Gould
GCPG
Tijuana, Mexico
Gilberto Celiceo, Paulina Graciano
Genter Schindler
Cambridge, Massachusetts
Chris Genter, Susanne Schindler
Gr33n Architects
West Caldwell, New Jersey
Ayvind Karlsen, Mounir Tawadrous
Group of Jin-Hua
Douliu, Taiwan
Jin-Hua Huang
Grupo Parasol
Aventura, Florida
Eric Dubosc, Marco Imperadori, Margarita Blanco, Tania Torrentes, Linda Locatelli

H.I.A
Seoul, Korea
Hye Sook Jung, Ho Sung Won, Sang Jin Lee
Hangar Design Group NY
New York, New York
Juan Matiz
Hatch
Brooklyn, New York
Ani Schaeffer, Henry P. Miller, Jennifer Gurney, Daughtry Carstarphen
Henault-Truong
Paris, France
Fabrice Henault, Pierre Chanh-Van Truong
HIDETO HORIIKE + URTOPIA,INC.
Tokyo, Japan
Hideto Horiike
HMS Architects
New Orleans, Louisiana
Charles Montgomery, Keith Steger, Damien Job, Scott Welty, Louise Legardeur, Ben Montgomery
Hong-Ik First
Seoul, Korea
In-Jae Kim, Jun-U Lee, Gyung-Seng Lee
Hs WorkShop-ASIA
Osaka, Japan
Kohki Hiranuma

I.A.P
Douliu, Taiwan
Chi-Hsuan Lai
[in]fuse
Snoqualmie, Washington
TJ Hoving, Daniel Brown

Jameson Terry
Blacksburg, Virginia
Jameson Terry
jamie blosser cd+d
Santa Fe, New Mexico
Jamie Blosser, Deirdre Harris, Roy Wroth
JEDRZEJCZAK-CARDON
Nancy, France
Piotr Jedrzekczak, Antoine Cardon
JP Emery
Tucson, Arizona
Jonathan Emery
Judith Kinnard, Architect
Charlottesville, Virginia
Judith Kinnard, Kenneth Schwartz, Noel Murphy, Katie Wood, Noel Murphy

K2R+ Architects
Kusatsu, Shiga, Japan
Kiichiro Komatsu, Kotaro Horiuchi, Yasushi Hasegawa, Yuji Kaneko
Katz & Shearer
Chicago, Illinois
Steven Shearer, Gila Katz

KFaB
New York, New York
Jonathan Benner, Mike Faulkner,
Chris Kao
Khalili + Henthorn
Evanston, Illinois
Parsa Khalili, Brett Henthorn
Konyk Architecture
Brooklyn, New York
Craig Konyk, Timo Koeppe,
Jonathan Louie, Ivan Sorensen
Kuality Architects
Ann Arbor, Michigan
Mike Styczynski, Michael Hopkins,
Hnedel Maximore

LA NOUVELLE AGENCE
Parempuyre, France
Ait Mehdi Samira, Latizeau Sylvain,
Schmeltz Benoit, Begou Julien,
Pillaud Veronique
Ladicius
New York, New York
Yvonne Choy, Inigo Cobeta
Larvender
Douliu, Taiwan
Pi-Ju Tang, Yeuh-Cheng Chen
Laughing Dog Studio Architecture, PLLC
Charlotte, North Carolina
Carrie Gault, Bruce Berberick, Darryl Hall,
Mike Romot, Ryan Justak, Donna Cole
le coq studio
Torino, Italy
Massimiliano Secco, Simona Scotton,
Alessandro Rigazio
Lehrstuhl Bauplanung und Entwerfen, TH Karlsruhe
Karlsruhe, Germany
Walter Naegeli, Gudrun Wiedemer,
Michael Merrill, Nadine Clauß,
Johannes Eck
LIANG-TA CHEN
Taichung City, Taiwan
Liang-Ta Chen
Licht&Wülfing
New York, New York
Nanna Wülfing, Thomas Licht
Los Angeles Team
Los Angeles, California
Hussam Salama

M.E.N.
Milford, New York
Eliza Higgins, Michael Rogers,
Nicole Desjardins
M3
West-Newbury, Vermont
Martha Doerfler
Mai Friend Dianna
Worcester, Massachusetts
Dianna Pozdniakov
Marie Yates
New York, New York
Marie Yates
Marissa Gregory
San Diego, California
Marissa Gregory
Mars
Douliu, Taiwan
Chia-Ching Lin
Mass Works
Chicago, Illinois
Jerico Prater, Francis Cooke
Masze
Darmstadt, Germany
Georg Voigt, Lars Geis
ME AND ME
Las Palmas de Gran Canaria, Spain
Carlos A. Gonzalez Aleman
ME.ET
Berlin, Germany
Holger Jansen, Remo Lotano,
Christine French
Meacham and Apel Architects
Dublin, Ohio
Jon Stevens, Mark Daniels,
Josh Doehring, Greg Jackson,
Seth Oakley, Doug Clay
Metropolitan Planning Collaborative
New York, New York
Aaron Young, Catherine Lynch,
Georgia Borden, Richard Ramsey
MH Collaborative
Virginia Beach, Virginia
Darryl Moser, Wesley Herlan
MHM
Cambridge, Ontario, Canada
Monika Harte-Maxwell
Michael Sorkin Studio
New York, New York
Michael Sorkin, Makoto Okazaki,
Britta Degn, Camilla Giotto Levy
MMG
Chicago, Illinois
Richard Blender, Marcin Szef, Geoffrey
Elander, Geoffrey Elander, Mathew Jecha,
Rosalio Arellanes, Mathew Majack

MMM Design Group
Norfolk, Virginia
Brian Turner, Greg Simon,Robert Williams,
Dranan Sparks Brad Ellis, Ron Williams
Rebecca Holden, Ned Carr Errol Plata
Taylor Gould
Morcol Soygenis Tong Istanbul, Turkey
Murat Soygenis, Ertugrul Morcol, Togan
Tong, Erdal Aydin, Togay Ozkaraduman
MUTT
Columbis, Ohio
Lisa Tilder, Stephen Turk, Ji Young Yoon,
Adam Tomski

Naseeb
New York, New York
Kayzad Shroff
NDSU
Fargo, North Dakota
Mohamed Elnahas
Next Phase Studios
Jamaica Plain, Massachusetts
Rick Ames, Martin Werminghausen,
Lisa Hiserodt, Elizabeth Stifel, Anabela
Niedda, Scott Payette, Chris Gervais
Nick Hammer
Raleigh, North Carolina
Nick Hammer
NRA
New York, New York
Joel Napach

Oruga
Buenos Aires, Argentina
Eduardo Cociffi, Isabel Basombrío,
Ernesto Sanchez, Pablo Carucci,
Federico Jack, Patrick Mcclure

P2P
Charlottesville, Virginia
Duckjune Park, James Joyce Pressly
Paul Lessard—Architects
Salem, Massachusetts
Paul Lessard
Paul Michael Davis
New York, New York
Paul Davis
PINK
Douliu, Taiwan
Yu-Peng Lai, Hsing-Hua Tsai

Prodes Inc
Montreal, Quebec, Canada
Pierre Jampen

Ring
Seoul, Korea
Kim Ji Youn
RKStudio+HGDesign
Ann Arbor, Michigan
Robert Kleyn, Harry Giles
RRAM
Rome, Italy
Spyridon Andrikou, Cecilia Ratini,
Maria Russo, Nicoletta Muscara

Scott Henderson Design
Fano, Italy
Scott Henderson
Seminar Brezar
Domzale, Slovenia
Larisa Capuder, Martina Grizancic,
Nina Kolaric, Lea Prezelj
SLP
Brooklyn, New York
Sydney Mainster, David Chin,
Lauren Gropper, Tara Delaney
Snehal Intwala Architect
Providence, Rhode Island
Snehal Intwala
SO
San Francisco, California
Pasak Ongwattanagul, Tysonn Silva
SPARE
Perth, Australia
Eddie Tran, William Thomson,
Tom See Hoo, Cian Keith Davis
Standing Architecture
New York, New York
Alastair Standing, Mairim Dallaryan
STeM
New York, New York
Teresa Ball, Sofia Castricone,
Marc Perrotta
Studio Antithesis
Charlottesville, Virginia
Justin Hershberger, Nathan Petty,
Justin Sculthorpe
Studio C
Portland, Oregon
Jim Walker, Cami Walker, Brian Bennett,
Amy Vohs

Studio de Seis
San Diego, California
Dominic Ballerino, Sergio Flores,
Anne Lee, Baldwin Madriaga,
Manuel Moreno, Peter Ling
Studio Dwg
Brighton, Massachusetts
Mo Zell, Marc Roehrle, Andy Grote,
Steve Fellmeth
Studio La Nasa Parikh
Houston, Texas
Rajiv Parikh, Michael La Nasa
studio projects
Northhampton, Massachusetts
Joseph Krupczynski, Samantha Wood,
Adam Folta, Hernan Barufaldi,
Gustavo Pardo
Sun
Douliu, Taiwan
Yi-Yan Wu

Tai Ming Moy
New York, New York
Tai-Ming Moy
Team X
Seongnam-Si, Gyeonggi-Do, Korea
In Joong Kim, Kye Hyeong Lee,
Kyu Hyung Kim, Taek Ki Lee
The 3
Brooklyn, New York
Alexander Levi, Amanda Schachter,
Simeon Seigel
The DAAPers
Cincinnati, Ohio
Michael Wagner, Benjamin Crabtree,
Drew Kleman
The Think Shop
Brighton, Michigan
Keith Phillips, Ching Van
Thurlow Small Atelier
Pawtucket, Rhode Island
Maia Small, Andrew Thurlow
Turtle Team
Lincoln, Nebraska
Cedric Chone

VINET
Fontaine Les Dijon, France
Rudolf Vinet

Watershed
Richmond, Virginia
Damon Pearson, David Day, Patrick Farley,
Kristen Becker, Rob Ventura, Shari Perago
Williamson-Andrachuk
Brampton, Ontario, Canada
John Williamson, James Andrachuk
Withee Malcolm Architects
Torrance, California
Carolina Chacon, Paul Lee

Yolo Design
Anaheim, California
Albern Yolo
Yuan / Landscape Urbanism
Houston, Texas
Ding Yuan

Zan Bross
Cambridge, Massachusetts
Zan Bross

Appendix
Contacts of Projects' Architects and Developers

Abruzzo Bodziak
Brooklyn, New York
abruzzo-bodziak.com
Anderson Anderson Architecture
San Francisco, CA / Seattle, WA
andersonanderson.com

Blue Studio
Seoul, Korea
not available
Boyarsky Murphy Architects
London, UK
boyarskymurphy.com

CAN Architecture
Brooklyn, New York
Anna Dietzsch
anna@annajubs.com,
Carlos Salinas Weber
salinaswerber@earthlink.net,
Mauro Bianucci
maurobianucci.com
Carlo Carbone + JLP et Associés
Montreal, Canada
jlp.ca
Casa Familiar
San Ysidro, California
casafamiliar.org
CIM Group
Los Angeles / San Francisco / Bethesda, MD
cimgroup.com
Citizens Housing Corporation
San Francisco, California
citizenshousing.org
City of Los Angeles
California, Small Lots Ordinance
lacity.org/pln
City of Portland
Oregon, Living Smart Project
livingsmartpdx.com
City of Santa Cruz
California, Accessory Dwelling
Unit Ordinance
ci.santa-cruz.ca.us/pl/hcd/ADU/adu
Civic Enterprise
Los Angeles, California
civicenterprise.com
CK-Architecture
Los Angeles, California
ck-architecture.com
Community Corporation of Santa Monica
California
communitycorp.org

Dattner Architects
New York, New York
dattner.com
David Baker + Partners Architects
San Francisco, California
dbarchitect.com
David Foster
Santa Cruz, California
fosterbane@earthlink.net
DIRT Studio
Charlottesville, Virginia
dirtstudio.com
Drisko Studio
Santa Monica, California
driskostudio.net

ecoMOD, University of Virginia
Charlottesville, Virginia
ecomod.virginia.edu
Eskew + Dumez + Ripple
New Orleans, Louisiana
studioedr.com
Estudio Teddy Cruz
La Jolla, California
estudioteddycruz.com

Frederick P. Rose Fellowship
rosefellowship.org
Fung + Blatt Architects
Los Angeles, California
fungandblatt.com

Genter Schindler
Boston / Rotterdam
genterschindler.blogspot.com
Global Green
Holy Cross Project
globalgreen.org/neworleans/holycross
Grimshaw & Partners
London, UK
grimshaw-architects.com

Habitat Group Los Angeles
Los Angeles, California
habitatgroupla.com

Jamie Blosser
Santa Fe, New Mexico
aosarchitects.com
Jonathan Rose Companies
New York, New York
rose-network.com

Koning Eizenberg Architects
Santa Monica, California
kearch.com
konyk
Brooklyn, New York
konyk.net

Lloyd Russell
San Diego, California
lloyd-russell.com
LOHA Architects
Culver City, California
loharchitects.com

Metropolitan Planning Collaborative
New York, Washington D.C.,
San Francisco
metropolitanplanning.com

Oakland Community Housing
Oakland, California
ochi.org
Office dA
Boston, Massachusetts
officeda.com
Ohkay Owingeh Housing Authority
New Mexico, P.O. Box 1059,
Ohkay Owingeh, NM 87566
Onion Flats
Philadelphia, Pennsylvania
onionflats.com

PARC Foundation
New York, New York
parcfoundation.org
Paul Tebben / Studio IDE
Chicago, Illinois
studioide.com
Piedmont Housing Alliance
Charlottesville, Virginia
piedmonthousingalliance.org
Prairie View Homes
Portland, Oregon
prairieviewhomes.net
Pugh + Scarpa
Santa Monica, California
pugh-scarpa.com
Pyatok Architects
Oakland, California
pyatok.com

Russell Katz
Washington, D.C.
momidc.com
Small Lots,
Smart Designs Competition
Los Angeles
smallbutsmart.org
Smith and Others
San Diego, California
not available

Tektonics
Richmond, Virginia
tektonics.com
The Phipps Housing Group
New York, New York
phippsny.org
The Three
New York
Alexander Levi and Amanda Schachter
sloarchitecture.com,
Simeon Seigel
simeon@turettarch.com

Utile
Boston, Massachusetts
utiledesign.com

Van Amburgh + Pares Architects
Muir Beach, California
homepage.mac.com/vanamburgh
Vargas Greenan Architecture
Berkeley, California
vargasgreenan.com

Watershed Architects
Richmond, Virginia
watershedarch.net

Zoka Zola
Chicago, Illinois
zokazola.com

Credits

Urban Habitats Competition

urban-habitats.org

Competition Partners

Habitat for Humanity of Greater Charlottesville
501 Grove Avenue
Charlottesville, VA 22902
cvillehabitat.org

Overton McGehee, Executive Director
Lynne Conboy, Chair, Board of Directors
Kelly Eplee, Development Director

Charlottesville Community Design Center
100 5th Street NE
Charlottesville, VA 22902
cvilledesign.org

Katie Swenson, Executive Director

Staff and Interns
Maria Brinski, Azzura Cox, Serena Gruia, Spencer Haynsworth, Suzanne Dvells Morrish, John Semmelhack, Dan Zimmerman

Current and Former Board Members
Stuart Armstrong, William Atwood, AIA, Nisha Botchwey, Joe Celentano, AIA, James Grigg, AIA, William Morrish, Kristen Suokko (President of the Board), Matt Trowbridge, Karen Van Lengen

Volunteers
Cate Andrews, Craig Barton, Robert Batz, Ellen Cathey, Jenny Cox, Maurice Cox, Nathalie Gattengo, Brian Gerich, Evan Grimm, Liz Hoogheem, Jason Johnson, Toshi Karato, Will Kerner, Jim Kovach, Will May, Ben Montgomery, Pete O'Shea, Katie Wood

City of Charlottesville Staff
Jim Tolbert, Gary O'Connell, Ashley Cooper, Amy Kilroy, Mary Joy Scala, David Brown

Funders (Individuals)
Diane Schmidt, Diane Miller, Bob Hurst, Bill Edgerton, Gus Lorber

Financial Supporters

Anonymous

Blue Moon Fund
222 West South Street
Charlottesville, VA 22902
bluemoonfund.org

Enterprise Community Partners
10227 Wincopin Circle
American City Building
Columbia, MD 21044
enterprisecommunity.org

Piedmont Housing Alliance
111 Monticello Avenue, Suite 104
Charlottesville, VA 22902
piedmonthousingalliance.org

University of Virginia,
School of Architecture
Campbell Hall, P.O. Box 400122
Charlottesville VA 22904-4122
arch.virginia.edu

Allied Concrete
1000 Harris Street
Charlottesville, VA 22902
alliedconcrete.com

Growing Urban Habitats Symposium

Presenters

David Baker, Craig Barton, Lynne Conboy, Phoebe Crisman, Teddy Cruz, Robin Dripps, Julie Eizenberg, Andrew Gutowski, Russell Katz, William R. Morrish, Richard Price, Lawrence Scarpa, Katie Swenson, William Williams, and the Urban Habitats Competition finalists.

Financial Supporters

Anonymous

David Carley, Developer, Charlottesville

University of Virginia School of Architecture

Growing Urban Habitats Book

Authors
William R. Morrish, Charlottesville;
Susanne Schindler, Rotterdam;
Katie Swenson, Boston

Copy Editor
Juliette Spertus, New York

Editorial Advice
Kyle Copas, Charlottesville;
Tracey Hummer, New York

Design
Joana Mühlenbrock, Rotterdam

Finances and Administration
CCDC, Jane Fisher, Executive Director,
Amanda Burbage, Project Manager

Images

All images courtesy of the project architects unless noted here.

Photographs
Lawrence Anderson (77, 79 above)
Andrés Bäcker (26-27, 29, 31, 32–33, 39, 40–41, 232–233)
Hélène Binet (103, 105)